Worship Resources for Christian Congregations

A Symphony for the Senses

C. Welton Gaddy
Don W. Nixon

Smyth & Helwys Publishing, Inc.®
Macon GA

ISBN 1-880837-91-9

Worship Resources for Christian Congregations
A Symphony for the Senses
C. Welton Gaddy / Don W. Nixon

Copyright © 1995
Smyth & Helwys Publishing, Inc.®
6316 Peake Road
Macon, Georgia 31210-3960
1-800-568-1248

All biblical quotations are taken from the
New Revised Standard Version (NRSV) unless
otherwise indicated

Library of Congress Cataloging-in-Publication Data

Gaddy, C. Welton and Don W. Nixon.
    Worship resources for Christian congregations / a symphony for
the senses / by C. Welton Gaddy and Don W. Nixon.
        vi + 314   6" x 9" (15 x 23 cm.)
    ISBN 1-880837-91-9
    1. Worship programs. 2. Church year. 3. Baptists—Liturgy.
    4. Free churches—Liturgy. I. Nixon, Donald. II. Title.
    BV198.G33   1995
    264—dc20   94-41121
                                                          CIP

Floral arrangement photographs provided by C. Welton Gaddy.

Contents

91988

Soli Deo Gloria

For
our immediate families

Julia Mae Grabiel Gaddy, John Paul Gaddy,
and James Welton Gaddy;
Catherine L. Nixon and Jordan Burgess Nixon
and
our extended family in
Northminster Church
Monroe, Louisiana

Acknowledgments

Innumerable people encouraged the preparation and publication of this volume. Acknowledging each of these individuals by name would create a list much too long for inclusion here. The helpful involvement of certain persons, however, cannot go without recognition.

Scott Nash, Senior Vice-President for the Book Division of Smyth & Helwys Publishing, Inc., responded favorably the very first time I (WG) discussed the possibility of this project with him. Since that moment, Scott has not wavered in his interest in and support for our work by answering technical questions, brain-storming ideas, and waiting patiently (or impatiently) for us to meet a deadline.

Derin Tanyal, an art historian of the Art Resource in New York City, provided invaluable assistance in selecting photographs for the volume and securing permissions to use them.

The people at Northminster Church in Monroe, Louisiana, contribute daily to the kind of work reflected in this volume. This family of faith challenges us to plan experiences of Christian worship in which everyone present can participate and find meaning. Both the affirmations and complaints of these colleagues in ministry have enhanced our understanding of the essential (and inevitable) unity and diversity with which a church gathers to worship God. Their insistence on a variety of artistic expressions in worship constantly prods us to envision new and different media for praising God and proclaiming the gospel.

Members of our immediate families have supported our work on this project as well as extracted from us half-hearted promises that we will never again engage in such an undertaking. In addition to loving us through a long stretch of time-consuming, energy-draining work and trying to understand why we were doing it, Judy and Cathe—our wives—have read the manuscript and offered helpful suggestions for its improvement. Jordan (the Nixon's three-year-old daughter) has regularly interrupted our work to make us laugh and play, reminding us—even when we did not want to be reminded—that relating to people in love is more important than writing words. John Paul and James (the Gaddys' sons) have observed the project from a distance, periodically offering comments that kept us in touch with reality, and engendered within us either pride or humility.

For all of these individuals we are grateful. We gladly acknowledge their partnership in this publishing venture. Any errors that appear on these pages, however, are ours, not theirs.

Introduction

A Call to Worship

The worship of God is the most important responsibility of the people of God. Within the worship of God we discover the nature of our identity as well as the vision, inspiration, and strength for our God-commissioned ministry.

Worship that pleases God nurtures a healthy spirituality among individuals. Such worship enables each worshiper to live in conformity to the servant nature of Christ, realize forgiveness for failures in service, and find incentives to try again—and keep on trying—to live as a servant of God. Divine worship also motivates individuals involved to seek fellowship with other worshipers.

Over a period of time, communion with God in worship produces a community of faith. Conversely, apart from the worship of God as revealed in Jesus Christ, a congregation cannot be a church. Similarly, devoid of consistent, meaningful experiences of divine worship, a church cannot remain a church.

Every experience of corporate worship among Christians merits careful preparation by worship planners and holistic, focused participation by each person in the congregation of worshipers. The material on the following pages reflects two individuals' attempt to encourage and aid the realization of such worship.

Personal Confessions

For fifty-two weeks every year, we meet to plan services of corporate worship for the family of faith in which we minister—Northminster Church in Monroe, Louisiana. The sites of our planning vary as do the intensity and quality of our work. We make every effort to plan experiences of worship that will involve the whole congregation, whether standing in the hall by the water fountain or sitting around a desk in an office; whether weary from the press of other activities or rested and eager to get on with the task at hand; whether discussing the thirteenth Sunday of Pentecost or Christmas Day. The total personhood of every person in the congregation is envisioned in our planning.

Both of us stand squarely within the free church tradition, which we continue to appreciate. We know firsthand the fears of planning, structure, symbols, rites, litanies, and movement that persist in many congregations committed to this tradition. We have found, however, that planning for worship need not eliminate spontaneity in worship. Form can enliven every aspect of a congregation's encounter with God. Rather than drawing people's attention away from God, properly employed symbols and rites considerably intensify and enlighten worshipers' focus on God. Liturgical materials such as litanies and planned prayers enable every person present to participate in every phase of worship.

A careful study of the Bible and a rich history of personal experiences within the church have convinced us of the value of planned worship. When both sensitive to the leadership of God's Spirit and responsive to the needs of the people who gather for worship, planned experiences of worship employ memorable depictions of the awe-inspiring mystery of God. Such services dramatize captivating revelations of God's majesty, goodness, and greatness; involve a wide variety of instruments (musical, physical, and spiritual) to enhance the praise of God and evoke confessions to God; and utilize multiple forms of proclamation to ensure a meaningful, powerful communication of the gospel.

In the call to worship, God summons every worshiper to offer mind, body, and spirit to God; to commune with God via intellect, emotions, senses, and actions. Such total involvement does not always come easily. Carefully planning worship, therefore, carries great importance. Planning worship serves God and assists congregations by providing numerous appeals to each of the five senses that most worshipers' possess, and by assuring multiple opportunities for every member of a congregation to take part in every dimension of worship.

A Disclaimer about Creativity

In recent years, popular reactions to negative perspectives on worship and boring services have touted "creative worship" as a means of renewing worship and making worship exciting. Though the motivation behind an emphasis upon creativity in worship merits appreciation, the outcome of creative efforts often distorts the nature of worship.

When an interest in *creativity* serves as the starting point for worship planning, worship can easily degenerate into a means to an end. Creative individuals play with worship, tinker with its various elements, and insert numerous tricks into a service in order to assure novelty in worship. Personal ingenuity takes precedence over divine guidance. Achieving creativity in worship becomes more important than experiencing worship. This very practical danger borders on the sin of idolatry. Biblically understood, the worship of God is never a means toward another end—even if the end is creativity—but always an end in itself.

Creativity is a derivative of the worship of God, not a contributor to it. The creativity desirable in worship springs from an encounter with God that gives life a radical new impetus. Meaningful communion with God through worship appeals to every dimension of an individual's personhood, starts imaginative juices flowing, prods emotions, stimulates the mind to entertain new ideas, and motivates moral actions. Creative variations in worship grow out of the basic meaning and themes of worship. Worship is a stimulant to, not a product of, creativity.

Every element in a worship service should point worshipers to God. To insert a reading, piece of music, dance, floral arrangement, sermon, or any other item into a service of worship and then call attention to that item, compromises the fundamental nature of worship and threatens to supplant the congregation's focus on God. The aim of worship is God. Only God!

The Plan of This Book

We have found the metaphor of a symphony enables us to think, speak, and write about worship in a helpful manner. In the first section of the book, we explain the value of this metaphor in worship planning. Because a wealth of other materials focuses on more traditional aspects of worship—singing, praying, and preaching—we devote special attention to two important, though seldom addressed, art forms that can enhance meaningful worship inestimably: floral designs and liturgical movement.

The second section of the book consists of worship resource materials organized around the seasons of the Christian year. For each major period of worship in the Christian calendar, readers will find:

- A brief statement on the history and meaning of the season;
- A summary of the themes and emphases central to the season;
- Information on appropriate colors, fabrics, and floral forms;
- Biblical passages, sermon themes, litanies, and prayers;
- Recommendations on choral and instrumental music;
- Specific suggestions for corporate worship activities based upon our experiences;
- And, in some instances, a detailed discussion of one particular worship service.

In the Appendix to this volume, readers will find:

- A collection of orders of worship illustrative of the content and development of worship services discussed in the second section;
- A concise summary of the symbolism of certain colors, flowers, and images in Christian worship.
- A collection of banner designs for all the seasons of the Christian year along with brief notes on the general construction of liturgical banners;
- And a collection of instrumental music for each season of the year.

Our approach to worship represents a synthesis of free church practices and more liturgical forms of worship. We have exercised the freedom of our tradition to incorporate meaningful acts of worship from wherever we have found them. Thus, we have borrowed freely and gratefully from our brothers and sisters in other worship traditions. Consequently, the contents of this volume do not reflect "liturgical purity" when viewed from the perspective of any one particular tradition of worship.

Sources of Materials

Various church groups have produced worship materials that have great value for all Christian congregations. No reason exists to duplicate these resources. God's people do well to share the products of their labor. Wise worship leaders borrow from each other, adapting materials to meet the specific worship needs of their congregations.

This book is intended to serve as a complement to, but in no sense as a substitute for, the innumerable collections of very fine worship materials already in existence. We write with appreciation for and dependence upon worship ideas and practices that have been developed both within and outside our own tradition. To our colleagues in the free church tradition, we enthusiastically commend volumes such as *The Book of Common Prayer* (New York: The Seabury Press, 1977); *Book of Common Worship Daily Prayer* (Louisville, KY: Westminster/John Knox Press, 1993); *Fresh Winds of the Spirit: Liturgical Resources for Year A* by Lavon Bayler, (New York: The Pilgrim Press, 1986); *Whispers of God: Liturgical Resources for Year B* by Lavon Bayler (Cleveland, OH: The Pilgrim Press, 1987); *Refreshing Rains of the Living Word: Liturgical Resources for Year C* by Lavon Bayler (New York: The Pilgrim Press, 1988); *Fresh Winds of the Spirit, Book 2: Liturgical Resources for Year A* by Lavon Bayler (Cleveland, OH: The Pilgrim Press, 1992); *The Minister's Annual Manual for Preaching and Worship Planning* compiled and edited each year by Sharilyn A. Figueroa (St. Paul MN: Logos Productions Inc.); and *Handbook of the Christian Year* by Hoyt L. Hickman, Don E. Saliers, Laurence Hall Stookey, and James F. White (Nashville: Abingdon Press, 1990).

Section two of this book contains suggestions and specific materials for public worship during the major seasons of the Christian year. The writers' development of this material benefitted from recommendations, prayers, and litanies prepared by the following outstanding worship leaders:

❑ Recommendations of Choral Literature

Brazeal Dennard, Artistic Director, Brazeal Dennard Chorale, Detroit, Michigan.

Charles Jones, Retired Professor of Music, Carson Newman College, Jefferson City, Tennessee.

Mark Lawson, Minister of Music, Kirkwood Baptist Church, St. Louis, Missouri.

Donald Neuen, Choral Conducting Chair, Music Department, University of California Los Angeles, Los Angeles, California.

Frederick Swan, Organist-Choirmaster, The Crystal Cathedral, Garden Grove, California.

❑ Recommendations of Congregational Hymns

Harry Eskew, Professor of Music History and Hymnology and Music Librarian, New Orleans Baptist Theological Seminary, New Orleans, Louisiana.

Hugh T. McElrath, Senior Professor of Church Music, The Southern Baptist Theological Seminary, Louisville, Kentucky.

❑ Recommendations of Organ Literature

D. H. Clark, Organist, Northminster Church, Monroe, Louisiana.

James Good, Professor of Church Music, Southeastern Baptist Theological Seminary, Wake Forest, North Carolina.

❑ Recommendations of Piano Literature

Marj Stricklin, Pianist, Northminster Church; Piano Teacher, Principal Double Bass, Monroe, Louisiana.

❑ Recommendations of Other Instrumental Literature

Sherry Dees, Music Faculty, Arkansas State University, Jonesboro, Arkansas.

Collen Dibullion, Principal Viola, Monroe Symphony Orchestra, Monroe, Louisiana.

Roger Dibullion, past Concert Master; Teacher, Strings, Monroe, Louisiana.

Donald Gee, Ouachita High School Band Director; Principal Oboe, Monroe Symphony Orchestra, Monroe, Louisiana.

Marilyn Gibson, Principal Trumpet, Monroe Symphony Orchestra, Monroe, Louisiana.

Gary Greene, Music Faculty, Northeast Louisiana University; Principal Horn, Monroe Symphony Orchestra, Monroe, Louisiana.

Marcie Hall, Harpist, Monroe, Louisiana.

Ildeko Lusk, Music Faculty, Louisiana Tech University, Ruston, Louisiana.

Eugene Steinquest, Music Faculty, Northeast Louisiana University; Principal Flute, Monroe Symphony Orchestra, Monroe, Louisiana.

❑ Recommendations of Homiletical Themes and Sermon Titles

John R. Claypool, Rector, St. Luke's Episcopal Church, Birmingham, Alabama.

James W. Cox, Senior Professor of Christian Preaching, The Southern Baptist Theological Seminary, Louisville, Kentucky.

John Killinger, Distinguished Professor of Religion and Culture, Samford University, Birmingham, Alabama.

Nancy Hastings Sehested, Pastor, Prescott Memorial Baptist Church, Memphis, Tennessee.

William Willimon, Minster to the University and Dean of the Chapel, Duke University, Durham, North Carolina.

❏ Suggestions Regarding Banners

R. Keith Joiner, Free-lance artist; member of Northminster Church, Monroe, Louisiana.
Jan Richardson Stolfi, Free-lance artist; member of Broadway Baptist Church, Fort Worth, Texas.

❏ Prayers and Congregational Litanies

Kathy Manis Findley, Pastor, Providence Baptist Church, Little Rock, Arkansas.
William L. Hendricks, The Southern Baptist Theological Seminary, Louisville, Kentucky.
E. Glenn Hinson, Professor of Spirituality and John Loftis Professor of Church History, Baptist Theological Seminary at Richmond, Richmond, Virginia.
Bill J. Leonard, Chair, Department of Religion and Philosophy, Samford University, Birmingham, Alabama.
F. Robert Otto, Professor Emeritus, Mercer University, Macon, Georgia.
Kate Penfield, Pastor, The First Baptist Church in America, Providence, Rhode Island.
Sharlande Sledge, Associate Pastor, Lake Shore Baptist Church, Waco, Texas.

How to Use This Book

The first section of this book makes an appeal to the involvement of people's senses in Christian worship, provides basic insights into the use of artistic expressions for this purpose, and offers biblical, theological, and philosophical truths supportive of such usage. We encourage readers to interact honestly with the material. Appropriate our ideas as your own when possible. Where you disagree with us, give expression to your own theology and philosophy of worship regarding the inclusion of a variety of art forms in worship.

We encourage you to use the second section of the book as a reference for information, a resource for materials, and a prod for liturgical ideas. Adopt or adapt this material in the manner that will prove most helpful to your worshiping community. You will find personal confessions as well as liturgical suggestions.

Please know that we have no interest in trying to shape a form of worship applicable to every congregation. Honestly, we have enough difficulty trying to be faithful and responsive to the people whom we attempt to lead in worship each week.

We invite you to study the suggestions for worship included in each discussion of a worship season. In every instance, we suggest worship activities that have been tested and found meaningful in the laboratory of our own church. In offering these suggestions, however, our intent is to be provocative, not authoritative or comprehensive. If our ideas do not strike you as helpful, we pray that they will at least serve as a prod to move you in developing ideas of your own.

We write on worship not as experts, but as worship planners and participants always eager to discuss ideas and discover new materials that can enhance the corporate worship of God. Never would we suggest that anyone consider our ideas normative; at best, they are suggestive. Our sole interest in producing this volume is to aid persons who plan worship by encouraging the use of materials that engage the whole congregation and the total personhood of each member in Christian worship.

Christian Worship

A Symphony
for the Senses

A New Way of Thinking

Christian worship is like a symphony. Worshipers employ a variety of media to re-enact the mystery of divine redemption. The metaphor of a symphony, however, brings new meaning and challenges to traditional approaches to Christian worship.

A Helpful Metaphor

A symphony consists of various movements that have themes and subthemes, episodes, and developments. All of them are important. Each movement, however, has its special time and place in the symphonic experience. Before a symphony concludes, all of the major themes in the movements find expression; sometimes in interaction with each other, sometimes as one falls silent in deference to another's emergence, and sometimes as all the instruments boldly speak the main theme in concert. No one idea completely dominates the whole event. A melding of themes is essential to a symphony's success.

The worship of God consists of various movements, themes, subthemes, episodes, and developments, each of which makes a special contribution to God and to the worshipers involved. Praise completely fills some moments in corporate worship: vocal praise, instrumental praise, choral praise, actional praise; disciplined praise, quiet praise, ecstatic praise. Other themes have to wait. God delights in receiving praise; praise that God deserves, and praise that worshipers need to offer. Eventually, praise to God gives way to confessions of personal sins; the mood changes. Penitent sorrow mutes joy as guilt and grief find meaningful expressions. Assurances of divine forgiveness, however, soon ignite thanksgiving and inspire worshipers to make an offering—a commitment of life, a financial gift, or a personal pledge to serve in a specific ministry.

A symphony requires contributions from a variety of orchestral instruments. Because of their genius and skills, both the composer and the conductor of a symphony create unity from diversity and construct harmony out of a variety of distinctive parts. Grand, glorious music fills the air when violins, piccolos, drums, trumpets, cymbals, clarinets, bassoons, flutes, and basses layer their distinctive instrumental sounds around a single chord or musical theme. The majesty of a symphony emerges by employing all kinds of musical instruments to appeal to the ears and the spirits of an audience. The breadth of instrumentation in a symphony guarantees the symphony's appeal to a diverse audience.

Worship, too, is symphonic. The worship of God requires contributions from an endless variety of persons with multiple needs, gifts, interests, and intentions related to worship. God moves among worshipers acknowledging and accepting differences between them. Then, out of the diversity that characterizes the worshipers, God creates unity—a community of worship. Though individual distinctions remain, enhancing the richness of the community and its expressions of worship, unity prevails. Worshipers respond to the holiness of God speaking in one voice and acting as one body. Christian worship is never more glorious than when numerous individuals set aside a pressing need to draw attention to themselves in order to unite in praising God.

Consider the nature of an individual worshiper. Most participants in worship possess five senses—five instruments with which to make an offering to God and five receivers to which the worship of God can (and should) appeal. Corporate worship among Christians ascends to its greatest heights when it invites a variety of instruments into its work and appeals to the multiple sensory dimensions of every person involved in its presentation.

Each of an individual's five senses has the potential to serve God as an influential instrument of worship. Reciprocally, meaningful corporate worship appeals to all five of the senses of humankind. Involving the whole person in worship pleases God and fosters greater spiritual maturity among the worshipers. Sensitive experiences of divine worship often evoke a spirited response from dimensions of an individual's life long considered dead to any possibility of serving God.

Consider details of the symphony metaphor that we find helpful when discussing, planning, and participating in worship.

Symphony	Worship
Composer/Conductor	God
Players/Instruments	Every dimension of the person in worship
Score	The order of worship developed on the basis of a biblical understanding of the components of corporate worship
Themes/Developments/ Variations/Episodes	Adoration, praise, confession, repentance, communion, God's word, offerings, commitment, and proclamation through a variety of media
Audience	God

Like any metaphor, this one fails at points. Press it too tightly and its usefulness diminishes. View it instructively, though, and both the meaning and challenges of Christian worship can be better understood.

Guidance from the symphony metaphor brings consistency to planners of worship. As "symphony conductors," worship planners build services in which numerous diverse individuals can be holistically involved in worship. Emphasis falls on cooperation. Efforts aim at establishing unity throughout the entire worshiping community.

Unity and Purpose in Worship

Viewing worship as a symphony grows out of our theology. Both the nature of God and the responsibility of Christian worshipers, biblically defined, suggest the symphony metaphor. Diversity is appreciated, but unity prevails.

Planners of corporate worship have no obligation to prepare a liturgical smorgasbord offering a variety of musical styles, entertainment, and biblical-theological themes from which people can choose favorites. Neither is pasting together a shabby liturgical collage a good idea. Worship planners need not attempt appeals to radically diverse personal tastes or try to incorporate disparate theological emphases in a service. Meaningful worship requires unity.

Every element of a worship service should contribute to the purpose of worship. No material should be included in a service just for the sake of entertainment or doing something different. Think how a symphony would sound if each of its instrumentalists played at will, if the movements of the musical work had no order, and if dozens of themes vied for attention. The discord, confusion, and chaos sure to develop would negate any possibility of enjoyment or benefit among either the performers or the audience. Likewise in corporate Christian worship, all participants must give themselves to the high purpose of addressing God with dignity, cooperation, and a sense of community.

No one service of worship can accomplish everything that needs to be done spiritually. Neither can a single symphonic score incorporate every potentially important contributor musically. In each instance, the purpose of the specific event should govern its components.

In service to the purpose of a particular symphony, brass players in the orchestra may have to mute their horns so as not to overpower the quiet, but crucial, hum of the strings. Similarly, an experience of worship during Lent often requires lowering a voice, hushing an organ, and quieting the colors in a banner in order to touch worshipers with the somber truths that prompt a confession of sins, a request for forgiveness, and a release of guilt.

Attempts to offer something for everybody in every service usually result in experiences that include little—if anything—to substantively help anybody. A purposeful approach to worship presses for a *raison d' etre* for every element in each service. No word or act belongs in worship simply because it has always been there or someone expects it. Does the material contribute to the meaning of this experience by enhancing the worship of God? Does the piece belong in this symphony? These questions point to the most fundamental issue.

Our approach to worship creates a potential for change and innovation. Worship planners repeatedly raise the question, "What is the best possible way to accomplish this particular act of worship in this specific service?" A flute cannot substitute for a bass horn if a symphony score calls for a strong, low-pitched sound. A casually spoken call to worship cannot suffice for the beauty of a choral summons to praise if a particular worship service needs to begin with a sense of majesty.

Can a dramatic monologue based upon a biblical parable contribute to a congregation's worship of God as effectively as a spoken sermon or a choral meditation? Can a kettle drum establish a symphonic theme with the same appeal as a quartet of clarinets? Correct answers to these questions depend entirely upon the purpose at stake in a specific experience—the purpose of a particular symphony, the aim of the worship service for next Sunday.

A symphony reaches its fullest potential when as many instruments as possible contribute to it. So does worship. Sometimes a sermon carries the theme of a worship service like no other component in the experience. At other times, the primary instrument of worship may be a dramatic reading, a dance, a banner, or an antiphonal presentation by a choir.

Perhaps, this unifying, purpose-oriented approach to worship sounds strange at first. Worship as a symphony? A new way of thinking may be required. The meaningful celebrations of worship that result from purposeful planning will more than compensate for any anxiety raised by entertaining new thoughts. Approaching worship with specific themes in mind result in greater communion among the worshipers and a more understandable encounter with divine revelation. Seeking to appeal to all of an individual's senses in worship as well as to involve all the members of a congregation in worship lead to the discovery of new forms of worship. With God's help, giving structure to new insights into worship can take congregational experiences of worship to previously unscaled heights of spiritual significance and commitment.

Sensuous Worship

A call to worship God constitutes a holistic as well as a holy summons. The call requests every person present to engage in worship. What is more, each sense possessed by a person is a potential medium of worship. The incorporation of all of a person's senses in worship is integral to a fulfilling experience of worship.

Rational and emotional dimensions of people's lives routinely receive attention in worship planning: Does the hymn tune convey *joy* appropriate to the fourth Sunday of Advent? Will the service be *uplifting*? Does the sermon for the day challenge shabby *thinking* about the presence of suffering in Christians' lives? Persons, however, consist of more than minds and emotions. We are holistic, sensual beings—individuals possessing senses—who value sensuous communication.

Holistic worship, then, involves worshipers' senses even as it does their intellects and feelings. Human senses serve both to transmit expressions of worship and to receive the benefits inherent in a worshipful encounter with God. Because authentic worship involves the total personhood of ever worshiper, sensual worship claims an importance equivalent to that of rational worship and emotional worship.

Sensuality and Spirituality

Sensuality affects spirituality long before most people become aware of its influence. Sam Keen points out that discrimination and judgment reside in people's eyes long before they are associated with the intellect. Likewise, the nose and ear pick up on differences between good and evil prior to the moral tutoring of a conscience. Even young children taste the world and find it pleasing or spit it out like milk that has soured.[1]

Meaningful experiences of worship require opportunities for the sensual involvement of worshipers. Anticipating the development of such a service requires asking several important questions:

- How will this experience make people *feel*?
- Will this order of service cause worshipers to *think*?
- What will worshipers *see* in this service?
- What will worshipers *hear*?
- What sensations of *taste* and *scent* will be present?
- Will worshipers be able to sense the holy by their *touch*?

Some people fear any mention of sensuality in discussions of spirituality. Such folks typically reflect a cultural short-sightedness that equates sensuality exclusively with sexuality. Thus, they argue against sensual considerations in Christian worship. The Christian community, however, finds no biblical or theological support for excluding issues of sensuality from discussions of Christian worship. The God revealed in Jesus Christ appeals to people's senses and delights in sensual offerings from each worshiper.

Separating the senses from worship results in a commitment to disembodied Christianity—an oxymoron philologically and a radical form of heresy theologically. Amorphous, abstract religion makes virtually no contribution in a world of embodiment. In fact, religions that disdain the senses tend to focus so intently on another world that they have no time or concern for the problems and needs of people in this world. Religious leaders who only value a person's soul generally have no help to offer people when social-physical issues so torment their bodies that thoughts about matters of the spirit appear either as a luxury or an impossibility.

Christianity respects the human body as a site of revelation from God and as a medium for communion with God. A fleshed-out faith stands at the epicenter of Christianity—"the Word became flesh" in Christ (John 1:14). The New Testament writer named John described the Christian revelation sensually: "That which was from the beginning, which we have *heard*, which we have *seen* with our eyes, which we have *looked upon* and *touched* with our hands, concerning the word of life" (1 John 1:1). Revelation!

Attempts to separate body and spirit in worship represent an ancient Gnostic distrust of the physical. Christianity celebrates the whole person and invites communion with God on the part of the whole person. We respond to what happens around us by what goes on inside us. Conversely what develops within our senses finds its way into our actions. Little wonder that primitives often expressed their faith through emotional dances rather than declared their beliefs through rational confessions. For the same reason, some moderns find that feeding a hungry person conveys their commitment to Christ more than ascribing to a creed.

Sam Keen raises a question that rightfully should be answered every time we gather to worship God. A disillusioned quest for an exalted God brought Keen into contact with a fundamental inquiry involving the senses: "Can my eyes see, my ears hear, my nose smell, my tongue taste, and my skin feel the sacred?"[2]

Yes! Christianity responds affirmatively to Keen's question. We can experience God with and through our senses. Moreover, biblically based worship consistently demonstrates this truth, involving all of a person's senses in each encounter with God. Sight, sound, taste, touch, and smell are precious gifts from God; these senses enhance life and properly serve as media for expressing worship to God.

Take a look at a typical order of worship for your congregation and ask Keen's question about the senses: What is here that invites and enables worshipers to use their senses of sight, hearing, taste, touch, and smell in their encounter with God?

Seeing the dramatic dispersal of darkness by a single flickering flame on a candle increases our heart rate as we ponder the birth of the Light of the world. *Touching* a piece of fine fabric prompts thoughts of the robe of Jesus and a vision of what happened to his robe as well as to him at a place called Calvary. *Tasting* a crusty fragment of unleavened bread sends the memories of our souls racing back to an upper room and inspires thanksgiving for a grace-full redemption. *Sniffing* a scent of precious perfume creates a sensation of our presence at the anointing of Christ and raises a question about the extravagance of our love for him. *Hearing* a long blast from a shofar fills our beings with images of the Day of Atonement and bends our spirits to express reverent devotion to the one who is our peace.

$\mathcal{S}cent$ . . . .

Nothing is more memorable than a smell. Scent, however, is the most neglected sense in most worship services. Smelling an odor triggers memory and prompts thought: "We think because we smelled."[3] Scents rouse us, pamper us, and warn us. They lure us into temptation, steep us in luxury, and fan our religious fervor.

Speaking of smells requires metaphors. Scents almost defy descriptions, especially to someone who has never experienced them. They are virtually impossible to name. At best we can speak of the effects of a smell—revolting, intoxicating, inviting, pleasing —or compare a smell to something else.

❏ What Does Worship Smell Like?

A variety of answers to that question emerges as different persons reach deeply into their religious experiences. Worship smells like a musty room (not necessarily a cathedral), new carpet, burning candles, a mixture of perfumes and colognes, or the fabric of a new garment. Other scents that come to mind depend on a person's associations between worship and scents experienced in places of worship, odors exuded by other worshipers, and smells related to the clothes that person customarily has worn to worship.

When measured only by an individual's scent associations, all experiences of worship may smell the same. A place of worship and familiar colleagues in worship define the nature of that scent. A broader exposure to worship—especially involvement in worship services planned with sensitivity to scents—produces an awareness of the glorious variety of odors in the worship tradition of the church.

❏ Not All Seasons of Worship Smell Alike

Consider how the season of Advent surrounds worshipers with the scents of freshly cut evergreens and lighted candles of hope. Christmas assaults the nose with the smell of the clean, soft skin of a newborn baby—the scent of new life. With the arrival of Epiphany comes odors from the East, like incense. Lifting through Lent is the smell of waste and the residue of repentance, especially ashes. Holy Week harbors scents of a rotten religion and a soured faith as well as fatigue, sweat, suffering, and death. In sharp contrast, Easter brings a smell of freshness and celebrates the scents of spring flowers, budding trees, and new grass. Pentecost exudes the innumerable aromas of a cosmopolitan marketplace; not odors repulsively vying with each other in conflict but odors wafting about in a pleasant, complementary peace.

Several writers of scripture suggest that *sanctity has a scent*. The author of Genesis describes God's pleasure over the smell of Noah's sacrifice (Gen 8:21). Conversely, Isaiah warns of the stench that accompanies the arrival of the Day of the Lord (3:24). Paul writes of a "sweet smelling" offering to God (Phil 4:18) and calls Christ a "fragrant offering" (Eph 5:2). In the Apocalypse, the writer refers to bowls of incense as prayers of the saints (Rev 5:8).

Poets like Kipling and Milton embraced similar ideas. Kipling declared that "smells are surer than sights and sounds to make your heart-strings crack."[4] Milton distinguished between odors that please God and scents that must come from Satan.

Worship planners rightly inquire: What scents should we provide as worship aids to the congregation and what scents should we place before God in (or as) worship in this particular service? Both theology and psychology play a role in answering that question; scents directly effect people's emotions. Real estate agents instruct clients seeking to sell a house to be sure that pleasant scents prevail when potential buyers come to their house to visit. Aromas either attract or repel. Scientists have documented how the smell of spiced apples actually reduces panic and lowers blood pressure levels raised by stress. By way of contrast, think of people's biological and emotional reactions to the odor of a rotten egg or an acrid acid.

How do scents in a worship center impact those who gather there? Do noticeable scents help or hinder experiences of worship? Are the scents pleasing or displeasing to God? Remember that the first gift placed before the Christ child was a scent offering—frankincense!

❧ . . . . *Touch*

Touch is the most urgent as well as the first developed and longest lasting of the senses. To lose touch is to feel apart from everything and everybody, a prelude to death. A complete loss of touch produces brain damage.[5] To know touch is to realize life and love. Babies who receive regular massages gain weight fifty percent faster than babies who receive no massages.[6]

The Old Testament assigns spiritual significance to the sense of touch, warning people what they should not touch if they intend to obey God. Conversely, in the New Testament, Jesus invites people to touch him and thereby discover his holy nature. Touch was the sense that led the disciple named Thomas to a splendid confession of faith in Christ following the resurrection. Touch was a medium of revelation for the author of 1 John who described the "word of life" as one "touched with our hands" (1 John 1:1).

During the ministry of Jesus, many people in the crowds wanted to touch him. One lady, in particular, found healing by touching the garments of Jesus (Mark 5:28). Other people, like a blind man at Bethsaida, wanted to be touched by Jesus, believing that his touch would bring wholeness to diseased and dysfunctional parts of their bodies (Mark 8:22).

Students of the senses tell us that touch is "ten times stronger than verbal or emotional contact."[7] A person's very first experience of emotional touching makes a life-long impression. A loving touch instills a memory of selfless love. Conversely a touch that conveys hostility, anger, and hatred instills durable dread, fear, and distrust.

How can a sense of such spiritual significance be neglected in the corporate worship of God? Historically, the sense of touch has not been neglected. Early Christians embraced each other lovingly and often greeted each other with a kiss of peace. When the early church gathered to set apart someone for special service, members of the congregation laid their hands on this person as a symbol of affirmation, support, and encouragement.

Among the reasons that baptism and communion have such an enduring impact on people is the importance that they place on touch. Neither is a spectator experience; both require touching. A new Christian remembers the feel of the water in which she was baptized. A troubled person finds great comfort in touching the loaf that a worship leader extends with the words, "This is the body of Christ."

Each year, one of the Holy Week services in our church focuses major attention on the sense of touch. We request Christians to move to the chancel area of the building where a shell filled with water sets accessible to them. After encouraging the worshipers to remember their baptisms and to rethink the commitment to Christ that they celebrated in the water, we invite every worshiper to touch the water again. Without exception, this is always one of the most moving moments of worship in the course of a year. As individuals file by the shell and touch the water one-by-one, the spiritual impact of the touching is palpable. Smiles appear. Tears flow. Renewal occurs.

Other touches also communicate spiritual truths. During Christmas, the feel of a burial cloth helps us understand the touch of swaddling clothes on the sensitive skin of the newborn Christ child. The touch of a fine fabric during Epiphany informs an idea of the majesty merited by Jesus. Similarly, to touch a splintery wooden cross, a sharp nail, or a prickly limb of thorns on Good Friday drives home the pain of the passion of Jesus as words and sights cannot do.

No substitutes exist for the touch of another person, however. An alarming number of people who attend worship exhibit a starvation for touch whether or not the problem is ever confessed aloud. What a shame it is for these individuals to depart from the intimate fellowship of God's people and not experience the personal touch they so desperately need—whether they receive a handshake, a kiss on the cheek, or a physical embrace.

Sensory experts speak of the use of touch as a substitute for hearing. People know "round" when they see it because they touch "round." What a wonderful thought that people will know love when they see it because they have been touched by love in worship. The same can be said of adoration, awe, and commitment.

Surely an experience of God's presence in worship prompts worshipers to an action akin to that of Mary Magdalene when she

threw her arms around the resurrected Christ to touch his body
and to kiss his feet!

$\mathcal{T}aste$

Virtually everything of importance involves taste. Hosts and host-
esses invariably serve food and drinks at major events. How, then,
can worship ignore tastes?

Jesus described enjoyment of the reign of God in terms of participation in a messianic banquet. He envisioned the reconciliation
of a lost son or daughter as an occasion for feasting on fine food.
Likewise, in one of the New Testament epistles, the author suggested that the kindness of God can be tasted (1 Pet 2:3).

The sense of taste is a test. Tasting serves a person as a trial, a
sampling, which assists the individual in deciding either to accept
or reject what has been tried. Food and drinks used in a celebration include items that have already been tested (tasted) and
found desirable. Multiple spiritual implications derive from this
reality.

Taste does not exist in isolation. Rather, a sense of taste inter-
acts with all the other senses. Sighting a piece of chocolate, for
example, can excite a person's emotions. Tasting the juice of a lem-
on can alter an individual's facial expression and prompt negative
body language. Pleasant tastes tend to calm a person's demeanor.
Bad tastes have directly the opposite effect on people.

Despite the importance of taste, describing a taste to someone
who has never experienced it is almost impossible. Understanding
occurs only when an unfamiliar taste can be associated with a
familiar taste; rhubarb tastes like a strawberry picked before it is
fully ripe. Communication discipline resides at the heart of worship, conveying to God the tastes of adoration and commending
to worshipers tastes that not all have experienced (for example, the
taste of holiness).

Try thinking of taste in a non-traditional manner. You know
how a piece of peppermint candy tastes. Now, try to describe the
taste of the color blue; or the taste of winter; or the taste of faith.

Such an exercise prepares us for heeding the biblical admonition, "taste . . . the Lord" (Ps 34:8).

What does God taste like? Searching for an answer to this question may lead to revisiting specific acts of divine revelation. The Hebrew escapees from Egypt experienced God's presence as manna in the wilderness. Later, God's people knew their Sovereign in the enjoyment of fruit and honey. Jesus spoke of God in relation to bread and fine wine. All of these people gave evidence that the taste of God is good!

Unfortunately, apart from the bread and wine of communion, taste receives little consideration by most planners of Christian worship. Consequently, a major source of interacting with God remains dormant, even lifeless. Since taste is a trial that leads to decisions of acceptance and rejection, taste merits integral involvement in worshipful encounters with God.

Experiences of taste make powerful contributions to corporate experiences of worship. In a vesper service one evening, meditation on God's faithfulness in keeping promises led naturally to each worshiper coming to the communion table to taste bread, milk, and honey. Those taste sensations sent people's thoughts racing back to Israel's entry into the promised land and forward to the day of our realization of God's promises.

Other tastes also can enrich worshipful encounters with God. Tasting bitter herbs facilitates a comprehension of the spirit of the Passover unattainable in another manner. Tasting vinegar shoves into the consciousness of worshipers a new dimension of identification with Christ during his crucifixion. A sip of cool water instills in people the importance of Christ's commission to minister among the thirsty. Sampling a bowl of gruel or bland rice accomplishes the same purpose in relation to persons who are hungry.

Worship planners do well to consider how certain truths impact people's taste buds. The tastes of worship can rightly foster praise for God and nurture a commitment that finds expression in obedience to God.

 *Sound*

Auditory sensations dominate most worship services. In many congregations, speaking and singing are virtually the only means of communication employed by worship leaders. Consequently, perception and interpretation among other worshipers are limited primarily to hearing.

Sounds make significant contributions to our lives. A shrill siren signals a potential danger before the danger can be seen. A campfire becomes more alluring and exciting when it begins to sizzle, hiss, and pop. Sea gulls screaming over the sound of waves crashing against a cliff-lined beach create sensations unprompted by the sight alone. We can never fully know the dynamics of a meeting only by reading minutes of its proceedings.

Without question, hearing is important. An inability to hear can cause a person to lose touch with logic. Sounds give meaning to sights. Some people, such as Helen Keller, even judge hearing to be more important than sight.[8]

❑ Sounds in Worship

Sounds interpret and communicate words. A vast difference exists between reading a word and hearing a word. How a speaker sounds a word provides insight into the intended meaning of the word. Take the non-liturgical term *really*. Seeing the word *really* touches no emotion; hearing it does. Heard as a declaration of agreeable response, *really* means "Yes, I could not agree with you more." Spoken with an inflection signaling interrogation, *really* means "I do not think I agree with you; are you sure?" Heard in a tone of voice that trails off into silence, *really* signals disgust. Spoken as a flat, emotionless comment, *really* indicates a recognition of truth, the way things are. Not to hear how someone says the word *really* prevents an accurate interpretation of what that person means by the word.

One word—the same word—can convey anger, sympathy, resentment, and agreement. How the word is spoken signals its meaning in a specific situation. Imagine the importance of the sounds that contribute to worshipers' understanding of words such as grace, love, commitment, repentance, and God.

The sounds of worship within a congregation reflect that congregation's theology. Listen carefully. How does the word "repent" sound? Does it sound like a joyous invitation to grace spoken with gratitude or like an angry mandate to escape punishment hurled in a threatening tone? And, what about other terms? Do the sounds that accompany commandments suggest loving provisions from God for a more meaningful life or harsh restrictions from God intended to make life less enjoyable?

Repeatedly the Bible calls attention to the importance of people *hearing* God's word. Nowhere is adherence to that instruction more important than in corporate worship. Every reading of God's word should be characterized by meaningful voice inflections and careful verbal articulation aimed at an understandable reception of the passage read.

Worship leaders do well to inquire periodically: What do worshipers conclude about the nature of God and the promises of Christianity on the basis of the sounds heard in our worship experiences? In what tone of voice is the Bible read aloud? Does a discernible note of enthusiasm pervade the congregation's involvement in prayers and hymns? In what sounds can worshipers sense understanding and compassion?

❏ The Sound of Music

Music assaults our emotions like nothing else. Little wonder it is such an important component in corporate worship. Music is a message from the inside, an external medium that enables worshipers to surface internal feelings in public declarations of faith and doubt. Why, music even recreates experiences. The majestic swell of an organ on Easter Sunday suggests the explosion of joy, which rightly greets news of the resurrection of Jesus. A fanfare of trumpets on the fourth Sunday of Advent readies a congregation for the "good news of great joy." At the opposite end of the auditory spectrum, the musicless silence of an Easter Vigil screams hurt, if not death.

Music's value in worship diminishes, however, if it lacks variety. Worship has many moods, each needing a musical medium for honest expression. The exultant hallelujahs sounded in response to a declaration of God's love are inappropriate as accompaniments to painful confessions of sin. A rousing choral anthem should not immediately precede a pastoral sermon planned to motivate quiet meditation. God revealed a desire for a variety of sounds

> Praise the Lord . . . with trumpet sound . . . with lute and harp . . . with timbrel . . . with strings and pipe . . . with sounding cymbals . . . with loud clashing cymbals (Ps 150).

In a moving story about early Anabaptists, Will Campbell perfectly describes the auditory experience to be hoped for in Christian worship. Speaking to Pieter and Goris about their relationship, Campbell has a character named Cecilia declare, "Until we came together we knew the words. Now we know the tune."[9] Yes! Meaningful worship moves people beyond a mere encounter with words and fills the sanctuary of the soul with the symphony of the gospel. Worshipers not only hear terms, they hear music— music that sends them out of worship humming, singing, dancing, and living the rhythms of the gospel.

❏ Seasonal Sounds

Different seasons of worship call forth different sounds. Music during Lent differs dramatically from music during Pentecost. Likewise, to sing about the crucifixion of Christ in the same tones, moods, and rhythms that characterize music related to Christ's birth either causes confusion or raises questions among worshipers. A lack of distinction between musical statements about two such emotionally polar events compromises the integrity of the music and clouds the true nature of the life of Christ. Different musical sounds communicate significant differences between the seasons of worship and, even more importantly, between the distinctive nature of each of the gospel events that gave rise to the seasons.

Sounds other than those created by speaking or singing voices and musical instruments powerfully impact worship. Animal sounds contribute to a service based upon biblical accounts of creation. A long blast from a shofar can enhance worship on the first Sunday of Advent. A worship service commemorating victims of the Holocaust benefits from the recorded sounds of air raid sirens.

God desires to be heard, and God wills to hear from us. The sense of hearing is a crucial medium in the worship of God.

Sight

Seventy percent of our sensory perception comes through our eyes. When we wish to be undisturbed, we close our eyes—as in praying or sleeping. We understand the world primarily through what we see.

For many years social visionaries advocated the concept of an interdependent world. Through both rational and emotional appeals, such persons repeatedly sounded warnings about the dangers of isolationism, the necessity of an international commitment to ecology, and the advisability of political cooperation between governments of the world. People heard the idea, but indicated little interest in a positive response. That changed, however, when astronauts returned from outer space with dramatic pictures of the earthen sphere. Sight accomplished what words could not achieve. One look at the relatively small blue sphere spinning in space—"space ship earth"—drove home the reality of the world as a global village.

Visual images trigger a wide range of sensory responses. For example, seeing a Christmas tree may cause the music of a carol to float through the mind, the flavor of a traditional fruit cake to tempt taste buds, the odor of fresh-cut evergreens to tantalize our sense of smell, and the feel of a prickly piece of holly to tease our sense of touch. No wonder visual images linger in our minds and memories long after a word or phrase has been lost for us.

The Bible certainly values sight. Though warning that nobody could see God and live (Exod 33:20), the scriptures encourage readers to open their eyes (2 Kgs 6:17, 16:20; Job 19:26) and *see* the work of God (Exod 34:10; Ps 66:5). Persons seeking God were told to *look* for God: go to Bethlehem and *see* (Luke 2:15); *see* the Son of Man coming (Matt 16:28); *see* the place where the Lord was laid (Matt 28:6); *see* Jesus in Galilee (Mark 16:7). Various individuals spoke of *seeing God* in the face of a brother, in the flames of a burning bush, in the mist of a hovering cloud, and in the wind that swept a mountain.

Perhaps sight finds its greatest delight in colors. Most individuals identify from 150 to 200 different colors. These colors inform, inspire, excite, soothe, and disturb us, triggering a broad variety of physical and emotional responses. Scientists actually research physical responses to certain colors by measuring the hormonal output of the penial gland and blood enzymes. Color laboratories find that a person's blood pressure, body chemistry, pulse beat, and body temperature reflect reactions to different colors. Experiments demonstrate a difference of five to seven degrees in the subjective feeling of heat or cold between people in a workroom painted blue-green and individuals in one painted red-orange. Blue-green colors slow down circulation while red-orange colors speed up circulation.[10]

Interior designers carefully consider the emotional consequences of various colors as they beautify different spaces. Red stimulates the appetite and makes time seem to move rapidly. Grays foster creativity. Artists find grayed blues ideal for their studios. Yellow is a stimulant that can create anxiety. Green almost always evokes positive responses.

❑ Using Sight in Worship

Sight monopolizes the senses; in life, if not in worship. What a powerful contributor to and participant in worship sight can be, however. Visuals such as floral arrangements, dramatic presentations, paintings, dances, sculptures, photographs, and films can strengthen worship inestimably. Colors carry liturgical significance as well as emotional impact.

The "look" of a place of worship instantly communicates insights into a congregation's view of worship—everything from the architectural design of the room to the cleanliness of the space; the positioning of the pulpit, communion table, and lectern to floral arrangements that are visible; the clothes of worship leaders to banners on display. Visuals present their own declarations of theology, interpretations of scripture, and expressions of congregational priorities.

Disruptions or distractions in worship occur when sights do not complement sounds and other sensual perceptions. When a soloist sings of the crucifixion of Jesus with a huge smile on her face, listeners may well conclude either that the soloist is emotionally out of touch with her music or that the killing of Jesus was really insignificant. When a minister speaks of God's love through a demeanor of anger, people tend to view God negatively. Should a liturgical dancer dress inappropriately, the visual created overwhelms the truth of the message contained in his movements.

Cezanne, the artist, often pondered for hours before putting a stroke on a canvas. He understood the power of a visual, believing that a properly done visual can even cause viewers to sense a particular odor. Cezanne believed that each mark he made on a canvas should "contain the air, the light, the object, the composition, the character, the outline, and the style."[11]

How can the visuals of worship be planned less carefully, or left out of worship thoughtlessly? What people see in worship affects their spiritual gifts to God and their personal spiritual growth as much as what they hear, if not more.

Worship and the Arts

Sensually dead worship, or worship that involves only one of the five senses, communicates untruth about the importance of worship and the nature of God. Worship is a symphony for the senses. Worship services that appeal to all of a person's senses, however, require careful planning and hard work.

Art enters in: all forms of art, every medium of art. What better way to incorporate the senses into worship—both as transmitters and receivers of communion with God—than by means of artistic expressions?

Much of the world's great art grew out of worship and contributed to worship. In the early centuries following Christ's ministry on earth, artists retold the story of salvation and attempted to bring glory to God through almost every artistic medium imaginable—literature, music, tapestry, engravings, movements, sculpture, drama, and images. Images were created on pottery, atop columns, on frameable canvases, across vast expanses of walls and ceilings, and even on such articles as water spouts, sarcophaguses, keys, and coins. The emphasis of art in (or as) worship changed during and after the Protestant Reformation.

Well-meaning but overzealous reformers attempted to correct what they considered abuses of ecclesiastical art in a manner that represented another form of abuse. Warning against idolatry and wary of aesthetics, marauding reformers ruthlessly stripped worship centers of all artistic expressions leaving sanctuaries bare, sterile, and boring. The spoken and sung word ascended to a preeminent position in worship leaving room for little else except in traditions that continued to assign importance to the bread and wine of communion.

At the same time, many artists moved away from the church, freeing themselves from the restraints of ecclesiastical art. Artists began to pursue beauty for the sake of beauty rather than as a means of serving God. Consequently, the seemingly happy, long term marriage between religion and the arts underwent an excruciating divorce, which left both parties in need of the other's company.

Those of us who grew up in the free church tradition—children of "divorced partners"—inherited a well-near paranoid suspicion of the value of artistic expressions in worship. Faithful to the radical components of our reformation heritage, we have continued to block from our worship centers art that enhances the worship of God and strengthens commitment to Christ.

Enough! Reconciliation is in order. The time has long passed for Christians to restore the arts to a position of importance in the church's life and to recover the glory of the arts in Christian worship. The arts contribute to the development of sensual worship like no other phenomena.

Synesthesia and Grace

Diane Ackerman, a skilled student of the senses, finds that senses correspond to each other. A sound can be translated into a smell, a sight into a taste, and a touch into a sound. Mix the senses in each of those phrases in a different manner and the truth of the sentence remains the same. The stimulation of one sense results in the stimulation of one or more other senses as well. Out of this synesthesia (a togetherness of the senses) comes perception.

Ackerman believes that all arts are parallel translations of a singular fundamental mystery.[12] The same can be said of the senses in worship. In an encounter with God, each sense parallels every other sense in expressing the meaning of the experience and perceiving the message of the experience.

A utilization of the senses as media for worship and receptors of worship results in perception among worshipers—insight, encounter, and an experience of the holy. With an interesting choice of words, Ackerman labels perception a "form of grace." Indeed! Perception is absolutely crucial in worship, as is grace. Experiences of grace motivate us to worship God and grace is another name for God.

Notes

[1]Sam Keen, *Hymns to an Unknown God: Awakening the Spirit in Everyday Life* (New York: Bantam Books, 1994) 130.

[2]Ibid., 120.

[3]Diane Ackerman, *A Natural History of the Senses* (New York: Vintage Books, 1990) 20.

[4]Ibid., 11.

[5]Ibid., 76.

[6]Ibid., 73.

[7]Ibid., 77.

[8]Ibid., 191.

[9]Will D. Campbell, *Cecilia's Sin* (Macon GA: Mercer University Press, 1983) 82.

[10]Faber Birren, ed., *The Elements of Color: A Treatise on the Color System of Johannes Itten* based on his book *The Art of Color*, trans., Ernst Van Hagen (New York: Van Nostrand Reinhold, 1970) 45.

[11]Ackerman, 267.

[12]Ibid., 291.

Truth in a Vase

Suppose someone said to you, "As an act of worship, present the truth of the gospel in a memorable manner. Make the truth clear; declare it with beauty and creativity. Do not, however, use the sense of sound." How would you respond? To what medium, or media, would you turn to convey wordless insights into the nature of God and the good news of the gospel?

Flowers offer wonderful possibilities for meeting that challenge. Throughout the history of religious ceremonies, people have used flowers to adorn places of worship. Adornment alone, however, is a much too restrictive use of flowers in worship. Flowers offer worship planners rich resources for conveying insights into the divine nature, expressing praise and adoration to God, encouraging a particular spiritual posture among worshipers, and declaring a variety of biblical truths.

The flowers that cover the earth represent a sacred trust from God. These divine gifts provide worshipers a holy means of responding to God and proclaiming God's word. In our congregation, floral arrangements make an inestimable contribution to services of worship; not as adornments to the worship center but as media of worship.

Guidelines for the Worship Leader as Flower Arranger

Daring creativity benefits any worship leader, especially one who arranges flowers for (and as) worship. Within a church, the task of floral design differs little, if any, from the responsibility for musical leadership or the preparation and delivery of a sermon. Personal gifts serve the cause of divine truth, revealing the face of God to all searching for a holy vision.

Just as a good host refuses to serve a guest the same food each meal, a worshiping congregation avoids setting the same flowers and floral designs before God and parishioners week after week. The challenge to change evokes one's best efforts—the only kind of efforts appropriate in service to God.

Intentions cannot compensate for a lack of skills in liturgical floral artistry. A working knowledge of ecclesiastical traditions and basic principles of floral design are essential. Mastering the fundamental "how to's" of flower arranging must precede creative experimentation and variations on a theme.

❏ Shapes and Theology

Be aware that certain shapes in floral arrangements reflect different aspects of Christian theology. For example, many designers associate an *equilateral triangle* with the Trinity. A *circle* represents the everlasting love of God and the inclusiveness of bonded relationships among God's people. A *vertical* design conveys people's reach toward God.

Sensitivity to small, seemingly insignificant, details regarding shapes in floral arrangements explains the importance of certain traditions within the church. Little wonder that during Advent the church uses a wreath—a circle representative of God's eternal love—to measure time. Floral design communicates the theological truth, important for all seasons, that God's love is never-ending, eternal by nature.

❏ Color and Symbolism

In flower arranging, as in any of the other visual arts, color fulfills a symbolic as well as an aesthetic function in communication. In floral art, however, artists place colors in juxtaposition to each other rather than mixing them together. Thus, an arranger of flowers must understand proper combinations of colors to prevent "holes" in the message—the arrangement—and to assure the achievement of a desired effect.

At least a minimal knowledge of the theories and systems of a color wheel proves beneficial in harmonizing colors. Floral designers, for example, profit from knowing that *yellow* placed deep within an *all white* arrangement brings enough depth to the composition to make the whites in front appear as if light is moving through the piece.

When worship plans call for a flower arrangement to appear from a position of considerable distance from the congregation, a designer needs to know which colors carry best in that particular setting. *Blues* are a waste in such a situation; they cannot speak beyond their position.

How the colored faces of flowers appear is an important concern in expansive settings. Proper placement of flowers' faces provides impressive coverage even when using only a few flowers. For instance, worshipers see altar flowers much better when the flowers are placed on a slight angle with faces leaning toward the nave of a church than when arranged in a rigid vertical design.

Sandra Hynson, the master floral designer at the National Cathedral in Washington, D. C., has devoted much of her life to issues of color and symbolism in floral arrangements. Working in the massive expanse of the cathedral and learning by trial and error, Hynson has found what is and is not effective in liturgical flower designs. Both novices and experienced floral designers can receive invaluable instruction from Hynson's book, *Homage in Flowers*.[1]

☐ Accessibility and Suitability of Flowers

Flower designers work with certain givens. Given the nature of today's flower markets, temperature controlled greenhouses, and rapid means of transportation, almost any flower can be purchased anywhere at any season. You will need, of course, to be willing to pay the price of purchase. I (DN) prefer, however, letting nature decide what flowers are available on a certain occasion. Tulips in the fall are confusing; I do not know whether to think about new birth and spring or the decay and dying of autumn.

The cycle of life exists for good reason. Worshipers should experience, appreciate, and find meaning in what nature provides during every season of the year. To ignore or neglect what surrounds us and gives us life constitutes a dreadful mistake. At any given time of the year, I like to construct my floral arrangements from nature's provisions.

Creativity involves bringing viewers into a close encounter with the most unlikely or even the most obvious. *Garlands of autumn leaves* and *sheaves of grains* or *grasses* convey beauty even as does *a bundle of roses*. Ecclesiastical floral designers do well to bring inside the worship center all the wonderful offerings of nature and allow these gifts from God to enhance people's worship of God.

My principle of using flowers available in nature presents me with problems during Lent. I have to exercise great restraint not to draw from the unbelievably beautiful flowers of spring. I find myself asking, "Who scheduled Lent?" and thinking, "Whoever placed Lent in the middle of spring obviously never consulted gardeners." Another question quickly follows, however: "Is the close proximity of the beauty of spring and the somberness of Lent one part of the lesson to be learned during this season?" Truth dawns. Discipline is one of the major themes of Lent.

❏ Forms of Flowers

Floral arrangers also benefit from a knowledge of the various forms of flowers and how certain combinations of these forms create memorable designs. Basic flower forms include *spike, fillers, rounded, subordinate,* and *dominant*.

Unless a floral designer recognizes that a *delphinium,* a *liatris,* or a *larkspur* is a spike flower, problems will arise when no other flowers are available and an arrangement needs to be rounded with *nosegay shapes.* Efforts to communicate an upward reach to God require more than *gardenias. Heather* makes great filler material for arrangements in large urns, but—apart from innovative mechanics—it cannot be used as an outer-line material. Floral artists need to keep in mind that an *amaryllis bloom* (size) and a *geranium bloom* (color) dominate other flowers in a design. Conversely, *alstroemeria, azaleas,* or *fressia* in single stems become subordinate in larger scaled arrangements.

❏ Texture

Designers of liturgical flower arrangements should know that the texture of a flower determines what that flower communicates visually. The *delicate* nature of a *champagne rose* conveys a completely different message from that presented by the *thickened, faceted* character of the *protea*. In floral art as in all art forms, communicating a specific message—which is usually the intent of a worship leader—requires an artist to select the materials to be used with great care. Otherwise, a single arrangement may have as many different interpretations as there are people who see it.

❏ Containers

A practical but absolutely essential concern in effective floral design is the container used to hold the flowers. Personally, I (DN) use everything from *broken clay pots* to *gilded candelabra, urns of concrete* or *no container* at all. Whatever enhances an arrangement's communication of scripture, elaboration of a theological theme, or application of a teaching point is appropriate to use.

More than good looks must be considered when determining the appropriateness of a container for use in a place of worship. The choice of a container should take into consideration the biblical texts, the lyrics of the music, and the theme of the sermon around which a service has been constructed. For example, be sensitive to how out of place it would be to arrange flowers in a recently inherited *porcelain mantel vase* for a worship service focused on Jesus' instructions about caring for the poor and feeding hungry people. A time may come when this expensive vase will be appropriate for a service.

Floral artists do well to inventory the flower containers available in their church. Knowing what is available prompts learning the mechanics for doing arrangements in these vessels. Artists, however, should never feel limited to the use of traditional *brass vases* found in most church buildings. An unlimited variety of shapes and textures of containers is available to enhance displays of flowers.

In our church, an abiding interest in communicating truth through floral designs has led to collecting a variety of containers. We regularly present flowers in *concrete urns* set on high pedestals. Pedestals can also hold flower trees or topiaries; pottery; earthen jars; glass vases; brass vases; fabric wrapped pots; oversized baskets; fruits and vegetables cut to serve as flower holders; and large floor candelabras adapted to function as holders. Sometimes the nature of a particular worship service dictates that no visible container for flowers be used. When this happens, we arrange flowers in *oasis cages*, which set directly on the top of a surface. These cages can also be chained together for a garland effect or hung as plaques on a wall, the lectern, or the pulpit.

❏ Summing Up

The quickest way to achieve incredible beauty in floral arrangements is to observe fundamental principles of floral design. Become familiar with the principles of line, form, space, pattern, texture, color, scale, proportion, and balance—symmetrical and asymmetrical. Learn the rhythm and movement of floral designs. A basic understanding of a few technicalities frees designers to creatively express sentiments of their souls in floral art.

What about Artificial Flowers?

The psalmist repeatedly called for everything with life and breath to praise God (Ps 150:6). Nowhere in the Psalms, or in any other part of the Bible, do you read about anything artificial voicing praise to God.

A long-standing rule in the local art guilds of Episcopal Churches prohibits the use of artificial flowers within the church building. At one time, I thought the mandate unduly restrictive; I no longer feel this way. A study of the role of flowers in worship and the utilization of flowers as expressions of worship brought me into complete agreement with the Episcopalian principle.

Why should artificial flowers even be considered by a congregation? Budget restrictions are often cited as the reason for using artificial arrangements. A lavishly massed bouquet every Sunday requires heavy financial underwriting. Alternatives exist, however. Nature provides unlimited possibilities. I regularly use weeds, wild grasses, Queen Anne's Lace, quince, and pear blossoms in our worship center. These plants are abundant and inexpensive.

Gardeners in the congregation delight in having the products of their labors used as offerings to God.

Practical Considerations in Floral Designs for Worship Services

- Know the architectural design of the room in which worship occurs, and become familiar with the surfaces with which you must work. Inspiration can be defeated by a lack of knowledge about the worship center and available equipment.

- Know the areas of the worship center where flowers are prohibited. Unnecessary hassle as well as valuable time can be saved by such knowledge. Certain denominations do not allow adornments on specific pieces of furniture that have importance in their services of worship. Prohibitions against floral arrangements in the chancel area of a church building should not defeat a designer. Church buildings provide innumerable locations in which flowers can be displayed for the benefit of worshipers and the glory of God.

- Know whether or not your church follows the calendar of the Christian year. If so, you will need to become familiar with liturgical guidelines related to flowers. Floral arrangements consisting of flowers and colors associated with a season of penance will not contribute to a church's festive celebration of Easter.

- Know which symbols, if any, have been used by the church within the various seasons of the church year. New possibilities abound. Shells can be used in a service of baptism. A fishnet or a ship visually suggests a church's willingness to help people in stormy times of struggle. An anchor expresses steadfast hope. A seven-branched candelabra serves as a symbol of Christ as the light of the world.

Floral Possibilities for the Chancel and Altar of a Church Building

❑ For the Chancel

- Place a floral sermon on the chancel steps.
- Outline architectural features or ecclesiastical furniture (pulpit or lectern) located on the floor of the chancel with garland-like designs.
- Place floral arrangements on pedestals set on the floor level of the nave embracing the chancel.
- Hang plaques of flowers in succession within the nave of the exterior walls.
- Place floral arrangements or towering cathedral trees in urns set atop pedestals located on both sides of the communion table.
- If the communion table sets raised above the level of the nave, construct flower arrangements on the front corners of the table.
- Construct a freestanding shelf unit to stand behind the altar or choir rail, and place flowers there.

❑ For the Altar

- Complement and balance traditional vase arrangements with candlesticks or candelabra.
- Place flowers in low planter boxes that run the length of the rear of the table.
- Use flowers in crescent designs with the bottom of the crescent pointing inward towards the cross on the communion table or reversed with the body of the flowers outlining the cross and the bottom of the crescent pointing beyond the table.

- Arrange flowers in the shape of an "L" or a right triangle without using a vase. The height of the "L" should embrace the sides of the cross, which sets on the communion table.
- Using planter boxes on the communion table and boxes on pedestals beside the table, create a curved garland with flowers. The flow of the flowers can be broken on either side of the cross on the communion table or curve to its lowest points as it passes in front of the cross.
- Copy a National Cathedral design that arranges flowers in a fan shape behind the cross on the communion table, thus highlighting worshipers' focus on the cross.
- Use wire tomato stakes to form beehive or conical-shaped topiaries as a complement to the cross, which sets on the communion table.

Floral Colors as Liturgical Symbols

Over the course of history, certain flower colors have taken on symbolic religious meaning. An awareness of the symbolic significance of these floral hues significantly aids the proclamation of truth through a flower arrangement.

The more common flower colors with special symbolic meaning are the following:

- *Blue* communicates truth and humility. The color is routinely used during the season of Advent.
- *Purple* denotes penance and is used during both Lent and Advent as a visual aid to the prayer and preparation inherent in these seasons.
- *Violet,* also a penance color, bespeaks sorrow, passion, and suffering. The color appears during Advent as well as on Ash Wednesday and Palm Sunday. Some liturgical traditions use violet flowers throughout the season of Lent.
- *Red* represents royalty, fire, and martyrdom. Red flowers are generally associated with Pentecost. Though some traditions never use *orange* flowers on Pentecost, a combination of *red, orange,* and *yellow* flowers creates a breathtaking

floral design of the fire so integral to Pentecost Sunday. Traditions that observe saints days also use red flowers on these occasions.

- *Green* connotes longevity, growth, and eternity. The color is used during the Sundays following Pentecost.
- *Gray* represents mourning or penance, and is a key color for floral arrangements during Lent and Advent.
- *White* communicates purity, faith, and joy. Most all liturgical traditions use white flowers on Christmas Eve, Christmas Day, Epiphany, and Easter. White is also the color for Ascension Sunday, Trinity Sunday, and All Saints Day. Additionally, white flowers are appropriate for funerals, baptisms, ordinations, and weddings.

A Long Personal Pilgrimage and a Weekly Liturgical Task

Countless times in my life I (DN) have entered a worship center for a religious gathering and have been numbed; I sit motionless. I go through all the rituals and litanies, saying the right words but never sensing a revelation of truth. Needing to be in a place where I can wrestle with questions in community, I enter the worship center longing for peace and direction. Words bypass me. Music passes through me. Only the structure of the building gives me a sense of the security of God's loving embrace. My eyes and soul beg for a resting place.

An important truth became clear to me in such a setting. The beauty of an arrangement of flowers embraced by a simple cross on the communion table captured my gaze. I recalled a verse of scripture that I had learned as a child—the New Testament lesson about God's care for the lilies of the field. Looking more intently at the flowers on the altar, I realized that the arrangement did more than adorn the worship center: the flowers visually interpreted the New Testament lesson. What imagination! What creativity! What a gift! What a sermon to me! I then realized that every aspect of worship should have meaning and purpose.

A life-altering experience in worship taught me that sensitively developed floral arrangements become art forms and create lasting impressions with worshipers. I felt called to use my gifts this way. This reality has hounded—and sometimes haunted—me for years.

Being true to my calling, however, has provided me with unbelievable opportunities for conveying gratitude and acknowledgment to the Giver of my gift. Who would have thought of the possibility of flowers becoming more than aesthetical adornments in worship? Then again, who ever would have imagined that a common loaf of bread could represent the body of Christ? Jesus frequently chose the most simple, unlikely objects to reveal the greatest theological truths. As an artist, I never know when God will use one of my floral offerings to provide life-altering inspiration for a struggler who happens into a service of worship, as I did many years ago.

Now each week brings with it an opportunity to incorporate floral designs into the worship of God. On one occasion, the scripture passage for the service related the story of the woman whom Jesus met at a well. I knew the kind of earthen vessel the woman must have been carrying. What struck me most was the brokenness of her being. In the biblical text, the woman appears as a shattered creation unable to hold anything of substance. I immediately thought of pieces of broken pottery and an old broken bird bath, discarded because of their lack of usefulness. Then, I gathered the shattered pieces of pottery and placed them on a palate of sand, which contained wild grasses growing along the base and around the larger broken bird bath. There was the sermon! Earth's gifts served to glorify God.

People who came to the worship service preoccupied with rejection, brokenness, and defeat in their lives could rest their eyes on the overwhelming truth that the great and good God will never let us go or cast us aside because of our fractured condition.

Thanks be to God!

Notes

[1]Sandra Hynson, *Homage in Flowers* (Keedysville MD: Fellfoot Publishers, 1990).

Meaningful Movement

Life without movement; try to imagine it. Gone would be the ability to express in actions profound sentiments. Devoid of freedom to move, we could not nod our heads to acknowledge a friend on the other side of a room; we could not enjoy the intimacy of physical contact with a lover; we could not shake the hand of a new acquaintance to convey our pleasure in meeting him; we could not embrace a family member aching for attention to demonstrate compassion; we could not place our hand on the shoulder of a colleague to comfort her. Deprived of a capacity to move, the blare of emptiness would deafen us. Absence of movement suggests death; movement indicates life.

Questions about movement in worship should be set in that context. Do the movements in a service of worship—or the lack of movements—communicate an encounter with God brimming with life or a spirituality passively yawning on the edge of death?

Movements that enable us to advance, communicate, and enjoy a meaningful existence comprises the journey of life. At birth, we enter the world squirming and kicking. Gestures and actions fill our lives. Every morning we get out of bed to wind our way through a day and enjoy an opportunity for rest in the evening. Our society measures achievement and success by movement—how far up "the ladder" a person has climbed. Movement is such a natural part of our existence that we respond to essential calls for movement almost thoughtlessly, instinctively.

How ironic that movements fill the most important hours of our days with the usual exception of Sunday. Then the singular most important function of our existence as Christians occurs apart from any serious consideration of movement. We bring to worship a suspicion of movement, often questioning the appropriateness of movement in worship.

The Bible speaks repeatedly about the movement of God. In creation, "the spirit of God swept over the face of the waters." Indeed, decisive actions dramatically revealed the God of creation: God "separated the light from the darkness," "made the dome," "made the two great lights," "made the earth and the heavens," "formed man," "breathed . . . the breath of life," "planted a garden," "brought her (a woman) to the man" (Gen 1 and 2).

Likewise, the redeeming nature of God became apparent through the movements of God and the actions of Jesus: God kept promises, demonstrated love to the world, and sent the Messiah; Jesus moved across Galilee, lifted children, healed sick people, washed feet, served a meal, offered himself as a gift, died, and broke the chains of death. Movement!

Movement conveys truths about God in a manner unequaled by words and music. What could be more appropriate for worshiping God and proclaiming the nature of God within worship than purposeful movements?

Liturgical Movement

Even congregations that protest the importance of liturgy engage in liturgical movements when they meet for worship. As soon as a worship leader announces a call to prayer, members of the congregation bow their heads and close their eyes. Liturgical movements! A bowed head symbolizes reverence for God. Eyes closed in prayer represent a desire to focus on God alone. These movements are not mandated by theology. We believe God hears the prayers we offer with our heads turned toward the heavens and our eyes wide open just as readily as those we speak with heads bowed and eyes closed. We bow our heads and close our eyes to pray because we want to convey a spirit of humility and an attitude of devotion as we approach God in prayer. Movement communicates meaning.

Standing to sing a hymn constitutes another form of liturgical movement. Obviously, we can sing while seated. Standing, however, makes a statement and is a symbolic gesture. When we stand to sing before God, we demonstrate a desire to extend our beings to their utmost limits for the glory of God and a commitment to devote the entirety of ourselves to praising God.

Liturgical movements can be found in virtually every congregation of worshipers. Reflection on these common movements in worship can open the door to new forms of movement in worship, movements equally meaningful in our relationship with God. Over time, newer liturgical movements in worship occur as easily and naturally as bowing to pray or standing to sing.

❑ The Body

The Bible refers to people committed to the lordship of Christ as the body—*the body of Christ* (1 Cor 12:27). How incredulous is the thought of that body without movement! In reality, the true identity of God's people comes to light as a result of their activity: caring for the sick, making peace, preaching the gospel, welcoming strangers, loving outcasts, comforting the grieving, eradicating prejudices, and extending grace. Surely the worship practices of this body should reflect the same dynamism in movements that characterizes its redemptive presence in the world.

Liturgical movements can express and interpret the worshipers' relationship to Jesus Christ. Embracing the age-old stories of faith and seeking to share the message of redemption with others, Christians search for actions that bridge the distance between then and now and move seekers-of-faith across that bridge. Worshipers, therefore, stretch upward, bow low, kneel, and reach outward; stand to sing, sit up to listen, and bend over to pray; shake hands to extend fellowship, embrace to convey compassion, and lay hands on a person's head to commission the individual for service. Through such movements, worshipers point to the revealed truth that makes them one body.

Individuals seeking a relationship with Christ and fellowship within a church look for a body that moves. No one wants to become a part of a stagnant, rigid, or inflexible family of faith. Worship experiences should at least hint at the major movements that characterize the message and mission of the church. The absence of such movement within a church risks observers concluding that the church is lifeless.

❑ A Model

As we plan for worship each week at Northminster, we seek to assure meaningful movements throughout the service—movements of sounds, sights, and people.

In a typical worship service in our congregation, worship begins with the sound of the organ or the piano (or both) coming from the *front* of the sanctuary. The next sound, however, comes from the opposite direction. The choir makes its first musical contribution to worship from the *distant narthex*. Caught *between* these two sounds, members of the congregation are called to worship. Their senses are set on edge by anticipation of a wonderful experience in which the Spirit of God arrives from *all directions* to assure God's presence where ever they may be on their spiritual journeys.

From the lectern, a layperson from the congregation speaks either a reenforcing invitation to worship or a summons to praise; sound comes again from the *front* of the sanctuary. Usually the choir responds from the *back* of the sanctuary, no longer in the distant narthex. These movements of sound at the beginning of worship dramatize the possibility of all people, regardless of where they come from and the spiritual condition of their lives, moving into the worship of God.

After a prayer of adoration and praise, which may occur either from behind or in front of the congregation, the choir offers a festive choral expression from the back of the sanctuary, sensitizing all present to the nearness of God. The organ, located at the *front* of the sanctuary, takes up the sound from the choir and swells into a majestic introduction to the processional hymn. During the processional hymn of praise the choir and ministers *move forward*, directing worshipers' attention to the chancel from which the next sounds of worship will emanate.

Our worship center was constructed with a divided chancel. Each reading from the Bible takes place at the lectern, which stands on the *right side* of the chancel. Usually the choir, which is positioned behind the pulpit on the *left side* of the chancel, responds to the reading of each text. Often the choir offers a meditation that moves worshipers from the Old Testament lesson to the New Testament lesson. Regardless of how it is done, a conscious, deliberate movement, takes place.

On many occasions the reader of the gospel stands in the center aisle in the *middle* of the sanctuary, to dramatize God's word in our midst. Members of the congregation stand for this reading, which concludes with the reader declaring, "The holy gospel of our Lord Jesus Christ" and the congregation responding, "Praise be to thee, O Christ." The movement of sounds dramatizes the ongoing dialogue between God's word and our words.

If a worship service contains a pastoral prayer, a minister makes that offering on behalf of the people from the *pulpit*. If the morning prayer is a "prayer of the people," a member of the congregation usually speaks that prayer from the *lectern*.

Proclamation begins with a musical expression from the *choir*. The pastor continues the preaching event from the pulpit. Following the sermon, focus is placed on the communion table, which stands at the *back center* of the chancel. The worship leaders responsible for serving communion in the service walk to the communion table, break the bread and pour wine into the cup, take the elements of the Lord's meal from the communion table, and move down the steps of the chancel to stand *in front* of the congregation. The movement of the worship leaders symbolizes God's humble movement toward us in the coming of Christ. Members of the congregation *move forward* to receive the broken bread and to drink from the cup. Each worshiper's movement signals a willingness to accept God's gift. Communion concludes with the unconsumed bread and wine returned to the Lord's table.

Worship moves toward its conclusion as the pastor, often standing at the *front* of the chancel, extends an invitation to discipleship or to church membership. Then, the pastor speaks a commission and reminds all present that the children of God are called not to remain in the safe confines of a sanctuary but to *move into the world* to share acts of love.

The choir's recessional directs people's thoughts back to the different worlds in which we live, work, and play. A spoken prayer of benediction comes from the *back center* aisle. The sounds of worship are now leaving the room and drawing the worshipers out with them. Finally, the choir sings a musical benediction from the narthex, once again *distantly removed* from the people. The brief musical expression, therefore, ends a memorable cycle of movement and concludes worship.

The cycle of movement in our worship services reflects the rhythmical movement that constitutes the life of our church. Our fellowship constantly moves into and out of worship—into the sanctuary for experiences of corporate worship and into the world for ministries to people in need. This congregational movement is inspired by the Spirit of God who constantly moves among us. To all who observe us, our movement bears witness that we are not dead but alive, vibrantly alive as the breathing, moving, serving, worshiping people of God.

Responding to the Lord of the Dance

"Let's include a dance in the service for the first Sunday of Advent this year." We were planning worship and I (WG) heard Don speaking. The word *dance* sent my thoughts sprinting into a time in my ecclesiastical past when dance was considered a bad word and dancing a morally questionable activity. Then, I filtered through what I knew about the potential value of dance in worship. Don's suggestion led to a service that opened with a dancer studiedly, slowly, beautifully, and gracefully removing a thin purple veil from the communion table. Through movement, the dancer invited worshipers to enter into the mystery that gives meaning to the season of Advent and the celebration of Christmas.

Innumerable people evidence a reticence to include dance in the worship of the church. Not so long ago, proposals of incorporating drama and congregational singing into worship received a similar response. Many of our negative prejudices toward new forms of worship generally, and movement in worship specifically, spring from the continuing influence of old taboos left unchallenged by the insights of biblical literature, theological truth, and the reality of what God can do with movements to proclaim the gospel of Christ. God can reveal the Word through flesh again and again if the church allows God's Spirit to move freely and creatively through its people.

Old Testament writers recognized the spiritual value of expressing feelings and thoughts in a patterned, rhythmical manner. They called for dancing in worship. Addressing the assembly of the faithful regarding the praise of God, the psalmist wrote: "Let them praise his (God's) name with dancing" (Ps 149:3) and "Praise him (God) with tambourine and dance" (Ps 150:2).

We have evidence that in earlier times the people of God danced their faith. Certainly King David engaged in such a dance according to 1 Samuel 29:5 and 2 Samuel 6:14. So did a prophetess named Miriam, who led a whole group of women to dance for the glory of God (Exod 15:20).

Though the New Testament contains no specific appeals for dancing, numerous texts imply the appropriateness of dance as a form of worship. Jesus apparently recognized dance as a normal means of expressing joy: "We played the flute for you and you did not dance" (Matt 11:17), he said on one occasion. In one of his most beloved parables, Jesus specifically referred to dancing as a natural response to the recovery of a son who had been lost. Faithful to such thought, the apostle Paul insisted on people recognizing the body as a temple of the Holy Spirit (1 Cor 6:19-20), thus viewing the human body as an instrument for glorifying God.

Conscientious worshipers seek signs and symbolic acts with which to convey their belief in God, love for God, penitence before God, and will to serve God. Dance provides a wonderful option. Dance can be a total mind-body-spirit expression of the worth of God and the worshiper's obedience to God. When offered to God as an act of worship, dance becomes a form of prayer as well as proclamation.

I (DN) remember well my first serious consideration of including dance in a service of corporate worship. A young dance instructor in the community came to our church building to attend a civic meeting. After we met, I inquired about her interest in dance and its acceptance in our community. I marveled at the opportunities she had to use her talent in the community, but felt for her as she described her inability to use these God-given skills within her home church. She described her frustration and longing for opportunities to offer her artistic gift in worship. Humbly, yet confidently, the woman shared with me, "Within my heart, I know that God has given these talents to me and I know the potential of their offerings. Someday, someone will come along and dare to risk having me offer my talent to God in worship."

The conversation with the talented woman altered my perspective on the use of dance in worship, and has led me to incorporate the movements of many skilled dancers into public services of worship. Invariably, the talent of these people serves as a powerful medium for communicating the gospel and praising God.

One experience, in particular, stands out in my mind. When asked to plan a worship service for a national convocation of religious leaders, I wanted the congregation to take communion. Like many worship leaders, I wrestled with how to make communion meaningful among people for whom the "breaking of bread" was a frequent experience. Finally, I decided that music-accompanied dance offered the best resolution for this dilemma.

In the second movement of John Rutter's *Gloria*, the composer provides a holy moment. Transcendent sounds prevail. Our choir sang this part of the Rutter piece while a friend of ours—a graduate of the Tisk School of Dance in New York—removed the covering from the communion table in reverent dance. Two art forms merged and the truth of the table became clear. Reverence gave way to assurance as members of the congregation focused on the symbols of hope and security made available for all who would partake.

Dance, however, will not contribute to the holiness of an experience if the dancer distracts from a focus on transcendence among the worshipers. The dancer must be skilled in abilities to move in a manner sensitive to the nature of worship. At the convocation, the intent behind the worship service was a meaningful experience of communion, not an impressive performance of dance. The goal was accomplished. Those who participated in the service often recall the grace of revelation received through communion; dance and music served God in worship.

Intentional movement gives wings and windows to messages for the soul like no other expression. The artistry of a human body can open worshipers' eyes to a world and a relationship in a manner unapproachable by verbal expression alone.

Evaluating Movement and Other Art Forms in Worship

Certain forms of movement in worship raise questions in some people's minds and stir controversy in others. For that reason, we want to be very clear about our suggestions for expanding worship-related movements beyond traditional ones.

The focus of worship is God. All that takes place in worship should aid that focus and bring God glory. No movement—more generally, no art form—belongs in worship unless it reflects the face of God. We have all witnessed elements of worship that did not belong in a service oriented to God. In a self-gratifying manner, these acts tend to draw attention to the personalities involved or their accomplishments. Such actions can be highly effective in a recital hall but they do not belong in a service of worship.

Secular art forms—rhythmic movement, rhetoric, or music—do not become holy simply because they are carried into a sanctuary. Insensitivity at this point has prompted a major suspicion regarding the place of the arts in worship. The artist whose work is incorporated into worship must understand the nature and purpose of worship and the role of the art form in worship. The most effective liturgical dancers, for example, are people who have a personal relationship with the God whose nature they hope to reveal.

Movement in worship, like so many other art forms, begins with high, holy intentions. Over the years, however, misuse and abuse destroyed people's confidence that these media could be used for the glory of God. Unfortunately, many worship leaders found removing these art forms from worship to be easier than correcting their perversions. As a result, many congregations have been denied an opportunity to experience expressions of worship that make the body—as well as the mind and emotions—an instrument of worship. The time has come for change.

We enthusiastically commend to you the importance of intentional movement in corporate worship. Purposeful movements among a worshiping congregation can bring unparalleled excitement and exhilaration to people. A variety of liturgical movements that help worshipers discover God and worship God with the entirety of their beings, contributes inestimably to worship as a symphony for the senses.

Christian Worship

Resources
for the Church Year

ADVENT

Advent: A Season of Waiting

Waiting . . . looking back over our shoulders . . . and waiting . . . peering as far into the future as possible . . . and waiting. The Christian year begins with waiting; waiting in darkness, waiting for light to break, and waiting for the birth of Christ.

Advent waiting is not a passive, twiddle-your-thumbs, sleepily yawning kind of waiting. The waiting appropriate for the beginning of the Christian year is an active, eyes-wide-open, alert, standing-on-tiptoes kind of waiting. The year-long pilgrimage of Christians' worship of God begins not with the kind of fretful, fearful waiting associated with standing alone in a graveyard, but with the kind of hopeful anticipatory waiting prompted by a visit to a nursery. An active memory stirs expectation.

History

Advent, a word that means "coming" or "arrival," began at the initiative of Christian missionaries surrounded by persons devoted to annual observances of pagan festivals. True to the tradition of the early church, Christians living amid non-Christian celebrations sought to adopt secular symbols for Christian purposes. Followers of Christ seized for Christian purposes the images of light and emphases on life in a new year, which were important to the winter solstice festivals held among fourth-century Germanic tribes. The church spoke of Christ as the light of the world and the source of life. Excesses in the pagan celebrations, however, overshadowed Christian emphases. Subsequently, Christians set aside a specific period for preparing to celebrate the birth of Christ.

The first celebrants of Advent patterned the season after Lent and organized it around the six Sundays prior to Christmas. In the late sixth century, church officials in Rome reduced the number of Sundays in Advent to four. Eastern Christians do not follow the Advent worship tradition of the Western church.

Many contemporary observances of Advent devote each of the four Sundays of the season to a special theme: hope, peace, joy, and love (in that order).

Sensations ....

Advent causes believers to stand on the tiptoes of their souls, intently peering into an increasingly illuminated horizon to catch a glimpse of how God is coming among them again. Advent may prompt us to rub our eyes as we seek to adjust to darkness being dispelled by light; to rethink predictability as we observe the surprising movements of God; to set aside despair as we discover the reality of hope; to recover the worth of a promise as we find God faithfully fulfilling divine promises of the past; and to ready our spirits for a life-transforming encounter with love.

Traditionally, two major themes serve as the threads running through all observances of Advent—*preparation for the celebration of Christ's birth* and *preparation for the second coming of Christ*. Each of these emphases, however, prompts other significant themes—subthemes, perhaps—such as: the importance of a forerunner like John the Baptist; the role of Israel in the fulfillment of God's promise of salvation through the Messiah; God's regular appearances in our lives through scripture and communion; the end of an age; the beginning of a new age; repentance; the labor of birthing; the primacy of apocalypse. Behind all the themes of Advent stands the gracious nature of God, which inspires daily living characterized by gratitude in relation to the past, hope regarding the future, and faithful grace in the present.

An often neglected dimension of Advent is actually more tangible and obvious than the more popular themes. We refer to the *coming of Christ into the world in which we live*. Frankly, many congregations fear this emphasis because it defies structure and maximizes freedom. Many worship leaders find it safer to remember Christ's coming in the past or to anticipate Christ's coming in the future rather than greet Christ in the present.

Advent prepares us to meet Immanuel—God with us—*today*. When we look at Christ as one who impacts our lives in the present, Advent takes on an importance that moves us far beyond getting ready for a season. The real issue of Advent is who each of us is as a person—a person ready or unready to allow Christ to be born in us.

❑ Colors

The colors of Advent convey inbreaking light. A deep *blue* or *purple* best reflects the somber, penitent nature with which worshipers begin a pilgrimage toward Christmas. Those colors, however, change week by week.

By the second Sunday in Advent, the primary color of blue should be combined with the other primary color of *red* to produce a beautiful *purple*. As *white* joins the colors of the season in week three of Advent, a *rose* color emerges. The addition of more white in week four produces a *pink*, which serves as a prelude to the burst of total white on Christmas Day.

However colors are used in Advent worship, they should assist worshipers in moving through the various emphases of the season and opening the totality of their lives to the coming of light—the Christlight.

❑ Flowers

Advent begins with a *bare* branched tree exposing only one *green* blade of new growth at its base. The sight screams prophecy—promises of the first advent of Christ, and more. One look and worshipers receive assurance that amid the barrenness of our lives God provides at least a hint of renewal and new life. Hope stirs. The message of the entire season of Advent unfolds around the bare branched tree.

Using a common base for the floral arrangements of Advent enables an easy dramatization of the pace of the season and the distinguishing characteristics of each Sunday. Worshipers readily identify with the obvious continuity before them as well as recognize the unfolding beauty that characterizes a pilgrimage to Christmas.

During a recent Advent service, worshipers in the congregation were led through a series of floral compositions using this approach. The basic design consisted of four bare *tree stumps* about four and one-half inches high. The tree stumps were secured in four garden urns that had been placed at the four corners of the altar. The urns were weighted with bricks for security and disguised with sheet *moss*. Each Sunday of the season the appearance of the trees changed to reflect the emphasis of the day.

On the Sunday of hope, a variety of *budding bulbs* appeared at the base of each barren tree, creating a sharp contrast between the starkness of the dead branches and the promise of the bulbs. Clippings of fresh *curly willow* were wrapped around one or two of the tree branches also signaling the hope of new life. These floral pieces pulled the vision of the worshipers upward, away from the base of the tree.

On the Sunday of peace, *liatris* and *sego palms* were used to create abstract suggestions of winged creatures within each of the trees. In the tree branch located closest to the pulpit, a round sphere was created on one of the wings. The ball was constructed of *vining* with *frenched carnations* (*small white flowers*) encircling its middle. This visual suggestion of the earth riding on the wings of peace inspired worshipers to desire the fulfillment of that image in our time.

A desire to depict an eruption of joy guided the floral arrangement for the third Sunday of Advent. *Trumpet lilies* extended from the base of the dead branches to herald the news carried by the shepherds. The fresh lilies had been handpainted with enough *gold leaf* to convey their future purpose. Disguised floral mechanics were used in arranging the lilies so they appeared to be bursting forth from the tips of the dead trees. Placing *brass herald horns* alongside a small amount of *crocus* at the stump of each tree also contributed to the unquestionable declaration of joy.

The eternal love of God, the theme for the final Sunday of Advent, is often represented by *green trees*. Thus, on the Sunday of love, *green foliage* covered the dry branches of the four trees. *Baged poinsettias*—traditional symbols of the messianic promise—encircled the base of each tree. The circle is a symbol used in expressing God's eternal love.

Another possibility for the final Sunday of Advent is to apply green foliage only to the outer branches of the trees. Place *gladiolus* rising from the base of the trees and reaching beyond the tops of their trunks. The colors of the gladiolus should graduate from *deep purple* at the base to *lavender*, to *pink*, to *light pink*, and to *white* at the top. Such a progression of colors reminds worshipers of the truths of the entire season of Advent.

❑ Banners

Possibilities for Advent banners abound. Because of the uniqueness of each Sunday and the numerous symbols associated with the various themes, combinations seem unlimited.

Basic logistical decisions have to be made before the creative work begins. How many banners will be made? Do you construct one banner for each of the four Sundays or one for the entire season? Where will the banners be displayed? Answers to these questions determine the best construction and method of expression for the banners.

Specific themes from each of the four Sundays of Advent make the development of four different banners an attractive idea.

> First Sunday: Prophets, hope, expectation
> Second Sunday: Shepherds, peace, proclamation
> Third Sunday: Angels, joy, purity
> Fourth Sunday: Mary, love, visitation

Each banner can be presented on the appropriate Sunday and then be removed for the season. If adequate hanging space is available, however, each banner can remain in place throughout the season. For example, the first banner should hang closest to the nave, perhaps on the edge of the balcony over the entrance to the chancel. The second banner should appear deeper in the chancel or maybe on the back wall over the choir loft. Banner three should be placed parallel to the front banner on the other side of the nave, and banner four, in the deeper location opposite banner two. To add a new banner to the worship center each week creates an effective visual interpretation of the unfolding season.

If only limited hanging space is available, four different banners can still be used. Construct each of the four in a manner that produces one large banner when they are hung together. Obviously, the large banner would not be complete until all four Sundays of the season have passed. Banners constructed in this style are less flexible in their usage but very dramatic in their overall effect. This manner of construction, however, requires a great deal of planning and creativity. Symbols and colors must be carefully coordinated so each of the banners makes a statement of its own as well as contributes to the whole. Imaging the complete four-part banner and planning how to divide it into four individual banners are the most demanding aspects of this method of construction.

Only one or two banners can contribute significantly to Advent worship. For instance, a more general approach to themes and symbols can be used effectively. Banners such as these may best focus on attitudes for Advent rather than specific interpretations of the liturgy. A word of caution is in order. When using a minimal number of banners, take care of the amount of symbolic material included. Banner-makers often attempt to do too much. Too many designs on a banner compromise its impact and may even cause distraction or confusion among viewers. Worshipers' eyes wander because they find no place to rest. Generally, simplicity in expression is best.

The fabric colors selected for the construction of a banner significantly help or hurt the banner's effectiveness. A wrong decision about a color can compromise the value of a wisely chosen symbol if that color overrides the intention of the symbol. The liturgical colors for Advent offer the best colors for use in Advent banners—purples, violets, and blues.

The specific content of a banner can take form around a symbol important to Advent:

Alpha and Omega; Tree of Jesse; Chi Rho; Olive Branches; Trumpets; Mangers; Angels; Christmas Rose; Star of David; Books of Prophecy.

Banner content can also include a phrase important to Advent:

"The people who walked in darkness have seen a great light"; "Unto us a child is born"; "Come Thou long expected Jesus"; "In the beginning was the Word"; "And the Word was made flesh and dwelt among us"; "Behold I bring you good tidings of great joy"; "Unto you is born this day in the city of David, a savior, which is Christ the Lord"; "And the darkness declares the glory of light."

Or, the banner can communicate a single word integral to Advent: "Alleluia"; "Hodie"; "Gaudete"; "Rejoice"; "This Day"; "Comfort"; "Immanuel."

The interpretation of a banner's content should be immediately obvious to worshipers. The overall appearance of a banner must not obstruct worshipers' understanding of that banner's message.

Sounds

The sounds of Advent move our spirits toward an encounter with Christ touching all of our senses and stirring a wide range of emotions as we journey. Haunting sounds prompted by unspeakable hope and meditations on awesome mystery give way to the sounds of rejoicing, which accompany a recognition that light really is increasing.

❏ **The Word of God**

Sunday I

Old Testament	Psalm	Epistle	Gospel
Isa 2:1-5	122	Rom 13:8-14	Matt 24:36-44

| Isa 63:16-64:8 | 80:1-7 | 1 Cor 1:3-9 | Mark 13:32-37 |
| Jer 33:14-16 | 25:1-10 | 1 Thess 3:9-13 | Luke 21:25-36 |

Sunday II

Isa 11:1-10	72:1-8	Rom 15:4-13	Matt 3:1-12
Isa 40:1-11	85:8-13	2 Pet 3:8-15	Matt 1:1-8
Mal 3:1-4	126	Phil 1:3-11	Luke 3:1-6

Sunday III

Isa 35:1-10	146:5-10	Jas 5:7-10	Matt 11:2-11
Isa 61:1-4, 8-11	(Luke 1: 1: 46b-55)	1 Thess 5:16-24	John 1:6-8, 19-28
Zeph 3:14-20	(Isa 12:2-6	Phil 4:4-13	Luke 3:7-18

Sunday IV

Isa 7:10-17	24	Rom 1:1-7	Matt 1:18-25
2 Sam 7:8-16	89:1-4, 19-24	Rom 16:25-27	Luke 1:26-38
Mic 5:2-4	80:1-7	Heb 10:5-10	Luke 1:39-55

❏ Choir Literature

Sunday I

"Let All Mortal Flesh," John Ferguson
"Oh, Come, Oh, Come, Emmanuel," Arr. Roupen Shakarian
"Comfort, Comfort," John Ferguson
"E'en So Lord Jesus," Paul Manz
"Of the Father's Love Begotten," Paul Wohlgemuth
"Behold a Star From Jacob Shining," Mendlessohn

Sunday II

"The Questions Asked," Roderick Nimtz
"*Dona Nobis Pacem*," Carl Nygard
"A Gaelic Blessing," John Rutter
"In the Beginning Was the Word," Michael Ryan-Wenger
"I Was Glad," Hubert Parry

Sunday III
"Torches," John Joubert
"Companions All Sing Loudly," John Mochnick
"Glory to God in the Highest," Pergolesi
"Fling Wide the Door," John Yarrington
"Shepherd's Pipe Carol," John Rutter

Sunday IV
"*Gaudete*," King Singer Choral Series
"*Ubi Caritas*" (*Quatare Motets*), Maurice Durufle
"The Joy of Mary," Don Neuen
"*Ave Maria*," Franz Biebl
"Song of Mary," Harold Friedell
"*O Magnum Mysterium*," Thomas Luis de Victoria

❏ Organ Literature

Sunday I
Nun komm, der Heiden heiland (*Come, now, Savior of the Nations*) Ornamented Chorale. J. S. Bach
Nun komm, der Heiden heiland (Organ pleno, Cantus firmus in pedal), J. S. Bach

Sunday II
Fantasy in C major, Cantabile Cesar Franck (Dover, Bourneman-Paris, Durand-Paris)
Chant de paix (*Song of Peace*), Jean Langlais (Bornemann, Paris)
Wachet Auf (*Wake, Awake, for night is flying*), Emma Lou Diemer (1979, Augsburg)

Sunday III
Settings of *In dulci jubilo* by J. S. Bach in *Orgelbuchlein*; Dello Joio, *Five Lyric Pieced for the Young Organist* (Belwin), Geomanne (Belwin) and others
Any setting of *Schmucke dich meine liebe Seele* (for example J. S. Bach and Brahms)
My Faithful Heart Rejoices, J. Brahms, from *Eleven Choral Preludes*, op 11 (H.W. Gray (Novello)
In dir ist Freude (*In Thee is Joy*), J. S. Bach from *Orgelbuchlien*

Sunday IV

Chorale, "*Nun komm, der Heiden Heiland,*" ("Savior of the Nations, Come") BWV 659, J. S. Bach

Chorale Fughetta, "*Nun komm, der Heiden Heiland,*" BWV 661, J. S. Bach

(Both available in J. S. Bach, *Orgelwerke,* Series IV. and 2, Leipzig: Deutscher Verlag Fur Musik)

Chorale, "*Nun Comm, der Heiden Heiland*" ("Savior of the Nations, Come"), Dietrich Buxtehude

(Buxtehude, *Samtliche Orgelwerke,* Vol IV, ed. Josef Hedar, Copenhagen: Wilhelm Hansen Musik {3928})

Chorale Improvisation, "*Nun komm, der Heiden Heiland,*" Paul Manz

(Manz, *Improvisations for the Christmas Season,* Set 1, 13–15. St. Louis MO: Morningstar Music Publishers)

❑ Piano Literature

Sunday I

"O Come, O Come Immanuel," Arr. Ron Boud, from *Piano for All Seasons,* Nashville: Broadman Press

"Savior of the Nations, Come," Bach-Busoni BWY 659

Sunday II

"Sarabande from 'Pour le Piano,' " Debussy

"Prelude" Op. 31 No. 1," Bliere

Sunday III

"Jesu, Joy of Man's Desiring," Bach, Arr. Myra Hess

"O, Come All Ye Faithful," (duet) Dello Joio

Sunday IV

"Good Christian Men, Rejoice," Arr. Ron Boud, from *Piano for All Seasons,* Nashville: Broadman Press

"Lo, How A Rose e'er Blooming" Op. 122, No 8, Brahms

☐ Congregational Hymns

Sunday I

"Lo! He Comes, With Clouds Descending," Charles Wesley, REGENT SQUARE Henry T. Smart

"Let All Mortal Flesh Keep Silence," Latin, Tr. Gerald Moultrie, PICARDY French Carol

"The Lord Will Come and Not Be Slow," John Milton, ST. MAGNUS Jeremiah Clark

Sunday II

"Come, Thou Long-Expected Jesus," Charles Wesley, HYFRYDOL Roland H. Prichard

"O Come, O Come, Emmanuel," Latin, Tr. John Mason Neale, VENI EMMANUEL Plainsong

"To a Maid Engaged to Joseph," Gracia Grindal, ANNUNCIATION Rusty Edwards

"Hail to the Lord's Anointed," John Montgomery, ELLACOMBE Adapt. W. H. Monk

Sunday III

"Wake, Awake, For Night Is Flying," Philip Nocolai, Tr. Catherine Winkworth, WACHET AUF Phillip Nicolai

"Lord Christ, When First You Came to Earth," Walter Russell Bowie, MIT FREUDEN ZART from the Unitas Fratrum

"On Jordan's Bank the Baptist's Cry," Charles Coffin, Tr. John Chandler, WINCHESTER NEW German Tune, Adapt. W. H. Monk

Sunday IV

"Lift Up Your Heads, Ye Mighty Gates," Georg Weissel, Tr. Catherine Winkworth, TRURO Thomas Williams

"Saviour of the Nations, Come," Martin Luther, Tr. William M. Reynolds, NUN KOMM, DER HEIDEN HEILAND Harm. J. S. Bach

"Lo, How a Rose E'er Blooming," German, Tr. Theodore Baker, ES IST EIN ROS Harm. Hichael Praetorius

"Tell Out, My Soul, the Greatness," Timothy Dudley-Smith, WOODLANDS Walter Greatorex

❏ Homiletical Themes (For the whole season)

Preparation; expectation; longing; hope; fulfillment of prophecy; waiting; John the Baptist; God's impossible dreams; laboring to new life; the Incarnation; God's presence; repentance; recovering a sense of wonder; the end of the age; the beginning of a new age; death and rebirth; apocalyptic prophecy; and peace.

❏ Sermon Titles

Sunday I
"In Those Days" (Jer 33:14-16) (Cox)
"What Time Is It?" (Willimon)
"Why Are We Never Ready for Christmas?" (Killinger)

Sunday II
"Creative Expectations" (Claypool)
"Apocalypse Now: Come Peace of God" (Gaddy)
"Are You Giving Any Christmas Presence This Year?" (Killinger)

Sunday III
"The Day of His Coming" (Mal 3:1-4) (Cox)
"Jesus Is Coming" (Willimon)
"The Homelessness of Christ" (Killinger)

Sunday IV
"God's in the Birthing Room and All's Wild
With the World" (Sehested)
"The Original Christmas Gift" (Killinger)
"A Question About Hallelujahs" (Gaddy)

❏ Prayers

Sunday I

God of Promise and Fulfillment:
We can hardly speak of hope without starting to
sing or pray, "Come Lord Jesus, quickly come."

Good intentions have failed us.
We cannot sustain positive thinking in the
face of harsh tragedies.
Human potential offers scant promise amid
human failures.
Medical science leaves us wanting; a new
treatment for one disease ends up creating
more physical problems.
Civic planning frustrates us as preparing a
site for the construction of new houses
results in the displacement and homelessness
of more people.
Even religion offers little help as it
perpetuates the sad tradition in which law
supersedes grace and inflicting guilt seems
more holy than activating forgiveness.
God, if we're going to have any hope, we're going
to have to get it from you. Come, Lord Jesus.
Fill us with the hope that sends us scurrying
to give hope to others by
caring for the ill whom we cannot heal
feeding the hungry who cannot feed themselves
building houses for those who live in the
streets
challenging religion with the good news, which
is the Gospel.
In praying, "Come, Lord Jesus" we sense stirrings
of the hope that threatens all that is wrong in
the world.
We need hope. Come, Lord Jesus. Amen.

(Gaddy)

O God, this season can create in us an overwhelming desire for the things our money can buy. Through our Advent preparation, create in us a single-minded hunger for you alone. And through the sharing of our gifts, may people in need catch glimpses of your Light breaking into the world. Amen.

(Sledge)

Sunday II

We risk, O Lord, the journey to Bethlehem.
We earnestly seek
The community of shepherds and wise men.
For the star we look,
And await the Song.
For it is what the heart loves
Which draws to the truth.
This glad Season we venture to believe.
Help, Thou, our unbelief,
That our hearts may be strangely warmed. Amen.

———————   (Otto)

Peace, God? Peace? Is it possible?
On this Sunday of peace, the meditations of our hearts
    and the confessions of our prayers center on peace, O God.
But, is it futile?
Come peace of God and dwell again on earth—
    prejudice prevails
    arguments aggravate
    jealousies jaundice
    doubts destroy
    conflict consumes
    suspicions suffocate
    war kills.
Come peace of God and dwell again on earth!
Come peace of God and rule within our hearts—
    We are pessimistic, if not fatalistic, about peace.
    So much can go wrong. So many problems persist.
    Just when we think all is well, something goes wrong
    and we mutter that we knew it would.
Come peace of God and rule within our hearts!
    Honestly, God, even as we offer this prayer, we admit
    questions—Can it happen?
    Is it possible?
    Is there any assurance?
God of Advent, turn us again toward the Prince of Peace
    and let us sit at his feet and learn. He brought peace
    to fractured personalities
    to demented, tormented minds

to a lake whipped by winds into a churning
cauldron
to emotions gone berserk.
Of course, he was and is your Son. And you have been
about peace-making as long as you have been about
world-making and person-shaping.
You spoke of peace amid thunder.
You pointed to peace out of a whirlwind.
You brought peace to a frantic man in a wilderness.
You made peace possible by means of a violent
crucifixion.
It can happen! It is possible! You have given
assurance. Come peace of God and dwell again on earth.
Come peace of God and rule within our hearts.
We pray in the name of the One whose life has the
potential to be a sword but whose life was given that
all might know peace—Jesus, crucified in conflict and
resurrected in peace. Amen.

(Gaddy)

—————

Sunday III

Joy, God! We speak to you of joy—joy, joy, joy—
the kind of joy known only in the fulfillment of
promises.
Please understand our periodic stammering. This is
rather new for us, God. We are much more familiar
with plans rejected than with plans executed, with
hopes affirmed than with hopes realized, with promises
made than with promises kept. This kind of radical
fulfillment has produced a whole new kind of joy
within us.
You promised a handmaiden of the divine and Mary
bore Jesus.
You promised a baby and away in a manger the little
Lord Jesus laid down his sweet head.
You promised light and even now a star shines.
You promised love and Jesus came to do poor sinners
good.
You promised deliverance and Christ was born to save
us from all that enslaves us.

You promised that creation would be one, so holly
and ivy intertwine, oboes rejoice with bagpipes
crying, ox and ass kneel before him.
You keep your promises, God, every one of them.
Fulfillment is certain. As a result,
our waiting turns to rejoicing,
hopefulness becomes thankfulness,
anticipation dissolves into celebration.
God, you have said "yes" to us and to our needs and
that "Yes" has been placarded across all of creation
as well as focused in Bethlehem. Joy—joy, joy, joy!
Joy to us.
Joy from us.
Joy to the world.
Christ has come! Amen.

——————

(Gaddy)

God of our waiting; Author of our hoping:
We continue to wait for Christmas—waiting and
waiting. But, honestly, we are more than a little
weary of it. It seems like that is all we ever do—
wait. We spend most of our lives leaning forward,
looking ahead, talking about what will be.
We get tired of waiting, always being on the verge
of everything. Sometimes we want to be in the middle
of something—something really special.
Teach us patience, God, genuine patience.
Enlighten us so that we will always know the
difference between hoping and hallucinating,
waiting and escaping,
praying and dreaming,
anticipating and fantasizing.
We are waiting; not with any particular virtue or
grace. We are waiting because we have to wait. We
are ready to receive the divine gift, to shout for
joy at a birth, to celebrate unbroken fellowship, to
delight in redemption. We are ready for Christmas to
arrive in our world and Christ in our hearts.
But we know it is not yet. Not quite yet. So we
wait. And while waiting we pray. Come, Lord Jesus. Amen.

——————

(Gaddy)

Sunday IV

Enable the prophet to speak to us, O God;
Remove the hardness of our hearts
That his words may find lodging
In that one place
Where Christ ever seeks to be born.
Grant us
That gift of faith
Which is both love of Thee and obedience. Amen.

_____

(Otto)

God of Advent and Christmas:
How should we pray to you on this Sunday before Christmas?
Oh, we know what is appropriate—
words of praise,
phrases of adoration,
scores of music,
crescendos in instrumentation,
hallelujahs everywhere.
That's what is appropriate and that is what we can do
if we look only at Christmas. But, dear God, surely
you understand our sensitivity to the world to which
Jesus came as well as our recognition of his coming.
The same emotional capacity that makes some people
shout for joy causes others to cry in sadness. We
don't like hurting and it is even worse when hurting
is so out of step with all the rejoicing. But, God,
we have to be honest with you—on this day for
rejoicing, some of us are really hurting.
Pain and tears are as much a part of this season as
happiness and smiles.
Loneliness is intensified amid the laughter of
fellowship.
Tragedy is made more traumatic amid talk about
fulfillment.
Anxiety is heightened to near despair in the face of
naive harbingers of hope.
Oh God, you know what happens to us.
As we become more aware of life, we become more
aware of death.

As we come to know real love, we long for that
    kind of love in our lives.
As we read and hear of angels, shepherds, wisemen,
    and kings traveling to a manger, we seek people
    who will worship with us.
All of us welcome the Christ. All of us desire his
    coming. Just please understand, good God, that
    we cannot all express ourselves the same way.
Some of us will greet you with tears while others
    lift cheers.
Some may gather somberly as others assemble happily.
Some may shout for joy beside the manger while for
    others simply showing up is significant.
How do we pray to you today, God? Any way. Any way
that we need to pray to you! You accept us as we are
and come to us whether we have lighted candles or
decided to sit in darkness. You will reach out to us
whether we are singing jubilantly or weeping bitterly,
whether we are soaring with hope or plodding with
resolve. You will come to us where we are, as we are.
Come on, then. Come on now, God.
    May our prayers meet you and our words provide you welcome.
Come, Lord Jesus! Amen.

—————————

(Gaddy)

Great God of all good gifts:
As you sent your Son to Bethlehem, send him now to us.
    That we may continue the shepherds' pilgrimage of
      faith.
    That we may join in the song of angels.
    That we may place gifts in his presence.
    That we may be people of light.
    As you sent your Son to Bethlehem, send him now to us
    that we may, in turn, be sent on redemptive missions
    by him.
    We pray in the name of the Word, the Light, the
    Messiah, the Christ. Amen.

—————————

(Gaddy)

❑ Congregational Litanies

Sunday I

Leader: Will you come to our world, God? It is not a silent night. Shrill sirens split the air. Gun shots ring out. Screams signal pain. Sobs bespeak grief. We need hope.

People: O come, o come Immanuel. Bring hope.

Leader: Will you come to our world, God? It is not a peaceful place. Neighbors shout insults at each other. Families fear violence. Gangs chant litanies of hatred. Armies activate rituals of destruction. We need peace.

People: O come, o come Immanuel. Bring peace.

Leader: Will you come to our world, God? There is not a lot here that evokes joy. Kids ruin their lives with drugs. Men and women die of AIDS. Broken families grieve over what might have been. We need joy.

People: O come, o come Immanuel. Bring joy.

Leader: Will you come to our world, God? It is not a site where love prevails. Some people live in the streets, if you can call it living. Children suffer from malnutrition. Prejudice runs rampant among the races. We need love.

People: O come, o come Immanuel. Bring love.

Leader: Come Immanuel. Come herald of hope. Come prince of peace. Come giver of joy. Come perfect love. Come Immanuel. Come to us.

(Gaddy)

_____

Leader: Wake up, people of God! The Word of God is coming to dwell among us.

People: O world, watch! Do not sleep! For the realm of God is near.

Leader: Prepare for the unexpected to break into your lives; be alert to the signs of the coming of God.

People: But we are exiles in a strange land, hoping for news of a Savior to help us.

Leader: Look for the Light that was with God in the beginning. Even while you are seeking your home, prepare a dwelling place for the Lord.

People: We will wait without fully knowing; we will rest in the stillness
with the company of faith, hope, and love.

Leader: Wake up, people of God! Look for the Light! Listen
attentively for the coming of the Word. (Mark 13:32-37; Isa
64:1-9)

———————

(Sledge)

Leader: The promises of God birth hope.

People: Our predecessors in faith held to the divinely-engendered hope
that the Messiah would come to their world.

All: We invite the Messiah to bring hope into our world.

Leader: The commission of God creates harbingers of hope among
people like us.

People: Our contemporaries in need long to hear, see, feel, and know
hope.

All: On our journey to Christmas, we embrace the hope of God
and commit ourselves to inspiring hope among the hopeless
people in our world.

———————

(Gaddy)

Leader: Wait upon the Lord? What is waiting? What does one do,
when one waits?

People: It is not in the waiting; upon what or whom one waits! That is
the essential thing.

Leader: Waiting is not waiting upon what happens. That is to depend
upon the inner logic of events, as though events drove
themselves.

People: And waiting is not waiting upon heroes, as though men of stat-
ure and power determined the flow of history.

Leader: Nor is waiting resignation, that mindless acceptance of what
is in hopeless subjection to fate.

People: Waiting is not escape into dreams of another world, rejecting
creation as beyond redemption, hoping for a holocaust to
destroy our present evil.

Leader: Waiting is waiting upon the Lord. A waiting that is a hoping
and seeking, a return to the Lord, from and in our anxiety
and stress.

People: To wait is to groan inwardly, full of pain and distress, yet
knowing this is not of God, hoping against hope.

Leader: To wait is to refuse the obvious, to deny the persuasion of what is. To wait is to be confident of salvation, to look beyond our finite possibilities.

People: To wait is to receive from the Spirit the power to persevere without validation. To wait is to have courage and strength, exercising love and justice where justice and love are not.

All: To wait upon the Lord is to have the eye of faith focused. We shall see the goodness of God.

(Otto)

Sunday II

Leader: What do you know of peace?

People: God gives peace. Christ embodies peace. God's Spirit nurtures peace.

Leader: What are the possibilities for peace in this community in which we live?

People: Peace accompanies justice and equality, keeps fellowship with mercy and love, travels with reconciliation and redemption.

All: As citizens of this community eager to celebrate Christ's birth, we give ourselves to the divinely-commissioned work of peacemaking on earth, starting right here at home.

(Gaddy)

Leader: We risk, O Lord, the journey to Bethlehem.

People: We earnestly seek the community of shepherds and wise men.

Leader: For the star we look and await the Song.

People: For it is what the heart loves which draws to the truth.

All: This glad season we venture to believe. Help, Thou, our unbelief, that our hearts may be strangely warmed.

(Otto)

Leader: Sing "Noel"

People: Sing *"gloria in excelsis deo"*

Leader: Out of your silent night
or your midnight clear
with all the heavens and earth.

People: Sing "Joy to the World"

All: The Lord is coming to bring us peace.

(Sledge)

Sunday III

Leader: O God of Glory, you invade our darkness with the glory of
            your celestial light. Split the clouds of our sin and fearfulness
            so that we may again see the star of your gracious love.

People: **O God of purest joy, you comfort us when we are mourning
        underneath our heavy loads of sorrow.**

Leader: O God of peace, you establish your reign among us as a reign
            of loving kindness and tender mercy. As we have been con-
            soled, so may we offer comfort to those who mourn. As we
            have been sought out, so may we seek out the lost and aban-
            doned. As we have been freed from the rod of the oppressor,
            so may we set the captives free.

People: **As the Son was born for us, so may we be reborn for others. As
        the Savior died to bring us light and life, so may we know
        that it is in dying that *we* are born to life eternal.**

Leader: The people who walked in darkness have seen a great light:
            those who lived in a land of deep darkness—on them has the
            light shined.

                                            (Findley)

Leader: We wait, O Lord, we wait.
        For the Joy of our desiring
        Is not the fruit of our wills
        Nor the work of our hands.

People: **We wait, O Lord, we wait.
        What we have been made for
        Does not come from ourselves.
        It is the gift of surprise and mystery.**

Leader: The light is Thy light.
        Into darkness it comes,
        Overcoming our darkness with that light—
        The holiness of Grace.

People: **The prisons teeming with their captives
        Shall be opened.
        Those with broken hearts
        Shall be healed.
        The poor shall hear Glad Tidings.**

Leader: The lips that know the dirge
        Shall sing the songs of joy;

>   The faint of spirit and weary of soul
>   Shall become oaks of Justice.

People: **Ah, Lord God, out of ashes
        Shall rise the cities;
        Out of the garden shall spring forth
        The Justice and song
        Which shall be a praise to Thy glory.**

All: **We wait, O Lord, with deep longing
        For Him, called to be Thy Servant,
        Anointed by Thy Spirit,
        The Miracle and Mystery of Christmas.**

—————— (Otto)

Sunday IV

Leader: O God of Love, Love Divine, we gather here
        To listen,
        To learn,
        To discern,
        To try to make sense out of our lives.

People: **Without Your Presence we will not go away
        renewed, refreshed, enlightened, changed.
        We will not have been renewed in commitment.
        We will not have been refreshed in hope.
        We will not have been enlightened in
        understanding.
        We will not have been changed in life.**

Leader: So, here we are, Eternal God,
        Parched ground begging for rain.
        Flowers opening to the morning sun.
        Deer panting for living streams.
        Beggars stretching out empty hands.

People: **Come, O loving God,
        Let us know Your Presence.
        Let us hear Your Word.
        Let us feel Your Love.
        And transform us into Your Own.**

—————— (Hinson)

Leader: All around us are signs of the significance of the season.

People: **The beauty of the room in which we worship subtly whispers a
hint of glory.**

Leader: Majestic music, choral declarations of the words of angels,
and the reading of a gospel text call to mind the message of
the ages.

People: **Burning candles reiterate the truth of in-breaking light.**

Leader: Everything seems to be in a state of readiness for Christ to
come.

People: **But, what about our hearts?**

Leader: What good are the sights and sounds, the beauty and the
lights, if Christ is not welcome in our hearts?

All: **Today—right now—God, lead us into an experience of worship which pleases you and makes our hearts ready to receive
the Christ. May he be born in us.**

_____   (Gaddy)

Leader: A voice cries in the desert: Prepare the way of the Lord!

People: **Make straight God's paths.**

Leader: O God, in your measureless love you have fashioned all of
us.

People: **Making us glorious by the image of your Glory.**

Leader: Through Abraham and Sarah you have promised happiness
to all who love you.

People: **Through Christ you have made your self known to your Church.**

Leader: When we wander in darkness, you do not leave us, but
restore us to the light of your forgiveness.

People: **Sanctify in love the whole body of your people, now and forever.**

_____   (Leonard)

Suggestions

- *Present a multi-media collection of gallery art* depicting the
events of the birth of Christ accompanied by seasonal anthems
from the masters and paraphrases of the Matthew and Luke
infancy narratives. Call the worship experience "Arts of the
Nativity."

- *Plan a worship time inspired by the visits of angels*—past, present, and future. Display a photographic exhibit of angel figures taken from tombstones, church architecture, and other structures. In another section of the worship center, provide a display of angels as presented in the paintings of the great masters through the ages. When we did this service, our choir presented anthems based upon visits from angels. People in attendance had the option of listening as they viewed the various exhibits or hearing the entire musical program seated among the pieces of art. We also used the occasion to premiere a permanent collection of art on display in the educational hall of our facility. A professional artist assisted our "angels"— children in our congregation—in the construction of watercolor works depicting various biblical stories. Since we scheduled the worship experience for a Sunday afternoon in Advent, it was called "Art, Angels, and Afternoon Tea."

- *Focus on a contemporary issue* to which the themes of Advent bring special meaning. One year, in cooperation with a local agency that works with HIV-positive persons, we exhibited four panels of the national AIDS quilt during the first two Sundays of Advent. Two of the panels hung in the narthex, one on the back wall of the sanctuary and one suspended from the rafters directly over the communion table. The unavoidable presence of the quilted panels in our place of worship reminded us of the difficulty of finding peace in difficult situations and of the controversial nature of God's love. We resolved not to lose hope and prayed for a time when joy could be experienced by all people. Worship that embraced our identification with grieving and suffering people during this holy season resulted in one of the rare treasures in the worship pilgrimage of our congregation.

- *Plan and conduct an ordination service* during the season of Advent. Advent is a perfect time for this rite of the church. The role of today's minister can be instructed by the "prepare-the-way-of-the-Lord" nature of John the Baptist and his ministry. A recognition, affirmation, and commission to the ministry of the gospel hold a rightful place at the heart of preparation for the revelation of God in the Christ whose name, nature, and work incarnated the ministry of God's good news.

An Advent Service of Worship
Contemporary Advent

Desiring for worshipers to experience realistic implications of Christ's presence in our world, we structured a worship service to explore the meaning of Christ-inspired hope, peace, joy, and love where we live. By sensitizing ourselves to the people around us most in need of Advent truths, we hoped to find ways in which our congregation can "reveal Christ" and serve as "inbreaking light" for these waiting, hurting individuals.

A barrage of unexpected sights, sounds, and scents enveloped worshipers entering the narthex of our building. A young cellist played "Sonata in C Major," by J. S. Breval (Joy!). Her music, however, was difficult to hear over of the loud hammering of a local Habitat for Humanity project. The irksome clickety-clickety-click of an old sixteen-meter movie projector threw bright images of drug abuse on a wall while a soundless video from a local television station told the story of recent crimes that had made the news. A rusty metal shopping cart filled with tacky necessities for survival brought to mind the ragged, tattered belongings of a homeless man. A display of self-help books triggered thoughts of the frantic search for inner peace that preoccupies so many people today. A shocking collection of drugs—from crack cocaine to marijuana—were displayed on a table alongside a disturbing array of weapons. Draped alongside these items were caps and symbol-bearing shirts collected from community gang members who had run into trouble with law enforcement personnel.

All doors to the sanctuary were closed. People seeking an experience of Advent worship had to wait among all the noise and disturbance—a true picture of the Advent situation where we live—before proceeding to any contact with the holy. Frankly, not all would-be participants in the service were patient or pleased.

At the announced time for the service to begin, the roar in the narthex diminished as the pastor began a litany inviting Jesus our world. Together, the choir, the congregation, and other worship leaders processed into the sanctuary singing "O come, O come Emmanuel."

The worship experience consisted of four major parts corresponding to the four primary themes of the Sundays of Advent. Each section of the service included choral presentations, scripture readings, a contemporary comment, and a prayer.

Our focus on hope necessitated a realistic look at people in our community aching for hope in their lives: prisoners without a friend to help them receive a second chance; victims of AIDS dying alone; people struggling against prejudices of race, class, or economic status; individuals so abused by "climbers" that they have given up on everybody; and suffering strugglers looking for a friend to help them cope with a devastating disease. A woman who works with HIV-positive people spoke to us of the importance of hope. We pondered whether or not the Bethlehem story could become a reality here.

A local police officer aided a consideration of peace-related issues in our community. Amid musical interpretations of peace, we listened to stories of needless killings and senseless brutality among people who have never experienced love and trust. We heard about some of our cross-town neighbors who are willing to die defending the colors of a gang because they have found acceptance and sensed significance within that warring group. Concerns about inner peace developed within the context of this awareness of the lack of social peace. Each worshiper was challenged to look carefully at the personal conflicts that create tensions and feed anxieties.

The joy inherent in our contemporary experience of Advent found expression through the spoken words and artistic movements of a professional dancer. She helped us reflect on the happiness evidenced through shouts of jubilation that come from artists—musicians, painters, writers, designers—when someone recognizes their talents as gifts from God and invites their contributions in worship. The dancer interpreted the name of Jesus in liturgical movements as members of the congregation contemplated the joy to be found in taking the risk to do what is right.

"Contemporary Advent" concluded with a look at love. A local ophthalmologist spoke of her desire for our community to be a place where people genuinely cared for God's creation and took actions accordingly. She regularly picks up trash along a major thoroughfare. A woman whose family has been chosen to receive a new house through Habitat for Humanity talked to us about the kind of love that responds to people desperately wanting to improve their living situations while facing seemingly insurmountable barriers to achieve improvements. We saw firsthand the results of love in action—a new hope, a renewed peace, a bursting joy, and unquestionable love.

Advent is about getting ready for an appropriate reception of the coming Christ. The worship service gave content and direction to contemporary Advent preparations by directing the worshipers' attention to the issues of hope, peace, joy, and love that have to be addressed as a part of an appropriate response to Christ's arrival where we live.

Floral Arrangements

The arrangement is designed for the first Sunday of Advent—Hope. The earthen vessel is filled with heavy vines and tree branches. Sprouting as new growth from the base of the stems are heather and statis in various shades of purple. Other symbols related to the Old Testament assist in communicating the prophecy associated with the first Sunday of Advent.

The floral arrangement is designed for the third Sunday of Advent—
Joy—and communicates the message of the angels. The visual founda-
tion is designed by using concrete statues supporting an evergreen
garland. The floral design consists of red and pink ginger, sego palms,
gold strelitzia, and herald horns of brass and copper.

The floral arrangement is also designed for the third Sunday of Advent. The arrangement communicates the joyful message of the angels and consists of red and pink ginger, sego palms, gold strelitzia, and herald horns of brass and copper.

Worship Banners

❑ The First Sunday of Advent: Hope ❑

❑ The Second Sunday of Advent: Peace ❑

❏ The Third Sunday of Advent: Joy ❏

❑ The Fourth Sunday of Advent: Love ❑

❏ **Additional Banners for Advent** ❏

❑ **Additional Banners for Advent** ❑

Eus in ad
iutorium
meum inten
de.

Domine ad adiu
uandum me festina
Gloria patri et filio
et spiritui sancto.

Christmas:
A Season of Fulfillment

A fanfare with trumpets! Lights, brilliant lights. A scent of ever-green. A resounding chorus of "hallelujahs." A touch of wonder. The taste of sweetness. Brightly burning candles. The majestic swell of a pipe organ. Bells pealing. A sense of mystery. Joy tempered by awe. Christmas! A festival like no other on the Christian calendar, Christmas assaults the senses, boggles the mind, bows the spirit, and inspires giving.

History

The early church had no fixed date for the celebration of Christ's birth. Some Christians observed Christmas, a word derived from the Old English "Christes Masse" or Christ's Mass, in May and others in June. Members of the Eastern Church consistently kept 6 January—now observed as Epiphany—as the day for commemorating the birth of Jesus.

The first known evidence for Christians observing 25 December as the date for Christmas arose in 354 A.D. Like the dates of so many other Christian festivals, this day was probably chosen because of the time off from work and opportunities for worship afforded to Christians by Roman activities related to the feast day for the Birth of the Unconquered Sun—a major pagan festival commemorating the winter solstice. Christians appropriated the feasting, merriment, and exchanging of gifts associated with pagan rites and used them in rejoicing over the incarnation of the "Sun of Righteousness."

Christmas Day begins the Christmas season and extends for twelve days, ending on the eve of Epiphany. No other Christian season enjoys the popularity and broad-based public participation devoted to Christmas.

$\mathcal{S}$*ensations* . . . .

At the center of Christmas stands a creche that holds a child named "Jesus"—a baby in whom God uniquely revealed the divine nature. Jesus was the long-promised "Immanuel," meaning God with us. In the person of Jesus we meet the *incarnation of God*!

The magnitude of the Christmas event prompts a vast array of responses among individuals. This happening in the past births great *promise* regarding possibilities for the future. *Hope* lives. *Joy* surges through our spirits and *"hallelujahs"* leap out of our mouths. A longing for *peace* intermingles with scents associated with a stable and finds comfort in the soft cooing of a child worshiped as the Prince of Peace. Every person with even a minimal under-standing of Christmas experiences the elation and receives an *assurance* that no person has to live alone. *God is with us*—all of us! Christmas declares that God joins our journeys.

Giving dominates the activities of Christmas: God giving the Messiah to us; we giving our lives to God; people sharing gifts with each other to commemorate the ultimate gift.

Surprise runs rampant. Who would predict that the ultimate revelation of God would come in the form of a baby born in an animal shelter located in an out-of-the-way place called Bethlehem! Why not in Rome? Or Athens? Why not in a palace? Why not a place of worship? Then again, who would think that God would show up amid the messes of our lives and reveal divine love in such non-religious settings! God *with us*; that is the message of Christmas.

Christmas confronts us with no small *miracle*. The miracle of God with us sets in motion other miracles: the miracle of salvation, the miracle of new possibilities, and the miracle of life through death. To arrive at Christmas is to visit a holy place where any-thing can happen.

Maybe the most descriptive word for Christmas is *mystery*. A look at the events, message, and meaning of Christmas make me think of *a mystery wrapped in a mystery that is covered with mystery*. Can anyone speak with patent certainty about how Christmas happened or happens, how God came among us, and how the Christ child brings the possibility of salvation to all people?

Personally, I (WG) still enjoy majestic services of worship during Christmas, the crescendo of an orchestra straining to present the miracle of the season, Handel's magnificent "Hallelujah Chorus," and combined choirs singing "Joy to the World." How I delight in the scintillating odors, tastes, and touches of Christmas. Sometimes I want to shout a "hallelujah," though I do not always do it. More and more I am preoccupied with the magnificent mystery of Christmas. Such mystery impacts me with a force that reduces my words to whispers. Christmas incites *reverence* and moves me to the *awe* associated with standing on holy ground.

A little girl named Sharon captured the sensation most definitive of Christmas for me. John Shea relates how Sharon concluded her retelling of the Christmas story. "Then the baby was borned," Sharon said. "And do you know who he was?" the little girl asked. "The baby was God," she whispered just before she leaped into the air, spun around, and dove into a sofa where she covered her head with pillows.[1]

Sights

❑ Color

The liturgical color of Christmas is *white*; the color for all feast days that center on Christ. White symbolizes purity and joy.

❑ Fabrics

Fine fabrics make a substantial contribution to celebrations of Christmas Day. Typically *brocades* and *silk* seem most appropriate for pulpit hangings and table coverings. Such fabrics convey the royalty of Christ, bespeak worshipers' adoration of Christ, and dramatize worship leaders' intentions to give the very best of everything to the holy one from God. Keep in mind, though, that offering the best is not to be confused with offering the most expensive.

If fine fabrics are used in a manner that suggests "hands off," rethink this use from the perspective of the theology of the day. At the center of Christmas Day stands the truth of God's availability. Jesus represented a touchable God. The simplicity that prevailed at the Bethlehem nativity of our Lord may be best recalled by simplicity in our worship centers. *White cotton* or *gauze textiles* can be effectively used as reminders of the swaddling clothes that figured so prominently in clothing baby Jesus.

❑ Flowers

Flowers for Christmas Day should represent the worshipers' encounter with splendor and mystery as well as their exultant joy over Christ's birth. *Flowering almond stalks, gladiolus, swallows,* and *poinsettias* can all be used for purposes of aesthetic beauty and liturgical meaning.

One Christmas Day, I (DN) covered the altar in the sanctuary of our church building with *a garland of Christmas greens* and hundreds of *red roses*. Symbols were placed of the communion table—a cross, a chalice, a paten with a loaf of bread, and lighted tapers. Roses ran around and alongside the symbols that set on the communion table as a reminder of God's love. The lighted tapers suggested the coming of the light of the world. If the excitement of the day robbed worshipers of attentive ears with which to hear, the flowers on the altar confronted them with the glory of God's love. The truth heralded by the flowers needed no explanation. Worshipers experienced the glory of Christmas with their eyes and felt moved to offer prayers.

Sounds . . . .

❑ The Word of God

Old Testament	Psalm	Epistle	Gospel
Isa 52:7-10	98	Heb 1:1-12	Luke 2:8-20
			John 1:1-14

❑ Choral Literature

"A *Hodie* Processional," Paul Manz
"*Hodie*," Healey Willan
"To Him We Sing," Robert Young
"Sing We Now of Christmas," Fred Prentice
"Sing We Noel," Noel Goemanne
"Noel (The Nativity According to St. Luke)," Randall Thompson
"Masters in the Hall," John Miller
"A Wondrous Mystery," Lloyd Pfautsch
"Christmas Trilogy," Allen Johnson, ed. Don Neuen
"Christmas Day," Gustav Holst

❑ Organ Literature

"*Divinum Mysterium*," ("Of the Father's Love Begotten") T. F. H. Candlyn
(Candlyn, *Prelude on "Divinum Mysterium,"* Boston MA: The Arthur P. Schmidt Co.)
Carillon de Westminster, Opus 54 IV, Louis Vierne
"Sussex Carol," Dale Wood
(Wood, Dale. *Woodworks for Christmas.* Dayton OH: The Sacred Music Press. 13-16, KK 454)
"*Giga*" ("*In dulci Jubilo*"), Norman Dello Joio
(Dello Joio, Norman. *Five Lyric Pieces.* 14–19. Melville NY: Edward B. Marks Music Corporation)

❑ Piano Literature

"Prelude in A Minor," Bach-Liszt
"Angels" from "Christmas Gifts," Rebikoff

❑ Congregational Hymns

"Gentle Mary, Laid Her Babe," Joseph Simpson Cook, TEMPUS ADEST FLORIDUM from *Piae Cantiones*, 1582
"Good Christian Folk, Rejoice," Latin, Tr. John Mason Neale IN DULCI JUBILO German Carol
"Break Forth, O Beauteous Heavenly Light," Johann Rist, Tr. John Troutbeck, ERMUNTRE DICH Harm. J. S. Bach

❑ Homiletical Themes

Incarnation; the God of surprises; promises kept and hopes fulfilled; salvation; light; and love.

❑ Sermon Titles

"Home for Christmas" (Killinger)
"Whispers of Christmas" (Gaddy)
"How Can This Be?" (Sehested)

❑ Prayers

God of Creation, Father of the Christ:
We come before you with no illusions of being angels
        no aspirations of being shepherds
        no credentials to be royalty, but
We come before you with a desire to worship you and to lay gifts before you.
        We offer the gift of our presence—as we praise you, we

prepare to live as your people.

We offer the gift of poetry—we lend our voices to the words of others that truth may be proclaimed and your
name glorified.

We offer the gift of singing—the music inspired by your coming falls from our lips as an offering.

Please accept our gifts, O God. More importantly, please accept us. Please accept us as we accept the Christ and all the gifts he offers. Amen.

――――――

(Gaddy)

Heads bowed, hearts uplifted, minds waiting, we gather to praise
    you who became one of us, O God,
    you who have shared our lot,
    you who have pitched your tent with us,
    you who have always come.
Self-centered, self-serving, sin-full, we gather to confess
    Both our faithfulness and our faithlessness,
    Both our dedication and our deviation,
    Both our dependence and our independence,
    Both our hopefulness and our helplessness.
Believing and doubting, wondering and wavering, we
    gather to thank you
    That you have never given up on us,
    That you have gone to such lengths to reach us,
    That you have come "in the fullness of time,"
    That you are not a God far off but Immanuel.
Full of memories, full of hopes, full of fears, we gather
    To hear again the story of stories, *your* story,
    To sing again the song of angels, your messengers,
    To come again with shepherds to Bethlehem, your city,
    To take part in the story of Jesus Christ, your Son.
A family of diverse and struggling sinners, we gather to
    pledge
    That we will try to live the Advent story better day
    by day,
    That we will make room for you to dwell among
    humankind,
    That we will keep space in minds and hearts for you,

That in us your kingdom may come and your will be done
on earth as in heaven. Amen.

—————————

(Hinson)

Faithful, Promise-Keeping God:
We are here, but we are not much into adoration and
praise. Oh, of course, we speak of adoration. But it's one thing
to say it and another thing to mean it.
    Why do we say, "We adore you"? We don't talk like that to
the people around us we love the most.
    And, praise? We fear if we praise other people too much they
will get the big head and we will look even smaller than we feel.
    Please God, in this moment intended for praise and adoration, please
understand our reservations.
    But, here is this nativity. We are facing into the meaning
of Christmas.
You showing up in flesh.
Comfort becoming a reality.
Salvation offered as a possibility.
Joy as a way of life.
God, we are not accustomed to anything like this, not even
to anything close to it. Help us to transcend the normal and to stretch our
attitudes.
    We adore you, O God—for your magnificent creativity
for your infinite patience
for your gifts of music and beauty
for your incomparable love
for your endless grace.
We praise you, O God—for not giving up on us
for forgiving us when we don't deserve it
for coming to live in our midst
for giving us hope in every situation.
Our frail words pale before your majesty. Our weak phrases tremble
as we see your strength. But, maybe, we've said enough for you to
know that like the angels, shepherds, and other worshipers on
another Christmas day, we worship you with praise and adoration.
Allelujah. Amen.

—————————

(Gaddy)

Great Loving, Giving God:
We come to this celebration of Christ's birth as persons in
need of forgiveness.
Forgive us for wishing we had been in Bethlehem to rejoice
over Christ's birth and failing to rejoice over Christ's
presence here and now.
Forgive us for reflecting so much on prophecies about the
appearance of the Messiah and refusing to offer ourselves
in service to the Lord who has come.
Forgive our sentimentality—our warm feelings—over
ideologies of love, joy, and peace if we are not willing to
make them actualities by living as love givers, peace
makers, and disciples of joy.
Forgive our pageantry—the processional, banners, anthems,
and other festivities of this day—if pageantry is divorced
from reality and our acceptance of the incarnate savior.
Forgive our singing of carols if singing is for entertainment
and self fulfillment and devoid of intentions of worship
and praise for you.
Forgive us, God.
Christmas Day contains as many opportunities for
hypocrisy as for authentic growth in Christian spirituality.
Lord Jesus, forgive us.
Lord Jesus, forgive us that forgiven we may come to you.
Lord Jesus, forgive us that forgiven we may come to you and
be forgiving to others.
Welcome into our lives Incarnate God. Amen.

——————— (Gaddy)

❏ Congregational Litanies

Leader: Man, and yet God.
            Infinite, and yet finite.
            The wedding of the temporal and eternal.
People: How may this be?
            Ah, Lord God.
Leader: In the presence of the Incarnate One,
People: We tremble on the borders of Mystery.
            There at the edge of Transcendence,
            We find ourselves.

Leader: And are discovered by our true destiny.
            Made of clay—shaped in the divine image;
            Returned to the dust—destined for the Tree of Life.
            Lives woven into the fabric of human history,
            But also servants of the Kingdom of Heaven.
People: **Who are we, Lord God,**
            That Thou shouldst be mindful of us?
Leader: Yet Thou hast made us little less than God.
All: **We praise Thee, O King of the Universe—**
            Thou didst become one with us,
            That we might become one with Thee.

                                    ————————   (Otto)

Sing: O little town of Bethlehem, how still we see thee lie! Above thy
          deep and dreamless sleep, the silent stars go by; yet in thy dark
          streets shineth, the everlasting Light, the hopes and fears of all
          the years are met in thee tonight.
Leader: God who makes all things new, our hearts turn to Bethlehem,
          which means house of bread, because we hunger for a place
          in this life where our hopes and fears meet and turn into joy
          deeper than comprehension.
People: **In the dark streets of the cities where our lives converge, we**
          yearn for a light that nothing can extinguish to burn away sin
          and sorrow, to blaze with hope for a transformation of our
          common life into a dwelling which is community.
Sing: For Christ is born of Mary, and gathered all above, while mortals
          sleep, the angels keep their watch of wondering love. O morning
          stars, together proclaim the holy birth, and praises sing to God
          the King, and peace to men on earth!
Leader: Your love, which encompasses eternity and time, from crea-
          tion when the morning stars sang together and all the
          children of God shouted for joy, to consummation when all
          angels and creatures encircle and sing praises to you, that
          very same love has come down at Christmas in the birth of
          a baby to save us.
People: **Wake us from our dreamless sleep, wake us from our nightmares,**
          draw us near to wonder at a baby in whose face we see at
          last how beloved and therefore lovely we are in your eyes,
          all of us together.

Sing: How silently, how silently the wondrous gift is given! So God imparts to human hearts the blessings of His heaven. No ear may hear His coming, but in this world of sin, where meek souls will receive Him, still the dear Christ enters in.

Leader: In the holy hush of Christmas this breathtaking gift of Jesus Christ has entered history and has seized our hearts with the wondrous possibility of healing and hope in a world made one and new.

People: **Prepare us to receive your gift by opening us to surprise, by opening us to solidarity with our sisters and brothers, by opening us to seek the peace of the city which symbolizes every configuration of human lives connected across our differences and enriched by our diversity.**

Sing: O holy Child of Bethlehem, descend to us we pray. Cast out our sin, and enter in; be born in us today. We hear the Christmas angels the great glad tidings tell; O come to us, abide with us, our Lord Immanuel!

Leader: To the one whose birth is our own into a glorious new dimension of life, we pray: Let there be born in and through us the new creation, whose birth pangs already announce a new day dawning.

People: **Gracious God, turn all your children to this holy child of Bethlehem; turn mourning to joy and darkness to light; turn his whole world into the city coming down out of heaven from you, where we shall forever see your face and worship you.**

All: **With the shepherds we make haste to Bethlehem to see this baby. With the angels we sing glad tidings of his birth. In Jesus Christ your glory has been revealed, and all flesh have seen it together. Amen.**

—————————

(Penfield)

Suggestions

- *Incorporate scents into the worship service* on Christmas Day. The Christmas season—especially Christmas Day—offers many possibilities for meaningful odors. Perhaps the smell of used hay and the body odor of working shepherds may be too realistic for most congregations to serve as aids to worship.

The smell of fresh greenery and burning candles, however, should easily remind all present of the everlasting love of God made known in the light of the world—Jesus.

• *Include a period of liturgical movement or dance* to dramatize the soul's elation on this special day. Seeing organized shapes created by a human body can transport worshipers into an encounter with the holy in a manner that music and words cannot equal. Unaccompanied dance provides an extremely powerful medium for enabling people to visualize the gospel, the truth of God incarnate.

• *Plan a Christmas Eve candlelight service* in which each worshiper lights a candle, reminding them of the coming of light into the world in Christ. Sing traditional carols and listen again to the ancient biblical texts that speak of the promised messiah.

• *Ask both children and adults to help* create a visual of the infancy narrative by bringing forward different pieces of a creche and placing them on the altar. This act of worship can be done on Christmas Eve or Christmas Day.

Other variations of presenting the figures of the creche merit adoption as well. Distribute various pieces of the church's creche among worshipers. At the appropriate time in the service ask them to bring together the uniform, scaled nativity scene. Or, call various members of the congregation and invite each of them to bring a specific character from their family creche. The uniqueness of a scene containing all sizes and shapes of figures can present an overwhelming message.

You may also invite members of the congregation to bring with them to worship a special character from their family creche. Then, as the nativity narrative is read from the Bible, invite these people to bring their creche pieces to an altar. An amazing number and variety of characters will appear. If more than one Christ-child character is permitted, use each one to create a new site in the room for another creche.

- *Adopt or modify a wonderful French tradition* that brings great meaning to a congregational collection of a creche. The French bring to the manger little figures that they call *santons*. Each figure represents a specific person within the worshiper's family, church, or community who has reflected love in a special manner to the worshiper. Time during the service is provided for statements of thanksgiving and an explanation of why a particular figure was chosen for the scene.

  A meaningful variation of this French tradition involves bringing to the service the person being honored by a figure placed on the altar as part of the creche. Words of gratitude can then be spoken both to God and to the person who has prompted the gratitude. As the honorees join those who have honored them while standing at the creche, they experience a powerful realization: "I was chosen to be at the manger." When the form of a living creche gathers around the creche-bearing altar, a simple commission and prayer of thanksgiving can be spoken. Conclude the service with a reminder of how "the *words* became flesh and dwelt among us."

  One addition to this service can prove meaningful. Following the postlude of the service encourage each worshiper who placed a *santon* on the altar during the service to pick up the figure and present it to the person it represents. The entire church family will be brought to a realization of how the influence of the Christ-child's coming continues to impact our lives.

Notes

[1]Barbara Taylor, *Mixed Blessings* (Atlanta GA: Susan Hunter Publishing, 1986) 32.

Floral Arrangements and Worship Banners for the Christmas season are found in section one of worship resources entitled *Advent*.

EPIPHANY

Epiphany:
A Season of Revelation

A small, thin column of aromatic, white smoke rises into the air and hovers cloud-like over a slender ring of burning incense. The invasive scent suggests the Far East and hints at mystery. All the while, larger streams of white smoke drift above flames, which dance atop seven golden candlesticks. Rays of light flicker across a room and bring clarity of vision to the people present. Light and incense, mystery and clarity, clouds and vision—these are the ingredients of Epiphany. The incarnation of God in Christ represents an impenetrable mystery. Who can explain it? The revelation of God in Christ brings clarity of vision regarding the messiah's identity. Who can miss it?

History

The Feast of the Epiphany actually antedates observances of Christmas. References to Epiphany appear as early as 200 A.D. Christians in the Eastern Church chose 6 January to celebrate the birth of Christ and the baptism of Jesus. By the year 300 A.D., remembering the magi's visit to the newborn savior had become a major part of Epiphany observances.

The Western Church borrowed Epiphany from its Eastern brothers and sisters in the late fourth century. Western Christians eventually dropped the commemoration of Jesus' baptism—as well as his first miracle in Cana and the transfiguration—and narrowed the focus of the season to the visit of the magi. These travelers from the East occupied a central place in Epiphany because, as non-Jews, they represented all Gentiles: Gentiles to whom the supreme revelation of God had also been sent.

The thematic meaning of the season of Epiphany resides in the literal definition of the word Epiphany. Derived from the Greek, Epiphany designates "an appearance" or "a manifestation." Precisely! During the season of Epiphany, Christians rejoice over the manifestation of God to all people—Jews and Gentiles—and ponder their own responsibility in presenting Christ to the world.

The season of Epiphany stretches across nine Sundays and ends on the Tuesday before Ash Wednesday (the day that ushers Christians into the season of Lent). Some people refer to this day as Shrove Tuesday because in a few traditions it was the time when priests "shrove" the people; that is, the priests heard their confessions of sin and offered forgiveness.

Sensations

Rational onlookers may well hurl caustic epitaphs at worshipers who faithfully embody the themes of Epiphany—*naive, crazy, child-like, flighty.* Who in their right mind would follow a star or dare to believe in the possible fulfillment of a fantastic dream? Epiphany encourages a spirit that prompts people to drop everything they are doing and embark upon a journey without knowing its destination. "Epiphany is *the festival of dreamers.*"[1]

At the center of Epiphany traditions stand the *magi* who traveled a great distance to see the Christ child, worship him, and present him with *costly gifts.* True to that tradition, during Epiphany we make sure *we move to meet the God* who is *moving to meet us.* No questions asked! When a promise of meeting God confronts us, it does not matter what time it is, what we had previously scheduled, or where we have to go. We quickly take off in the direction of the promise, leaving behind us whatever has to be left behind to start the journey.

The work of Epiphany is *manifestation* or *revelation.* God started it, revealing the divine nature in Jesus Christ and making sure both Jews and Gentiles saw the revelation. The people of God are to take it up. During this season, we see clearly what God is like and labor to be sure that everyone else knows as well. At this time of the year, Christians rightly assess their involvement in the manifestation of Christ through *missions* and *evangelism.* The gospel of Christ is *a universal gospel.* No one stands outside the love of God or beyond the redemptive reach of God. The message of the church is for all people.

In the Greek Orthodox Church, the season of Epiphany abounds with *pageantry*. Worshipers celebrate the showing forth of God to the world with elaborate gifts and regal processions. Often referring to Epiphany as Little Christmas or Three Kings' Day, worshipers exalt Christ as the "Light of the World."

The great truth of Epiphany sets before us the reality of *the continuing revelation of God in Christ today*. Worship services focus on the themes of what God has done in Christ, what Christ reveals about God, and God's merciful action on behalf of the salvation of humankind. The focus of the service is not in the distant past alone, but in the present, amid the humdrum activities of our daily lives. Churches devote special attention to incidents in the life of Jesus that make a major contribution to people's understanding of the nature of God: the baptism of Jesus, the first miracle of Jesus in which he turned water into wine, the healing miracles of Jesus, and the sovereignty of Jesus over life and death.

The great Brighton preacher of the nineteenth century, Frederick W. Robertson, caught the overwhelming truth of Epiphany in a sermon on Jesus' miracle in Cana of Galilee. Robertson made the point that the real glory of the Messiah resided

> not in the life of asceticism, but in the life of godliness—not separating from life, but consecrating it; carrying a Divine spirit into every simplest act . . . For Christianity does not destroy what is natural, but ennobles it. To turn water into wine, and what is common into what is Holy is indeed the glory of Christianity.[2]

Worship during Epiphany *expands people's vision*, feeds a sense of the bigness of the gospel, and stirs awe among all who grasp the meaning of the season. Feeling blessed by the gift of God, worshipers move toward a *commitment* to carry out their God-given responsibility to *share the gospel* with all people through both words and actions.

Sights

Epiphany's close association with the magi's visit to the Christ child brings a touch of royalty to this season. The ancient travelers from the East approached Christ out of a regal tradition and lavished extravagant gifts upon him. Thus, the sights of Epiphany suggest the kind of finery appropriate for a child who would redefine the nature of kingly rule.

❏ Colors

White best reflects the light, faith, innocence, and glory so integral to Epiphany. *Golds,* however, also convey an appropriate intensity and richness. Golds represent divinity, faith, and intelligence. *Yellows* suggest illumination, the brightness of the day, festivities of celebration, and the presentation of Christ to the world.

The Sundays following the day of Epiphany utilize the liturgical color that symbolizes growth, life, and hope—*green*. Visible sights of green in worship send worshipers' minds scurrying to the theological mandate regarding the church's mission.

No reasons exist why other colors cannot be used during Epiphany. If certain colors better communicate an interpretation of a scripture passage or the declaration of a theological theme, include the color in the worship service. Though purple usually signifies penitence, this deep, captivating color can also represent royalty. *Rich tones of purple* can be employed to convey the regal office held by Jesus' early visitors.

❏ Fabrics

Fine tapestries, silk, and *brocades* woven in a wide array of majestic colors convey the royalty of Christ's visitors and the extravagant gifts that his presence invites.

❏ Flowers

Several different floral arrangements help interpret the magi's visit to Christ. One of my (DN) favorite arrangements involves the use of three containers, each from a different nation. Arranging flowers representative of a nation in a container from that nation and setting the arrangements side by side bespeaks inclusiveness—Christ's availability to the entirety of humankind.

Another approach is to arrange three kinds of unusual flowers in a single container. Using exotic or regal-like flowers such as *ginger*, *birds of paradise*, or *protea* presents a richness of color and foliage suggestive of royalty. In addition, the gifts of the magi can be represented florally. Arrangers, however, should become familiar with the nature and meaning of each gift they seek to depict.

Ancient Jews used *frankincense* as an ancient balm for healing. Priests included frankincense among the ingredients in the *incense*, which burned in the temple to purify the sanctuary. Thus, a gift of frankincense to Christ symbolized Christ's purity. The gift, therefore, was a perfect visual form of adoration for one who was divine and merits representation in our worship. Because of its derivation from the crushed leaves of an Arabian tree with exotic color or foliage, a *large tree* or a *large plant* effectively represents frankincense to contemporary worshipers of Christ.

Myrrh also can be represented florally. The ancients obtained this valuable herb from a *thorny shrub*, which blooms with small flowers and produces a plum-like fruit. People used myrrh in the process of embalming and as an ingredient in the holy oil preserved for anointing. Not surprisingly, as a gift to Christ, myrrh anticipated the suffering and death the holy one would experience. Placing *thorny plants bearing plum-like fruit* at the base of an arrangement or within an arrangement conveys the most primitive depiction of myrrh. This ancient gift of the magi can also be recalled by placing *resin* in an antique burial urn.

❏ Banners

Two independent banners serve well during Epiphany—one for
the actual day of Epiphany and the other for the following Sundays in Epiphany.

The season of Epiphany offers numerous possibilities for banner construction. A banner can center on a symbol chosen from the
traditional symbols of Epiphany:

> An orb with a cross symbolizing Christ's triumph over the sin of
> the world; a shell and drops of water connoting baptism; hands
> with fingers extended downward indicate the presence of God or
> the blessing of God; and four overlapping Latin crosses point to
> the church's mission to the four corners of the world.

Or, the focus of the banner can be on a phrase integral to the season of Epiphany:

> "Arise for your light has come"; "the glory of God has risen
> upon you"; "nations shall come to your light and the kings to the
> brightness of your rising"; "the true light that enlightens every-
> one was coming into the world"; "I am the root and offspring of
> David, the bright and morning star"; "O morning star how
> bright, how fair."

A banner with an abstract design can be created by swirling
black and white in a manner that communicates the theme of light
overcoming darkness. Similarly, an all black (or dark) fabric can
form a banner's background split or cracked open to reveal the
newness of light or a brilliant white symbolic of the future manifestation of Christ.

ℭounds . . . .

❑ The Word of God

Old Testament (Epiphany)	Psalms	Epistle	Gospel
Isa 60:1-6	72:1-14	Eph 3:1-12	Matt 2:1-2
(After Epiphany)			
*Isa 61:1-4	29	Acts 8:14-17	Luke 3:15-17, 21-22
*Isa 421-9		Acts 10:34-43	Matt 3:13-17
*Gen 1:1-5		Acts 19:1-7	Mark 1:4-11
Isa 62:1-5	36:5-10	1 Cor 12:1-11	John 2:1-11
Neh 8:1-4a 5-6, 8-10	19:7-14	1 Cor 12:12-30	Luke 4:14-21
Isa 61:1-8	138	1 Cor 15:1-11	Luke 5:1-11
Jer 17:5-10	1	1 Cor 15:12-20	Luke 6:17-26
Gen 45:3-11, & 15	37:1-11	1 Cor 15:35-38 42-50	Luke 6:39-49
Isa 55:10-13	92:1-4, 12-15	1 Cor 15:51-58	Luke 6:39-49
Isa 49:1-7	40:1-11	1 Cor 1:1-9	John 1:29-34
Isa 9:1-4	27:1-6	1 Cor 1:10-17	Matt 4:12-23
Mic 6:1-8	37:1-11	1 Cor 1:18-31	Matt 5:1-12
Isa 58:3-9a	112:4-9	1 Cor 2:1-11	Matt 5:13-16
Deut 30:15-20	119:1-8	1 Cor 3:1-9	Matt 5:17-26
Isa 49:8-13	62:5-12	1 Cor 3:10-11, 16-23	Matt 5:27-37
Lev 19:1-2, 9-18	119:33-40	1 Cor 4:1-5	Matt 5:38-48
1 Sam 3:1-10	63:1-8	1 Cor 6:12-15, 19-20	John 1:35-42
Jonah 3:1-5, 10	62:5-12	1 Cor 7:29-31	Mark 1:14-20
Deut 18:15-20	111	1 Cor 8:1-13	Mark 1:21-28
Job 7:1-7	147:1-11	1 Cor 9:16-23	Mark 1:29-39
2 Kgs 5:1-14	32	1 Cor 9:24-27	Mark 1:40-45
Isa 43:18-25	41	2 Cor 1:18-22	Mark 2:1-12
Hos 2:14-20	103:1-13	2 Cor 3:1-6	Mark 2:18-22
**Exod 34:29-35	99	2 Cor 3:12-4:2	Luke 9:28-36

| **Exod 24:12-18 | 2:6-11 | 2 Pet 1:16-21 | Matt 17:1-9 |
| **2 Kgs 2:1-12a | 50:1-6 | 2 Cor 4:3-6 | Mark 9:2-9 |

*First Sunday after Epiphany; Baptism of Jesus.
**Last Sunday after Epiphany; Transfiguration.

❑ Organ Literature

Any arrangement or set of variations of *How Brightly Shone that Morning Star*. The Chorale Prelude setting by J. Pachelbel is particularly nice.
Es ist ein' Ros' entsprungen (Behold a Rose is Blooming), Brahms from *Eleven Chorale Preludes*

❑ Piano Literature

"In the Monastery," Borodin
"Chorale I," "Old Hundredth," Willard Palmer, from *Contemporary Album for the Young*, Publ. Alfred

❑ Choral Literature

"Arise For Your Light Has Come," David Danner
"The Three Kings," Healy Willan
"A Star," Gary Allen Smith
"Creator of the Stars at Night," Jeffery Honore
"If Not Us?" Sheldon Curry
"Jesus, Thou Joy of Loving Hearts," Claude Bass
"He Comes to Us," Jane Marshal

❑ Congregational Hymns

"As With Gladness Men of Old," William Chatterton Dix, DIX Conrad Kocher

"We Three Kings of Orient Are," John Henry Hopkins, THREE KINGS OF ORIENT J. H. Hopkins

"What Child is This," William C. Dix, GREENSLEEVES Traditional English Melody, Harm. John Stainer

"Brightest and Best of the Songs of the Morning," Reginald Heber, MORNING STAR James Proctor Harding

"Songs of Thankfulness and Praise," Christopher Wordsworth, SALZ-BURG Melody, Jakob Hintze, Harm. Adap. J. S. Bach

❑ Homiletical Themes

Revelation; light; dawn; Incarnation; Christ's mission; universality of Christ; the universal gospel; the world-wide mission of the church; recovering from Christmas exertions; baptism; prayer; journey inward; and the revelation of God in everyday life.

❑ Sermon Titles

"Undeserved Epiphany" (Willimon)
"Arise, Shine!" (Cox)
"The Wideness of Christ and the Narrowness of Christianity" (Killinger)
"Keeping the Lights On" (Sehested)
"Widening the Circle" (Claypool)
"Losing the Star" (Killinger)
"Drenched in Grace: Jesus' Baptism" (Sehested)
"Honk If You Love Jesus: Celebrating Epiphany With Integrity" (Gaddy)

❑ Prayers

Revealing, Redeeming God:
We thank you for the gift of the gospel of light. We like enlightening, inspiring good news and this is the best news of all. You have accepted us, acted to redeem us, and invited us into a relationship fit for all eternity. Thank you

brilliant God.

Even as you have blessed us with the gospel of light, you have
challenged us. You have commissioned us to become
bearers of good news sharing light with other people,
witnesses to the power of the gospel.

Help us, God.

Enable our minds to think creatively as we develop
strategies for sharing light.

Enable our words to impact powerfully those to whom they
lovingly convey the gospel news.

Enable our actions to convey illuminating insights into your
compassion.

With glad hearts we have received the gospel of light. With
firm resolve we seek to share the gospel of light with
others. Thank you for entrusting us with it. Make us good
stewards of it.

We pray in the name of the Light who is the essence of the
gospel—the person of Jesus Christ. Amen.

              ————————   (Gaddy)

"If we walk in the Light
As He is in the Light . . ."
O Lord God.
Even our blindness must flee before Thee.
The night cannot say nay
To the coming of Thy dawn.
Though we see not,
During the night shall we wait,
And sing with shouts of joy
For we shall see
From the mountainside of eternity. Amen.

              ————————   (Otto)

God of Abraham, Isaac, and Jacob,
God of Sarah, Rachel, and Mary,
God of Gentiles and Jews:
We come to you in search of faith.

All around us are promises of security—security that can
be bought or earned in some other way.

All around us are various philosophies of life—
philosophies of success, self-aggression, and the like.
We come to you in search of faith.
We seek hope as well.

    We are weary of self-sufficiency. We are leery of
    positive thinking.
    Life seems far too much closed in upon us.
    We're not looking for an injection of optimism, but for
    communion with authentic hope.
We come to you in search of hope.
We also seek love.

    Though interacting with people all the time, we long for
    relationships of depth, covenants with endurance, and
    genuine self-less care.
    We are worn out with mechanical associations, superficial
    friendships, and an etiquette that barely covers
    prejudice.
We come to you in search of love.
O God of Light, instruct us even as you encounter us with
faith, hope, and love through the One in whose name we
pray. Amen.

               —————   (Gaddy)

❏ Congregational Litanies

Leader: The true Light,
             Not borrowed,
             Not reflected from afar,
             Has come into our midst.
People: **The true Light,**
             Underived,
             The source of all that is,
             Has entered its own creation.
Leader: In Him may we have faith,
             The gifts of confidence and trust.
             And thereby are we the born of God.
People: **Children, sons, and daughters**
             Of the Eternal,
             Our names are not given us

	By flesh and blood.
Leader:	Born of God,

Leader: Born of God,
Our destinies are not ephemeral,
Washed here and there
By the ebb and flow of time.

**People: To us has the light given power,
The power of Light.
To us is it given
To be borrowed rays
Of the Light of creation.**

Leader: Created in Christ,
Ours is a borrowed glory,
Called to be the praise
Of His glorious grace.

**All: Come, O Christ,
Thou Light of God,
Dispel our darkness;
Set us free
In the obedience of good works.**

—————   (Otto)

Sing: Fairest Lord Jesus, Ruler of all nature, O Thou of God and man the Son, Thee will I cherish, Thee will I honor, Thou my soul's glory, joy, and crown.

Leader: Fairest Lord Jesus, the light who warms this winter weary world and shines hope into its dry and dark and desolate corners, we look to you as people yearning to blossom forth into all the promise planted in our beings.

People: Lord Jesus Christ, to you we turn as the one who shows us who God is and how much God loves us, and, therefore, the capacity of our souls for living into our destiny to shine with God's radiance.

Sing: Fair as the meadows, Fairer still the woodlands, Robed in the blooming garb of spring; Jesus is fairer, Jesus is purer, who makes the woeful heart to sing.

Leader: Gracious God, we pray to come alive like the meadows and woodlands as spring stirs everything into life and the sweet scent of the season fills the air.

People: O God, let the power of Christ's story and the life force of your Spirit touch the essence of who we are and burst into bloom

in lives so beautiful and fragrant that they glorify you and draw our sisters and brothers to you because they have sensed your presence in our presence.

Sing: Fair is the sunshine, Fairer still the moonlight, And all the twinkling, starry host; Jesus shines brighter, Jesus shines purer, Than all the angels heaven can boast.

Leader: Spirit of God, from the dawn of creation until the consummation of all things made new, your light summons all God's beloved daughters and sons to follow in the way of Jesus Christ.

People: For this whole world we pray a turning toward your light so powerful that no darkness can overcome it, until each shall behold the other in full recognition that we are all your children, and all shall live together in peace; by the grace of Jesus Christ in whose name we pray. Amen.

———————

(Penfield)

Leader: How many the differences that color our ways and decorate our days.

People: We call them tribes and nations, cultures and civilizations.

Leader: So are we divided into eras and periods, belief systems, folkways, and mores.

People: As creatures of cultural differences, we find ourselves foreigners to one another, puzzled by our differences of belief and behavior, of life and mores.

Leader: Foreign and alien, mysteries to one another—yet are we not one, dwellers in the same home?

People: Are we not faced with the same threats, led by the same needs, consumed by similar thirsts?

Leader: And over all our times and ages falls the voice of the Eternal. "Let us make creatures in our image." Thus are we all the creatures made for the Eternal.

People: "O Lord, how majestic is Thy Name." In the mystery of descending from Thy hand do we find our oneness.

Leader: Herein is the Mystery of God revealed: In Christ all—in heaven, on the earth, and under the earth—shall be united to the Creator's glory.

People: "O Lord, how majestic is Thy Name." In the mystery of being grasped by thy saving love do we find our oneness—with

Thee, with one another, with all the ages of thy sons and
daughters.

—————————

(Otto)

Suggestions

- *Provide a visual reminder of the gifts* that the magi presented
  to the Christ child. The easiest of the three to reproduce is *gold*.
  Think through how this gift was packaged for travel as well as
  how it was presented to the Lord. Guided by those thoughts,
  place either *gold nuggets* or *gold powder* in a wooden box at the
  front of the worship center. Worshipers will not miss the
  symbolic meaning of this precious metal and its implicit
  encouragement for making a precious offering to Christ.

- *Transform a table in the narthex* of the worship center into a
  palette for interpretations of the gospel truths at the center of
  this season. For example, Epiphany invites a serious look at the
  first miracle of Christ. A visual reminder of this event set
  before worshipers prior to their entrance into the sanctuary can
  greatly enhance their understanding of the gospel text once
  inside. Set six *earthen* or *stone-like vessels* filled with water on a
  table outside the sanctuary. At the base of this grouping of jars,
  lay a container on its side, looking as if everything once within
  it has been poured out. At the rim of the empty vessel, set a
  shallow bowl filled with red wine, which is visible to worshipers
  entering the sanctuary. Placing a *gourd-like dipper* on its side in
  the bowl enhances the visual impact even more. Add a *bridal
  veil* as an accent to the display; worshipers immediately think
  of the setting and meaning of Jesus' miracle at the wedding in
  Cana of Galilee.

- *The calling of the disciples* constitutes another major Epiphany
  theme. Use a table in the narthex to present a visual display
  that will prepare worshipers for an encounter with this gospel
  story. Since Peter, Andrew, James, and John were summoned

to discipleship from the fishing industry, cover the entire top of the table with *sand*. Place in the sand a collection of *sea jewels, shells, urchins,* and other objects usually found along a seashore. Towards the back of the arrangement, create a backdrop with a plant such as *sea-oats* or *pampas grass*. A simple *crudely constructed stool* can be set near the plant along with a *hand-sewn knapsack*. *Nets* can be mounded beside the stool as if left there when their repair had been interrupted by a fisherman suddenly leaving.

• *Light is crucial to Epiphany. Candles* can serve as great reminders of the light of the world, who is the Christ. To prevent people from taking light for granted, plan a worship experience without light, present a painting without the presence of light, or hold up a jewel in darkness. Worshipers begin to comprehend the importance of the simple truth of Christ as light. Not until light moves upon, through, and within these various objects does their beauty really become visible. Here is the central truth of Epiphany.

• *Schedule an art exhibit* in which the presence of light is a necessity for the art to find its fullest expression. Invite an *art historian* to present a *lecture* on the artistic influence of light through the ages. Secure an artist who can demonstrate how the source of light placed at various locations within a piece of art alters the entire composition.

• *Exhibit a collection of cut glass and jewels.* Worshipers can see how light affects the appearance of each piece.

• *Invite an interior designer to lecture* on the effect of light within our living environments and to explain how color and light directly influence our *attitudes* and *emotions*.

• *Use Epiphany to bring about interracial and intercultural understanding.* Plan joint worship experiences and dialogue sessions to bring together two local congregations that have very different racial compositions. *Choral services* based on *ethnic music* can help break down barriers that divide people. Getting together with people unlike ourselves can aid our realization that the manifestation of Christ was to *all people.*

• *Instead of using flowers in a service of worship,* place mirror boxes atop urns and other containers throughout the sanctuary. As people move around in the worship center, they see realistically what other people see as the lights of the world— an overwhelming insight related to each individual's role in the mission of the Christian community.

Notes

[1]John H. Westerhoff III, *A Pilgrim People: Learning Through the Church Year* (Minneapolis MN: The Seabury Press, 1984) 59.

[2]Cited in L. W. Cowie and John Selwyn Gummer, *The Christian Calendar: A Complete Guide to the Seasons of the Christian Year Telling the Story of Christ and the Saints from Advent to Pentecost* (Springfield MA: G. & C. Merriam Company, Publishers, 1974) 37.

Floral Arrangements

The altar arrangement is designed to present a visual of the gifts of the magi. The altar arrangement consists of a walnut box filled with yellow and gold fressia. The burial urn contains a wild thorny shrub with small red berries. A third container is a bronze relief cache pot massed with rubrum lillies. Standing behind the table, a backdrop of evergreens towers eight feet above the arrangement. The three gifts are supported with ornate fabrics, representing the robes of the kings.

*The floral arrangement also creates a visual of the gifts of the magi.
Contained within the composition of the design is a walnut box filled
with yellow and gold fressia. The burial urn contains a wild thorny
shrub with small red berries. Rising from the arrangement is smoke
from the burning incense. The three gifts of the magi are supported with
ornate fabrics, representing the individual robes of the kings. A banner
for Epiphany hangs behind the arrangement.*

Worship Banners

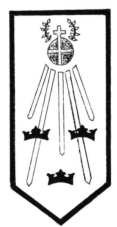

❏ Epiphany: Revelation ❏

Lent:
A Season of Penitence

Ominous, dark clouds boil up; if not on the distant horizon, then deep within our emotions. Frightening, strong wind currents erratically shift from one direction to another. A hint of betrayal sends a shudder through our souls. Trouble is in the air. Sounds of weeping assault our ears. Maybe Rachel is weeping for her children; perhaps it is the women in Jerusalem. More likely, however, we are hearing the sounds of our own sobs. Everything around us screams, "Crisis." Everything within us whispers, "Repent." We are entering the season of Lent.

History

Early Christians observed Good Friday and Easter Day—separated by a fast—as a singular observance of the crucifixion and resurrection of Jesus. This approach to the climactic events in the life of Jesus, however, quickly changed. By 100 A.D., Christian writings mentioned a period of fasting and praying called Lent.

The season of Lent developed as people recognized the importance of Easter celebrations. Christians developed a period of preparation adequate to ensure a proper observance of the resurrection event. During this period, the church devoted special attention to new converts to Christianity who were readying themselves for baptism on Easter Sunday. Members of the church prayed for the new Christians and also interrogated them in matters of doctrine. While everyone was expected to observe a Lenten fast to some extent, those awaiting baptism were instructed to fast for at least two or three weeks to demonstrate the kind of penitence that should precede baptism.

Different churches established different durations of time for Lent. Some congregations made it last three weeks, others six weeks, and still others seven weeks. In the Eastern Church, Lent remains a season of seven weeks excluding Saturdays and Sundays. Lent, however, does not include the Saturday prior to Easter known as Holy Saturday.

After Christianity became a legally recognized religion (about A.D. 313), many people entered the church devoid of devotion suitable for disciples of Christ. This grave situation gave added importance to Lent as a period of instruction in the Christian faith, development in discipline, and growth in discipleship.

Church leaders established Lent, also called Quadragesima (meaning "forty days"), as an exact forty-day period in the fifth century. A focus on doctrinal teaching, disciplined preparation for Easter, and renewal in faith remained in tact.

Since the resurrection of Jesus, Christians have observed Sundays as feast days, weekly celebrations of Christ's triumph over death. Not even an officially recognized, extended period of fasting could change Sunday from a feast day to a day of fasting. Liturgical literature, therefore, refers to Sundays during the period from Ash Wednesday to Easter as Sundays *in* Lent rather than Sundays *of* Lent.

 *Sensations* . . . .

Lent is a challenging season, perhaps the most difficult in the Christian year. Once again *preparation* is involved. Unlike the preparation of Advent, which builds to the crescendo of a heavenly birth, the preparation of Lent leads straight to a gruesome death. A resurrection will come, to be sure; but the only way to get to the resurrection is by going through a crucifixion.

Lenten worship brings us to a realization that what happened to Jesus during the last segment of his ministry in the first century most likely would happen to him in our day as well. *Good and evil are all mixed up together.* We see that truth more clearly than ever during Lent. Individuals who should have been among the first to accept Jesus took up prominent positions against him while many non-religious folks welcomed Jesus into their lives. Good people committed dastardly deeds while so-called bad people demonstrated heroic virtue. Left scratching our heads because of the confusion, we suddenly realize that we are a part of the confusing picture. Good and bad exist side-by-side within each of us. If a seemingly morally upright person could turn on Jesus with hostility in the first century, it could happen again. A capacity for betrayal resides deep within us all.

Confronting the stark reality of our potential for good and evil, Lent leads to *careful self-examination* through *long periods of introspection*; this is not an easy activity. We schedule times of *solitude* and *silence*. Of necessity, *discipline* becomes a major ingredient in our spirituality. Efforts to clear away distractions and to deepen our communion with God may require *healthy sacrifices*. The goal of Lenten worship, however, is not better self-awareness but a deeper, more faithful commitment to the lordship of Christ— *strengthening the spiritual life, experiencing spiritual renewal.*

John Westerhoff calls Lent *"the season of adolescence."*[1] During Lent, the dreamers of Epiphany run headlong into large, hard chunks of reality, like death. Partying gives way to contemplation and maybe even mourning. The aim is to bring about *intentional decision-making* that prepares us to live in a world where costly decisions have to be made about support for or opposition to the work of God.

Cognizant of a relationship between *physical hunger* and *spiritual desire*, traditionally the church has encouraged *fasting* or at least *abstaining* from certain foods during Lent. In more recent years, the practice of *self-denial* has reached beyond dietary considerations. Lenten worshipers commit to *giving up* something —an activity, an expenditure of money, a bad habit. Lent may also be properly observed by *taking on* something important such as a commitment to Bible study, a resolution to visit people in need, or a scheduled time for prayer.

Some Christian traditions designate Lent as a time to *re-establish contact with persons who have dropped out of the church* and to *dramatize the costly nature of forgiveness* by seeking a renewal of fellowship with individuals guilty of notorious wrongdoing. Great ways to understand the redemptive activity of God!

When true to the original purpose of Lent—abstinence from worldly amusements in order to prepare for a celebration of Easter —programs of personal social involvements decrease and programs in the life of the church increase. Program emphases for the church rightly focus on the development of *Christlike behavior.* Specific program emphases appropriate for the season include:

> Health issues; stress management; marriage and family relation- ships; coping with the stages of life; self-acceptance; racial issues; basic biblical studies; spirituality; biblical perspectives on social issues; a history of art and liturgy; aerobics; calligraphy; hym- ology; liturgy and worship; laity in worship; and liturgical movement.

Lent holds little overt attraction but great promise. Few people enjoy receiving an invitation to come apart for a while to mourn, contemplate death, engage in penitence, and make radical com- mitments. Only through such practices, however, do Christians ready themselves to respond obediently to the crucified Christ who said emphatically, "Follow me."

Sights

Flowers and flourishes are no more appropriate during the Lenten season than alleluias. Every element of Lenten worship exists to prepare worshipers for the festive season that follows. Just as altarware typically gets cleaned during Lent—in anticipation of Easter Sunday—worshipers prepare themselves as vessels fit to be filled with the truth of the gospel.

A *dancer* serves as an unlikely artisan of unusual worth in Lent- en communication. Dancers express a language of the soul that words cannot convey. Reflective pieces of dance can symbolize in shapes what people's hearts yearn to reveal. At its best, liturgical dance forms a visible prayer. Meditative movement provides an insight into the spirit's dance with God.

Sculpted pottery also serves as a helpful visual statement on the season of Lent. The very idea of clay shaped into vessels of use- fulness and beauty by an artist's hands sets before worshipers the great potential associated with God shaping our lives.

Displays outside the worship center, preferably in the narthex, can attract and stimulate the attention of worshipers before the first note of a prelude is played. Keep in mind that each visual must be purposeful, contributing to the worship of God and providing enlightenment for worshipers. Visuals in worship should be aesthetically pleasing, but their primary purpose is to point worshipers to the truth of the day.

Potentially helpful visual interpretations of key biblical narratives include the following:

- *The temptations of Christ.* A floral arrangement centered on a table outside the worship center can depict the wilderness temptation of Christ. *A large-scaled, bare-branched tree* with *wild overgrown grasses* and *old winter dried stalks* placed toward the back of the table create the impression of a wasteland. *Large stones mounded with dirt* and *moss* underneath them cover the entire front portion of the table. One of the stones appears split. This can be accomplished by using papier-mâché to shape a stone that matches real stones. *A half of a loaf of bread* set in the pocket of the split stone suggests the creation of bread from a stone, which was one of the temptations of Jesus. The bread should be sprayed or varnished so that it does not look like real bread

- *The healing of a blind man.* Create a reproduction of the sight of Jesus' healing of a blind man in one of the major intersections of worshipers' routes to the sanctuary. A child's wading pool serves as a *pool of water*. The plastic pool is disguised with *burlap fabric* around its outer edge and sprayed with *dark grey paint* on the inside. *Large stones, green plants,* and *wild grasses* are then placed around the pool. The edge of this reproduced landscape ends with real dirt. Beside the pool *a mound of fabric* is suggestive of the man's clothing. At the center of this visual is a *paste of clay* created in the dirt—a small mound of dirt gathered and moistened to a "dirt pie" consistency.

- *Money changers in the temple.* In the entrance way to the sanctuary, turn a large table on its side. Objects that normally appear on the table lie on the floor, perhaps broken. Scatter *foreign coins* across the floor. In the sanctuary, as well as at other points along the entrance way to it, turn over additional tables and disperse coin boxes on the floor. Dishevel pictures and rugs in the entrance way. Worshipers immediately know that things are not as they should be. These visuals create a teachable moment for experiencing the meaning of the gospel text.

- *A grain of wheat which must die.* The contents of a *long, sectioned, plexiglass container* in the narthex proclaim the gospel lesson, showing the life cycle of a grain of wheat. Section one contains *a shaft of wheat.* Section two contains *a grain of wheat,* such as that which falls to the ground. Section three shows a grain of wheat obviously dying. Section four contains *lifeless dirt.* Section five heralds the promise of new life. Section six contains evidence of new life. An accompanying meditation written in *calligraphy* enhances the display.

  Cling not to the things of the past.
  Realize the hope of the gospel.
  What you glean from the past will
  reveal fresh insights for new
  beginnings.

  In the sanctuary, arrange *fully mature stalks of wheat* around the communion table. Design the stalks of wheat in such a way as to give the impression that they are growing naturally on the floor.

- *The anointing of Jesus.* The *fragrance* of a *sweet ointment* fills the room. Burning *incense* can accomplish this goal quickly. A series of *pedestals* of various heights stand close to an aisle in the sanctuary where they cannot be ignored. On the pedestals appear a collection of *bottles* nice enough to be considered precious. Two or three of the bottles have been turned on their sides, obviously emptied of their contents. *Liquid* from one of the bottles appears spilled on a slab of marble set atop one of the pedestals. A *small dampened linen hand towel* lays near the spill. Devotion to Christ has been declared. Worshipers question, however, whether or not the display of affection was in order even though Christ was its object. The money from this display could have been used to feed the poor.

❑ Banners

Symbols for use on banners are as scarce for Lent as they are plentiful for Holy Week. The *cross* is simple and ample. Some traditions, however, choose not to display banners of any kind during this penitential period.

If a Lenten banner is constructed of fabric, *simple linens* or *cotton fabrics* should be used instead of expensive brocades or fine silk. Burlap is a good communicative fabric (sackcloth) out of which to make a banner for Lent.

A banner can be developed with a focus on a *key phrase*:

"Have mercy on me, O God"; "Kyrie Eleison"; "Create in me a clean heart, O God"; "Cast me not away from your presence, and take not your Holy Spirit from me"; "Restore unto me the joy of my salvation"; "Purge me from my sin and I shall be pure"; "Wash me, and I shall be clean indeed."

Or, the banner can center on *a single word*:

Recreation; Restoration; Renewed; Separated-Reconciled; Repentance; Woe; Wash; Penitence; Repent.

Sounds . . . .

❏ The Word of God

Old Testament	Psalm	Epistle	Gospel
Gen 9:8-17	25:1-10	1 Pet 3:18-22	Mark 1:9-15
Gen 17:1-10, 15-19	105:1-11	Rom 4:16-25	Mark 8:31-38
Exod 20:1-17	19:7-14	1 Cor 1:22-25	John 2:13-22
2 Chr 36:14-23	137:1-6	Eph 2:4-10	John 3:14-21
Jer 31:31-34	51:10-17	Heb 5:7-10	John 12:20-33
Deut 26:1-11	91:9-16	Rom 10:8b-13	Luke 4:1-13
Gen 15:1-12	127	Phil 3:17-4:1	Luke 13:31-35
Exod 3:1-15	103:1-13	1 Cor 10:1-13	Luke 13:1-9
Josh 5:9-12	34:1-8	2 Cor 5:16-21	Luke 15:1-3, 11-32
Isa 43:16-21	126	Phil 3:18-24	John 12:1-8
Gen 2:4b-9, 15-17, 25-3:7	130	Rom 5:12-19	Matt 4:1-11
Gen 12:1-8	33:18-22	Rom 4:1-5, 13-17	John 3:1-17
Exod 17:3-7	95	Rom 5:1-11	John 4:5-42
1 Sam 16:1-13	23	Eph 5:8-14	John 9:1-41
Ezek 37:1-14	116:1-9	Rom 8:6-19	John 11:1-53

(Ash Wednesday)

Joel 2:1-2, 12-17a	22:1-18	Heb 4:14-16 & 5:7-9	John 18:1-19:42 or 19:17-30

❏ Choral Literature

"The Best of All Rooms," Randall Thompson
"The Eyes of All," Jean Berger
"Be Thou My Vision," John Rutter
"Jesus, I Adore Thee," Stephen Carricciolo
"Set Me As a Seal," Rene Clausen
"Spring in the Dessert," Arthur Jennings

"*Cantique de Jean Racine*," Gabriel Faure
"Create in Me a Clean Heart," Carl Mueller
"My Shepherd Will Supply My Need," Virgil Thomson
"Blessed Are They," Ed. Jane Marshall
"Hush! Somebody's Calling My Name," Brazil Dennard
"Psalm 131," Jeffery Van
"The Lord is My Shepherd," Randall Thompson
"Cast Thy Burden Upon the Lord," Mendelssohn
"O Love How Deep," Everett Titcomb
"*Veni Jesu*," Cherubini
"Here's One," Arr. Mark Hayes
"When I Survey the Wondrous Cross," arr. Gilbert Martin
"Jesus, My Lord, My Life, My All," Bob Burroughs
"Precious Lord, Take My Hand," Arr. Roy Ringwald
"King of Glory, King of Peace," Harold Friedell

(Ash Wednesday)

"O Make Our Hearts to Blossom," Joseph Clokey
"Amazing Grace," Arr. Samuel Adler
"Jesus Loves Me," Arr. Doris Nelson

❏ Organ Literature

O Mensch Bewein (O Man, Bewail thy grievous Sin), J. S. Bach in *Orgelbuchlein*
Liebster Jesu, wie sind hier (Blessed Jesus, We are Here), chorale prelude by J. S. Bach
Chaconne, Louis Couperin (H. W. Gray-Belwin), St. Cecilia Series

❏ Piano Literature

"Sonata, Op. 13, 2nd movement, Adagio cantabile," Beethoven
"Organ Prelude in E Minor," Bach-Siloti

❑ Congregational Hymns

"Deck Thyself, My Soul, With Gladness," Johann Franck, Tr. Catherine Winkworth, SCHMUCKE DICH Johann Cruger

"Guide Me, O Thou Great Jehovah," William Williams, CWM RHONDDA John Hughes

"Breathe On Me, Breath of God," Edwin Hatch, TRENTHAM Robert Jackson

"Take My Life and Let It Be Consecrated," Frances Havergal, HENDON Henri A. C. Malan

"Jesus, Thou Joy of Loving Hearts," Bernard of Clairvaux, Tr. Ray Palmer, QUEBEC Henry Baker

"O For a Thousand Tongues to Sing," Charles Wesley, AZMON Carl G. Glaser

❑ Homiletical Themes

Confrontation with sin and death; self-examination; intentional decision-making; healthy sacrifices; mortality and hope; wilderness faith; lament; hopelessness; temptations; freedom; the cost of discipleship; repentance; amendment of life; re-entering; the inseparability of good and evil in the world; and learning to be quick and simple.

❑ Sermon Titles

"As It All Began" (Gen 2:4b-9, 15-17, 25-3:7) (Cox)
"Can These Bones Live?" (Sehested)
"Seeing the World Through Kingdom Eyes" (Killinger)
"The Narrow Way of Discipleship" (Willimon)
"The Meaning of Self-Denial" (Claypool)
"You—Old and New" (Rom 5:12-19) (Cox)
"Embracing the Exile" (Sehested)
"Learning to Let Go of the Past" (Killinger)
"A Walk on the Wild Side—The Wilderness Journey" (Sehested)
"What Counts in Religion" (Rom 5:1-11) (Cox)
"Where Have All the Heroes Gone?" (Deut 34) (Sehested)

☐ Prayers

The most difficult task, O Lord,
Is to throw away what we possess,
To come before Thee with empty hands.
     Nevertheless, that is our glory—
To receive ourselves from Thee.
Glory be to Thee, our Father.
When we do not possess ourselves,
When our very being
Is always a receiving from Thee,
Then nothing can dispossess us of ourselves.
     We are Thine, O Lord,
Claimed at the Tree,
Liberated by Thy Son's blood.
So, we shall rejoice in Thee
Through Jesus Christ, our Lord. Amen.

———————

(Otto)

God, forgive us for being asleep when you need us. You agonize over the world's hungry while we worry over the menu. You weep with the soul of one who is friendless while we wonder whom to invite to our home. God, forgive us for often taking your children for granted and not risking our security for their needs—for your sake. We know Christ's teachings. We know the needs of the world. We know ourselves. God, forgive us for not transforming what we have been taught into what we do. Amen.

———————

(Sledge)

We confess, our Father,
That we listen to our fears and dine on our despair.
We are too ready to seek safety behind locked doors, too
    reluctant to look unto Him who is the Author and Perfecter
    of our faith.
We accept the verdict of our fears, and forget Him who also
    looked into the Darkness and said, "Into Thy hands I
    commit My spirit."
It is a home made safe, which we seek for our faith.
Doubtful are we of peace and joy in the midst of the terror
    that tyrannizes by night and by day.

We are Thy faithless servants, O Lord, huddled behind locked
   doors in fear of the Darkness outside. Amen.

————————
                                                                     (Otto)

God, perhaps we don't walk toward Jerusalem as much as we
   rush through the motions of our days that we think will get
   us further along on our journey.
So catch us in our anxious scurrying, Lord, and hold our feet
   in the fire of your Lenten grace that we may begin to die
   anew to the things that keep us from living with you and
   with our neighbors on this earth.
Loosen our grip on our grudges and our indifference
         to certainties that smother possibilities
         to our insistence on how things have to be
         to our fears that
               eat away at the wonder of living today
               and the adventure of losing our lives
               in order to find them in you.
Catch us in our aimless scurrying, Lord
         and hold our hearts in this Lenten season.
Create in each of us a resting place, a kneeling place
There may we empty ourselves of our self-importance and
   become vulnerable enough to listen for your word to us.
There may we intercede for the children, youth, and adults of
   our world who have more pain in their lives than love.
Catch us in our scurrying, Lord, and hold our spirits
   in this Lenten season.
Grant us peace enough to want more peace and the will to
   submit to nothing less.
Help us set our faces firmly against friendly suggestions
         to live a safe, expedient life. Rather, let us follow
         the way of the cross where despair is transformed by
         the promise of new life.
When we are too eager to be "better than" . . .
When we are too rushed to care . . .
When we are too tired to bother . . .
When we don't really listen . . .
When we are too quick to act from motives other than love.
Catch our feet . . . our actions
         in your costly love. Amen.

————————
                                                                  (Sledge)

❑ Congregational Litanies

Leader: We entered into a Holy Lent, O Lord,
       and we look for new hope in our hearts
       with the coming of the springtime.
       For you, O Lord, give hope and joy where there is
       sadness.
       Have mercy on us, Lord, and hear our prayers and
       confessions.

People: **Have mercy on your people, Lord.**

Leader: Hear us in these forty days, O Lord, and give us
       cleansed lives.
       Hear our petitions, hear our fears, hear our
       sorrows;
       Hear us, O Lord; place within us new hope
       and fill our hearts with joy.

People: **Hear us, O Lord, and fill our hearts.**

Leader: And from our hearts of joy, may we praise you,
       Lord.
       For you are a compassionate and gracious God,
       slow to be angry with us and abounding in love
       and faithfulness.

People: **Great is your love to us, O Lord.**

Leader: We will praise you, O Lord, with all our hearts;
       We will glorify your name forever;

People: **For great is your love to us, Lord.**

Leader: Hear us, O Lord. Guard each of us and protect us.
       Bring us hope with the coming of spring.
       Grace us with joyful hearts.
       Grant us your promise of new life.

People: **Bring joy to your servant**
       for to you, O Lord, I lift up my soul.

Leader: And in this holy season of Lent,
       and in the fresh newness of spring that soon
       will come,
       may you find God's promise of hope, and joy,
       and new life.
       And may the peace of the Lord be with you all.

People: **And also with you.**

—————

(Findley)

Leader: God calls us to make ready for once again journeying through Holy Week, contemplating the cross of Christ, and celebrating his resurrection.

People: **Lent is the season of our preparation.**

Leader: With God's help, what do you plan to give up during Lent?

People: **Fornication, impurity, licentiousness, idolatry, sorcery, enmity, strife, jealousy, anger, selfishness, dissension, party spirit, envy, drunkenness, carousing, and the like.**

Leader: With God's help, what do you plan to take on during Lent?

People: **Love, joy, peace, patience, kindness, goodness, faithfulness, gentleness, self-control.**

Leader: Good! Do that with God's help and you will give up the "works of the flesh" and take on "the fruit of the Spirit;" disciplines important not only to prepare for Holy Week and Easter, but for all of life. Good journey. God's speed. (based on Galatians 45:19-20, 22-23)

                                                 (Gaddy)

———————

Leader: The day of betrayal is Wednesday

People: **Always Wednesday?**

Leader: No, just anyday
               In which gold glitters
                    More brightly than grace
               Or anxiety obliterates the face
                    of the Friend
               In whom we put our confidence
                    then turned again to self reliance
               And seal betrayal with a kiss
                    of feigned friendship

People: **Full from our lips**
               There drop the honeyed words
                    "Master, I will follow thee."

Leader: But He can see
               Betrayal on Wednesday
               on anyday
               on everyday.

People: **What shall he say,**
               the Betrayed,
               on that last great day?

Leader: "Even in betrayal
            I loved you all the way
            on Wednesday
            on Everyday."

                        _____   (Hendricks)

Leader: Since my people are crushed, I am crushed, says the
            Lord.
People: Is there no balm in Gilead? Is there no Physician
            there?
Leader: Why is there no healing for the wound of my people?
People: Is there no balm in Gilead? Is there no Physician
            there?
Leader: I will make a covenant with my people, says the
            Lord . . .
People: Not written on tablets of stone
            but upon the tablets of our hearts.
Leader: I will be their God, and they will be my people.
People: We will all know the Lord,
            from the least of us to the greatest.
Leader: And God will forgive our wickedness,
            and remember our sins no more.
All: There is a balm in Gilead to make the wounded
            whole.
        There is a balm in Gilead to heal the sin-sick
            soul. (From Jeremiah 8 and 31)

                        _____   (Findley)

Suggestions

- *Display pieces of art* that contribute to the reflective, penitential nature of the week. Gwen McClure's Tripticon Museum
  in Louisville, Kentucky, contains numerous artistic expressions
  that are available for churches to exhibit. Recently, we borrowed from this collection a set of large batiks known as the
  "Stations of the Cross" and displayed them during this season.
  Each stretched canvas, colored in various shades of the Lenten

palette, offered a contemporary interpretation of Jesus' journey to the cross.

We exhibited the collection of fourteen batiks throughout Lent, keeping our church open at special, publicly announced hours so people in our community would have an opportunity to see them. We provided printed scripture passages and a meditative commentary related to each piece, thus enabling viewers of the art to engage in a spiritual journey. I (WG) planned a brief but very concentrated homily on each of the major themes portrayed in the batiks and offered these in a series of vesper-type services.

During Holy Week many people walked the way of the cross by means of these magnificent pieces of art. Several parochial schools visited our building and led their students along this journey.

- Plan a service *recreating the crucial gospel event of Jesus raising Lazarus* from the dead. Bind each worshiper entering the sanctuary with a strip of torn white gauze fabric. During the service, particularly during the sermon, emphasize how we allow life to bind us and prevent us from enjoying the freedom of the Christian life. Following the sermon, at the time of the commission, remind worshipers that a part of the work of the church involves removing from each other the grave clothes that bind us. Then, provide each worshiper an opportunity to loosen the "grave clothes" (the piece of gauze) from another worshiper and return the cloth to the freed person. Invite the newly liberated worshiper to come forward and place the strip of binding it on a crudely constructed cross standing at the chancel. As the collection of binding fabrics grows, a haunting abstract sculpture emerges. The ghostly image of a cross establishes the necessity of its existence. By the death of Christ, we are set free.

- *Schedule special hours of worship* throughout the season of Lent. A brief worship experience once a week at noontime can work well. Such occasions of Lenten worship provide good opportunities to invite ministers from neighboring congregations to serve as worship leaders.

A Lenten Service of Worship
Ash Wednesday

Lent begins on Ash Wednesday, a solemn day for penitence, fasting, and involvement in corporate worship. Observed since the eighth century, Ash Wednesday takes its name from the practice of worshipers placing ashes on their foreheads as an act of penitence and a symbol of human mortality. These liturgical actions stand within the Old Testament tradition of using ashes to signify repentance and mourning.

When worshipers arrived for the early morning service (7:15 A.M.), they found the front of the portico of our church building draped in *billowing grey fabrics*. As they entered the narthex, they saw a table containing *an arrangement of piled embers* theatrically rigged with dry ice to produce *smoke*. Immediately, each person is confronted by the symbol of ashes and a real demand for sacrifice.

Somber sounds produced by a duet of *recorder* and *cello* greeted worshipers as they took their seats in the sanctuary. An unaccompanied *oboe* or *violin* can produce a similar confessional attitude.

Located on the main isle of the sanctuary, worshipers encountered a piece of *raku pottery*, grey with edges torn and jagged as if damaged by a fire. *Ashes*—traditionally made by burning palm leaves used in the Palm Sunday service from the previous year—spilled out of the pottery. The altar cloth had been replaced with a cloth graduating from bottom to top in colors from *black* to *dark, grey* to *light grey* to *powder grey*, and *light purple* to *dark purple*. The contemporary design of the cloth containing *layered teardrops* offered a stark reminder of the penitential nature of the day. Flaming torches stood in the urns embracing the altar as reminders of the ancient mystery associated with purification by fire.

Following the *organist's* presentation of Mueller's "Create in Me A Clean Heart," the pastor called people to worship saying, "Today's service of divine worship is quite simple, but in many ways the service is as difficult as it is simple. We begin the journey to the cross by taking upon our foreheads the sign of the cross. The sign is a reminder of who we are—persons created from dust who go back to dust. It is a reminder of what we can do—kill the Son of God. It is a sign of repentance. The sign of the cross is also a symbol of commitment."

A reading of Psalm 51:1-12 helps prepare worshipers for a *prayer of confession* in which each one is invited to share. The prayer can be a unison offering, a responsorial presentation, or a silent communication. Sometimes *visual reminders,* such as photographic slides of hurting people who have been neglected, aid the worshipers's statement of *kyrie, eleison*—"Lord have mercy."

The *imposition of ashes* may be done by worshipers moving to the front of the sanctuary and receiving the sign of the cross from the ministers or by congregants moving to the main aisle and imposing ashes on each other. *Physical contact* etches into the memory truths that last long after the sign of the ashes disappears. The person imposing ashes on the forehead of another usually comments while forming the sign of the cross, "Remember, thou art dust and unto dust thou shalt return" or "As in Adam all die, so in Christ shall all be made alive."

Worship leaders change the appearance of the sanctuary as the service concludes and a period of meditation begins. *Fine linens* are stripped away and replaced with *burlap* and *muslin.* The exquisite Saint Phillip's processional cross, which stands at the front of our sanctuary, is replaced with a *crudely constructed* and *severely weathered iron cross.* The large *altar candlesticks* are then removed and *candleholders of iron, pottery,* or even *large tree trunks* constructed to hold candles set in their place. The environment of the worship center reflects the *frailty of humankind. Earthen vessels* replace brass containers and *clay pots* set where magnificent urns usually stand. All that the worshipers see communicates dependency upon Almighty God.

We pray that each worshiper will incorporate experientially the sights and sounds that fill the worship center. All bear a *sign of the cross* smudged on their foreheads in gray. The content of their souls, however, matters more than the pigmentation on their skin.

The service concluded with the singing of "Jesus, I my Cross Have Taken" as the recessional hymn. In the *commission* to the worshipers, the pastor declared, "Go now as marked people—people claimed by Christ, people committed to the God who brings healing from suffering and life from death."

Notes

[1]John H. Westerhoff III, *A Pilgrim People: Learning Through the Church Year* (Minneapolis MN: The Seabury Press, 1984) 71.

Floral Arrangements

Shafts of wheat, clusters of grapes, and a garland of leaves communicate a visual "remembrance" during Lent. Burlap, purple gauze, cotton fabric, and a crown made of thorns heightens members' awareness of Easter.

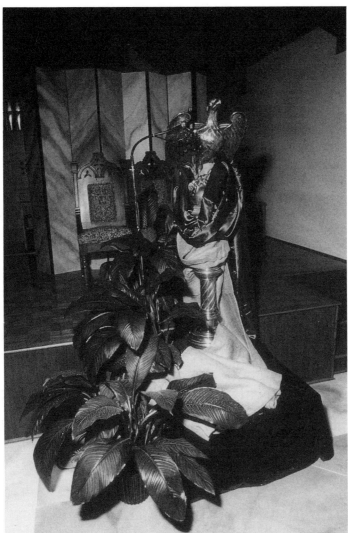

An arrangement of greenery graces the lectern for the Lenten season. Burlap, purple gauze, and cotton fabric enhance the design.

Worship Banners

SURELY he has BORNE OUR GRIEFS AND CARRIED OUR SORROWS

❑ Lent: Penitence ❑

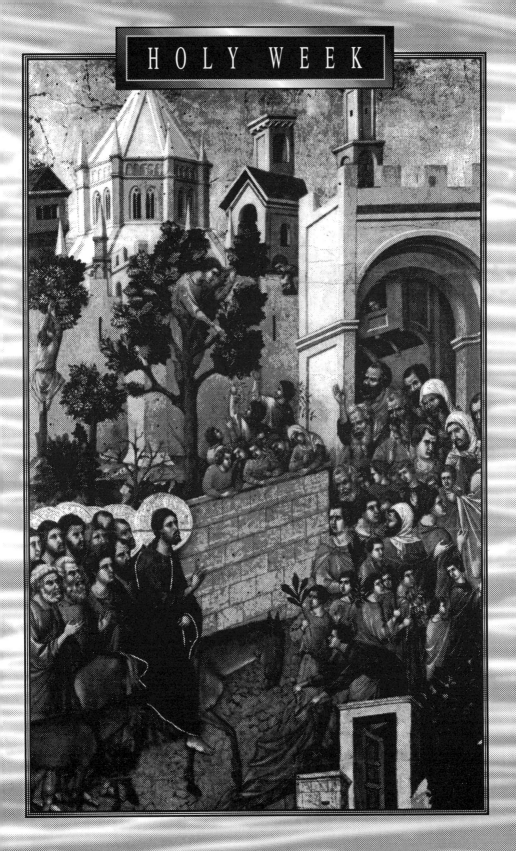

Holy Week:
A Season of Passion

Christians devote special attention to the last week of Lent, which is commonly known as Holy Week. The Great Week, the Week of Forgiveness, and the Week of the Holy Passion were other names used by early writers for the last week of Lent. During this seven-day period—not all traditions include Palm Sunday as part of Holy Week—Christian worshipers retrace the steps that marked the final week of Jesus' public ministry and finally carried his body to the place of his execution.

History

From the middle of the third century, Christians assigned unique spiritual significance to the week prior to the Pasch (Easter). No structure, however, had been prepared for worship during this time. Most likely, the structure in worship came from the church in Jerusalem in the latter part of the fourth century. By this date throngs of Christian pilgrimages annually crowded into Jerusalem before Easter to retrace the steps of Jesus and worship at various sacred sites associated with his passion. Church leaders in Jerusalem responded to the overwhelming interest in the passion by linking together key events in the last week of Jesus' ministry—when (the days) and where (the places) they occurred. The church leaders also provided meaningful forms of worship for this spiritually important season.

Though Holy Week had not developed as a liturgical season outside Jerusalem, the pre-Pasch observance quickly caught on in other places. Holy Week rapidly became a major occasion for Christian worship, and people realized the powerful potential of encountering Christ through fidelity to the Christian calendar.

Three major worship services attract most of the liturgical attention during Holy Week: Palm Sunday, Maundy Thursday, and Good Friday services. In addition, many churches host a *tenebrae* service on Wednesday evening. *Tenebrae* is a service of increasing darkness in which worshipers meditate on New Testament narratives of key events from the Last Supper to the entombment of Jesus. Numerous churches host an Easter Vigil on Holy Saturday night. Easter Vigil is a service celebrating the passion of Jesus and anticipating his resurrection.

Because of the distinctive importance of each service, Palm Sunday, Maundy Thursday, and Good Friday will each be treated separately.

Palm Sunday

Palm Sunday, also called the Sunday of the Passion, begins Holy Week and focuses the church's attention on the passion of Jesus during his last week in Jerusalem. The major liturgical events of the day had their origin in fourth-century Jerusalem.

In Jerusalem, early Christians traveled to the Mount of Olives during the afternoon of Palm Sunday, gathering on the summit of the mount. There, at 5:00 P.M., after an afternoon of hearing scriptures read and singing together, people listened once again to the gospels' account of Jesus' triumphal entry into Jerusalem. Still together, they slowly processed from the peak of the Mount of Olives into the Holy City. Each worshiper carried a branch of palm or olive and joined in the exultant singing of "Blessed is he that cometh in the name of the Lord."

Over the next eight centuries, Palm Sunday observances spread to Christian congregations all over the world, finally arriving in Rome in the twelfth century. Palm leaves were blessed as worshipers took them up and waved them during the processionals with which Palm Sunday worship services began. A gospel reading of Jesus' entry into Jerusalem occupied a central position in the liturgy for this day.

Little about Palm Sunday worship has changed from that time to the present. In many churches today, however, only children participate in the procession of palms.

Sights . . . .

Palm branches are integral to the visuals of Palm Sunday; they can be incorporated into the service in a variety of ways.

Processional banners constructed from *richly colored fabric* greatly enhance the pageantry of the day. A Palm Sunday banner can focus exclusively on a palm branch or incorporate other symbols that convey the idea of a parade. The pole used in carrying the banner can be wrapped and streaming ribbons in shades of violet and purple attached to the bottom of the banner. Gates can be used on a banner with, or instead of, palm branches to depict Jesus' entrance into Jerusalem. Another possibility for the content of a banner involves interweaving two crowns—a regal crown and a crown of thorns—to capture the realism of the day. If words are used on a Palm Sunday banner, good choices include "Shout aloud, O daughter of Jerusalem"; "Lo your king comes to you"; and "Hosanna, blessed is he that comes."

A hanging banner can be used as well as, or in place of, processional banners. Hanging a large *swag of fabric* at the front of the sanctuary or over each of the side aisles creates a beautiful and vibrant suggestion of celebration. Also, simple pieces of fabric cut in various designs on a banner provide a dramatic statement on the biblical events so crucial to this occasion. In each instance, however, the color palette of the banner should be limited to the liturgical colors of the season.

Dancers add a wonderful dimension to Palm Sunday by leading the processional into worship while holding *long flowing ribbon* or *fabric* in the *purple and violet* hues of the season. These colors prompt anticipation of the sorrow that lies ahead.

◀🎵▶ . . . .   *Sounds*

❑ The Word of God

Old Testament	Psalm	Epistle	Gospel
Isa 50:4-9a	118:19-29	Phil 2:5-11	Matt 21:1-11
			Luke 19:28-40
			11:1-11

❑ Choral Literature

"Lift Up Your Heads, O Ye Gates," William Mathias
"Go Not Far From Me, O God," N. Zingarelli
"Offertory," John Ness Beck
"Adoramus Te," G. P. Palestrina

❑ Organ Literature

Chorale Fantasia, *"Valet Will ich dir Geben"* ("All Glory, Laud, and Honor"), BWV 735, J. S. Bach
(Bach, *Orgelwerke*, Serie IV, Band III. Leipzg: Deutscher Verlag Fur Musik)
Hymn-Prelude, "Truro," Seth Bingham
(Bingham, Seth. *Twelve Hymn-Preludes.* Set 1, 14–16, NY: H. W. Gray)
Chorale, *"Valet Will Ich dir Geben"* ("All Glory, Laud, and Honor")
(Keller, Hermann, ed. *Eighty Chorale Preludes*, 106–107. NY: C. F. Peters Corp. 4448)
Chorale, *"Valet will ich dir Geben,"* Max Reger
(Reger, Max. *30 Short Chorale Preludes*, 22, NY: C. F. Peters Corp. 3980)

❑ Piano Literature

"Intermezzo," Op. 118, No. 2, Brahms
"Intermezzo," Op. 116, No. 6, Brahms

❑ Congregational Hymns

"All Glory, Laud, and Honor," Theodulph of Orleans, Tr. John Mason Neale, VALET WILL ICH DIR GEBEN Melchoir Teschner

"Ride On, Ride On in Majesty," Henry Hart Milman, ST. DROSTANE John B. Dykes

"Lift Up Your Heards, Ye Mighty Gates," George Weissel, Tr. Catherine Winkworth TRURO Thomas Williams' *Psalmodia Evangelica*

"Hosanna, Loud Hosanna," Jennette Threlfall ELLACOMBE *Gesangbuch*

"Alone Thou Goest Forth, O Lord," Peter Abelard, Tr. Bland Tucker, BANGOR William Tans'ur

❑ Homiletical Themes

Fickle faith; rejoicing and lament; show and substance; acceptance and rejection of Jesus; and mob spirituality.

❑ Sermon Titles

"Jesus' Jerusalem and Ours" (Claypool)
"Our Journey Behind Jesus" (Willimon)
"Festive Tragedy" (Gaddy)

❑ Prayers

God of Life and Death:
As we embark upon this pilgrimage of Passion, fill us with
    the Spirit which filled your Son.
Prevent us from relegating all truth to the past and
    escaping an engagement with truth in the present.
Present us with the contemporary claims of the way of the
    cross and provide for us the courage and discipline needed
    to accept them.
Prepare us for whatever we discover to be your will for us

in our Upper Rooms and Gardens of Gethsemane.
We venture now as pilgrims of the Passion, a bit uneasy
    about where we may be going but confident about the One
    who calls us, the one in whose name we pray. Amen.

—————————

(Gaddy)

Compassionate God:
We refer to this week as "Holy Week," knowing all the while
it is not necessarily any more "holy" than any other week.
The significance is in the focus. We seek to study the
practices of sacrificial love and unconditional servanthood
which made possible personal redemption. We try hard to
understand how it all fits together—
    the "Hosanna" and the "Crucify him,"
    the "I will not deny him" and the "I don't know the
        man,"
    the grace of God and the injustice of God's created
        beings,
    the forsakenness voiced in Jesus' plea to God for a
        sense of the divine presence in his dying and the
        forgiveness voiced in Jesus' plea to God for the
        realization of pardon among his killers.
The events on which we reflect are holy and we seek to learn
from them, to profit spiritually from them. There is a
problem, though. You know that most of the world does not
stop for this week. We have trouble staying focused.
People go on laughing, hurting, getting sick, dying, hating, profiteering,
studying, seeking, and losing. Please help us
find holiness in all of these experiences.
We know that holiness grows from the inside out; that we are
not holy because of where we are or how we look. Thus, God,
we pray for strength to incorporate into our beings that
which makes us holy and into our weeks that which makes *all*
of them holy. In the name of the Son of the Most High and
Holy God, we pray. Amen.

—————————

(Gaddy)

Good God!

On this Palm Sunday, Jerusalem seems like a terribly long distance away, and our measurement is not in miles and minutes alone.

We find ourselves wondering how Jesus must have felt after his grand entrance into that ancient, so-called "holy," city. Any exhilaration he experienced because of the Hosannas shouted by friends must have been tempered considerably by the keen disappointment brought on by seeing a place of worship that had been transformed into a den of thieves. God's house for worship had become a marketplace of human manipulation. Then, too, he must have pretty well known his days were numbered. Opposition was crystallizing. Traps were subtly set in place. Even the disciples were bickering over the uncertainty of the future.

Knowing what Jesus knew, we must confess that we can hardly fathom how he continued his ministry. However, knowing what you knew, we can hardly see why you sent him into all of this anyway.

Thanks be to you, O God, for instructing us as we wonder. We see. We understand. The events surrounding Palm Sunday teach us not only about ourselves, but about you. Here are commitment, faithfulness, courage, love, and redemption.

What a great God you are! What a great savior Jesus is!

Perhaps Jerusalem is not all that far away at all. Jesus comes to us even now exemplifying and offering commitment, faithfulness, courage, love, and redemption. What's more, the coming Jesus expects no less from us.

Help us to be responsible even as you teach us to be knowledgeable. Help us, O God. Please, please, help us. Amen.

(Gaddy)

_____

❏ Congregational Litanies

Leader: From Bethlehem to Bethany
              Required some thirty years
              From Bethany to Jerusalem
              Took but a week of tears.

People: A tree so full of foliage
        Its boughs with fruit should burst

> But unproductive nature
> Draws the creator's curse.

———————

(Hendricks)

Leader: Wait! Let singing turn to sad lament, and laughter turn to
            tears. Our song does not ring with the majesty of mighty
            deeds of conquest or fierce battles fought and won. For this
            man knew both shame and love's healing power, both the
            soaring joy of children joined in song and the sorrow of
            broken love.

Reader 1:   *But who can know the pain and anger of such a heart held out to*
            a blind and selfish generation, a generation of fickle followers, a
            generation of people confused. "Hosanna! Hosanna!" Hardly. The
            song is sounding hollow now.

People: But he rode into the city. One last gift brought to the altar of a
            blind generation, one last offering of his heart before a selfish,
            fear-torn people.

Reader 2:   *How many times has the king of glory ridden defenseless and vul-*
            nerable among a people of cold and hardened hearts, faithless people
            and fickle people? "Hosanna! Hosanna!" Hardly. They sing no
            more. The branches of palm have fallen from their hands. The
            parade could not hold their attention.

People: Every time we turn away from a brother or sister in need, or
            bring down judgment where mercy should have reigned—
            each time we do this our Christ again turns toward Jerusalem
            and begins the ascent of deep sorrow.

Reader 1:   *How long must he endure our lukewarm faith and our tepid*
            passion?

Reader 2:   *People of God, your Christ will not find entry into the holy place*
            of your heart until the inner voice of all your moments is accom-
            panied by your silent Hosanna!

People: Hosanna! Hosanna! Blessed is he comes in the name of the Lord!

Readers: *May God have mercy on us all.*

———————

(Findley)

Reader 1:   It starts and ends on high ground—
            All in between is low—
            From Hosanna in the highest
                Thru the passion he must go.

Reader 2: The accolades of Sunday
Were soon drowned by the din
Of the freed, stampeding animals
And the cries of greedy men.

                _____ (Hendricks)

Suggestions

- *Plan for a processional of children* to walk in front of a processional cross waving palm branches, which they lay on the altar. This is by far the most traditional form of presenting the palms in worship.

- *Try an attractive variation for a presentation of palms.* Line the main aisle with children who wave palm branches as other worship leaders move between them during the processional hymn.

- *Give palms to all members of the congregation* as they assemble for worship in the narthex. In this instance, every person is encouraged to participate in the processional and bring a palm to the altar. There a designer receives each palm and creates *large floral arrangements* from the individual branches. *Jade* or *emerald* greenery is preferred in these arrangements. The *long frons of the sego palm*, however, have more visual impact because they appear more authentic.

- *Attach palms to the ends of the pews* on the main aisle of the sanctuary. From the moment worshipers enter the worship center, they view a sea of greenery and conscientiously embrace the reality of Palm Sunday.

- *Create a dynamic offering in worship* by means of a more involved presentation of palms. A great deal of work is involved but the result is well worth it. The simplest construction begins with a waffle pad placed on the floor, the kind of padding used to prevent a rug from sliding. Next, a piece of *burlap fabric* cut the length of the aisle is laid on top of the padding. Palm leaves are then sewn to the fabric. Hot gluing can be done if the temperature control on the glue gun is low enough to prevent scorching the leaves.

• On Palm Sunday, *anchor bouquets of purple and violet helium balloons to the urns on the altar* of the worship center. If you choose such a dramatic variation, take great care in the presentation lest items be used for decorative purposes. All the visuals used in worship should contribute to a revelation of truth, not call attention to themselves.

Maundy Thursday

The Thursday of Holy Week—Maundy Thursday—takes its name from the Latin *Dies Mandati*, the Day of the Commandment, referring to Jesus' commandment for disciples to love one another (John 13:34). On this evening, Christians recall the events that transpired between Jesus and his disciples in an upper room in Jerusalem on the eve of his crucifixion.

Historically, Maundy Thursday worship has involved four major liturgical activities. First, and primary, worshipers remembered the Last Supper that Jesus shared with his disciples by breaking the bread and drinking the wine of Christian communion together. Second, church leaders and wealthy men washed the feet of other worshipers, imitating the humility displayed by Jesus as he washed the feet of his disciples. Third, money, food, and clothing were collected by worship leaders to give to the poor. And, fourth, worshipers stripped the main altar in the worship center of all fabrics, furniture, and flowers. These items were then washed. No decorations were appropriate on the following day, which was Good Friday.

In the Roman tradition, other ceremonies have persisted through the years. Some of the traditional liturgical activities have not survived in the free church tradition, although in some churches the rite of footwashing is receiving renewed attention.

Sights

Simplicity is the order of the hour in worship on Maundy Thursday. Inside the sanctuary, a quiet, meditative environment is created by overlapping the *burlap* base paraments of the Lenten season with *cloths and fabrics of purple.* These additional fabrics suggest something new without altering the traditional penitential interpretation of the day.

All fabrics should reflect the preferred liturgical color for Maundy Thursday, which is *scarlet,* or a *dark red* suggesting the blood of Christ. If any ornamentation or symbols appear on the fabric, they should be done in *black thread* and not gold, which is used at other times.

A banner constructed on the theme of "Instruments of the Passion" can be used appropriately on both Maundy Thursday and Good Friday, or from Monday through Saturday of Holy Week. Such a banner provides a visual interpretation of the entire week for viewers, which includes items associated with the trial, mockery, scourging, death, and burial of Jesus. Since all of the *symbols of the passion* of Jesus seldom appear together, the banner can have an especially dramatic impact on worshipers.

Because of the emotional heaviness of Holy Week, a banner on the passion of Jesus may be more effective if symbols—done in *purple* or *maroon* and accented in *black*—appear on a background of *violet.* The drabness and darkness of the banner convey the oppressive nature of this spiritual season.

Though *no flowers* should grace the altar, large arrangements of *natural bearded wheat* and a *mound of grapes* can be placed in urns set on both sides of the communion table. These raw materials provide great images of how common elements have come to possess profound spiritual meaning within the Christian faith.

Maundy Thursday communion should be taken from *a simple pottery chalice* filled with *wine* and *a pottery plate* containing *unleavened bread* set between *burning candles.*

 *Sounds*

❑ The Word of God

Old Testament	Psalm	Epistle	Gospel
Exod 24:3-8	116:12-19	1 Cor 10:16-17	Mark 14:12-26
Jer 31:31-34		Heb 10:16-25	Luke 22:7-20
Exod 12:1-14		1 Cor 11:23-26	John 13:1-15

❑ Choral Literature

"O Taste and See," Ralph Vaughan Williams
"Ave Verum Corpus," Mozart/Collins
"What Shall I Render to My God?" Austin Lovelace
"When Jesus Wept," Douglas Wagner

❑ Organ Literature

Psalm Prelude (Second Set, No. 1) Out of the Depths, Herbert Howells (Novello)
Postlude for the Office of Compline, Jehan Alain (This piece is also good for use in the Easter Vigil)

❑ Piano Literature

"Prelude in B Flat Minor" WTC I, Bach
"Adagio" from Concerto No 3 in D Minor for Oboe, Marcello-Bach BWV 974

"Capriccio on the Departure of the Most Beloved Brother," Adagio assai, J. S. Bach

❑ Congregational Hymns

"Bread of the World in Mercy Broken," Reginald Heber, EUCHARISTIC HYMN John S. B. Hodges

"Here, O My Lord, I See You Face to Face," Horatius Bonar, ADORO TE DEVOTE plainsong

"Christ, upon the Mountain Peak," Brian Wren, SHILLINGFORD Peter Cutts

"As He Gathered at His Table," Paul A. Richardson, STUTTGART Christian F. Witt

"When I Survey the Wondrous Cross," Isaac Watts, AVON Hugh Wilson

"'Tis Midnight, and on Olive's Brow," William B. Tappan OLIVE'S BROW William B. Bradbury

"I Come with Joy to Meet My Lord," Brian Wren, LAND OF REST or DOVE OF PEACE American folk melodies

❑ Homiletical Themes

Servanthood; betrayal; commitment; repentance; prayerful decision-making; the order of the towel; communion; bread and wine; the wilderness; drinking the cup; and surrendering to God's will.

❑ Sermon Titles

"What Jesus Thought About Prayer" (Killinger)
"Acceptance and Betrayal" (Gaddy)
"No Deals" (Gaddy)

❏ Prayers

Providing God:
On this Maundy Thursday, we are aware of the plethora of
your gifts to us—food and wine, yes; but also the very
essence of life and the promise of salvation.
Giving thanks to you seems both important and inadequate.
So, in addition to expressing gratitude, we commit ourselves
to finding ways to live out our devotion to you in
compassionate service.
    Give us vision, God.
    And strength as well as courage.
    Guide us that we may be faithful.
We pray in the name of the One who defined life in terms of
service and then demonstrated the definition in the breaking
of bread, the sharing of wine, and the washing of feet. Amen.

(Gaddy)

God of Love:
    We go now with only a taste of food and drink on our lips,
with only minimal nourishment in our stomachs, but with our
spirits fed, our souls nourished.
    We go now—not tentatively, but boldly
        not cynically but hopefully
        not sadly but joyfully—because tonight we have
        communed again with the One who provides for us compas-
        sionate strength and redemptive community forever.
    We pray in the name of Christ as we venture forth in the
name of Christ. Amen.

(Gaddy)

❏ Congregational Litanies

Leader: For I received from the Lord that which I also
            delivered unto you.
**People: With those who have gone before us, with those who
are with us now, with those who follow us, we share
this meal.**

Leader: That the Lord Jesus on the night when he was
 betrayed took bread,
People: **We confess our betrayals, but come at your
 invitation to take bread.**
Leader: And when he had given thanks,
People: **We thank you, Lord, for your bread.**
Leader: He broke it and said, "This is my body which is for
 you."
People: **It is for us.**
Leader: "Do this in remembrance of me."
People: **We remember.**
Leader: In the same way also the cup, after supper,
People: **Thank you, Lord, for the cup.**
Leader: Saying, "This cup is the new covenant in my blood."
People: **It is your blood for us.**
Leader: "Do this as often as you drink it, in remembrance of
 me."
People: **We remember.**
Leader: "For as often as you eat this bread and drink this
 cup, you proclaim the Lord's death until he comes."
People: **In the eating and drinking we remember your death,
 your promise, and are enabled to live again. Amen.**

———————

(Otto)

Leader: Do you eat some of the supper,
 Tasted lamb, unleaven bread?
People: **Bitter herbs seem to remind you
 Of the coming, awesome dread.**
Leader: Let unbroken hands the bread break
 Healthy lips partake the cup.
People: **Only when the kingdom comes in
 Will you eat and will you sup.**
All: Only when the kingdom comes in
 Will you eat and will you sup.

———————

(Hendricks)

Suggestions

- *Plan a Maundy Thursday service of Christian communion* in which the only words spoken are those of the institution—"This is the body of Christ" and "This is the cup of the new covenant." Provide each worshiper with an order of service that gives all the necessary instructions for a self-guided experience of worship. Include in this printed piece the texts of the litanies, prayers, hymns, and confessions that will be *read in silence.* Each worshiper can proceed through the service at his or her own pace. After the words of assurance following the prayer of confession, the order of service invites the worshiper to approach the chancel where ministers serve the bread and wine of communion.

- *Reproduce a Garden of Gethsemane for Maundy Thursday.* Because flowers should not be used in the sanctuary, this display will need to be located in the narthex. Create the garden out of a variety of *spring bulbs* and *flowering plants, dogwoods, daffodils, tulips, peonies,* and *narcissi.* The array of color draws the attention of worshipers entering the building and reminds them that Jesus also sought out a place to go and pray and find direction for his life.

Good Friday

Early Christian writers referred to the day of Jesus' death as Paschal Day. The day recalled the sacrifice of the Paschal lamb during the Jewish observance of Passover. Other terms for the day included Day of Preparation, Day of our Lord's Passion, and Day of Absolution. The name "Good Friday" developed among English Christians who judged the consequences of the day—not the crucifixion itself—as good. Eastern Christians speak of this day as Great Friday.

History

The city of Jerusalem was the source of the most meaningful acts of worship on this day. Historically, the slow processional from the Mount of Olives into Jerusalem did not arrive at its destination until light was beginning to streak across the sky on Friday morning. Worshipers stopped at the Sanctuary of the Cross and listened to a reading of the gospel account of Jesus' trial before Pilate. Then, all went to pray at a column that supposedly was the site where Jesus was scourged. After sunrise, worshipers made a brief visit to their homes before returning to the Sanctuary of the Cross for a rite venerating the cross. At noon, worshipers gathered in the courtyard of the Sanctuary and remained there until 3:00 P.M. listening to readings about the passion taken from both the Old Testament and the New Testament. Between readings, people offered prayers. At 3:00 P.M. the account of the crucifixion from the Gospel of John was read aloud and soon the service concluded. Later in the evening, worshipers gathered again to hear a reading of the gospel story of the burial of Jesus.

In the Roman tradition, Good Friday worship consists of a liturgy of the Word—readings from John, Isaiah, and Hebrews—followed by intercessory prayers. A veneration of the cross would follow as worshipers demonstrate their love for and allegiance to the cross of Christ by entering into the sanctuary with a cross. The celebration of communion, using elements that had been prepared on Maundy Thursday, brought closure to the service. Few Protestant churches have used this liturgy and, until recently, many churches did not observe Good Friday.

Probably the most popular Good Friday service has been a gathering planned to coincide with the three hours during which Jesus was on the cross. Traditionally, the services were from noon to 3:00 P.M. In the service, meditations and homilies on the seven last words of Jesus combine with prayers, hymns, silence, and scripture readings.

An act of worship within the Roman Catholic tradition that has become very meaningful to other Christians as well involves walking *the Stations of the Cross*. By means of artistic presentations of the Stations and accompanying devotional materials, Christians symbolically follow the steps Jesus took toward Golgotha. The traditional Stations of the Cross include:

> †"Christ is Condemned to Death by Pilate" (Matt 27:15-26, Mark 15:6-15, Luke 23:13-24, John 18:39-19:16a); †"Christ Receives His Cross" (Matt 27:31, Mark 15:20, Luke 13:25, John 19:16b-17); †"Christ Falls to the Ground" (Matt 27:32, Mark 15:21, Luke 23:26); †"Christ Meets His Mother"; †"Simon of Cyrene takes the Cross" (Matt 27:32, Mark 15:21, Luke 23:26); †"Christ's Face is Wiped by Veronica"; †"Christ Falls a Second Time"; †"Christ Tells the Women of Jerusalem not to Weep for Him" (Luke 23:28-31); †"Christ Falls a Third Time"; †"Christ is Stripped of His Garments"; †"Christ is Nailed to the Cross" (Matt 27:33-44, Mark 15:22-32, Luke 23:32-43, John 19:18-27); †"Christ Dies on the Cross" (Matt 27:45-56, Mark 15:33-41, Luke 23:44-49, John 19:28-37); †"Christ's Body is Taken Down from the Cross"; †"Christ's Body is Placed in the Tomb" (Matt 27:57-66, Mark 15:42-47, Luke 23:50-56, John 19:38-42).

Sights

On Good Friday, all eyes focus on the cross. The presence of a cross in the sanctuary increases worshipers' sensitivity to the centrality of the cross of Christ in readings from the gospels and in the living of their days. A *rough, wooden cross* serves well on this occasion.

If a banner on "Instruments of the Passion" has been displayed during the week, the visual statement should remain in place. In our church—whether or not other banners are visible—we hang a large *black banner* on Good Friday. It contains no other colors, symbols, or words. Yet, this banner never fails to speak to crucifixion-day worshipers in an overwhelming manner.

Because of the emphasis placed upon preparation for baptism among catechumens in the earliest observances of Lent, and because of a lack of emphasis upon a renewal of the baptismal covenant in contemporary congregations, we give prominence to water in Good Friday services. A *large shell basin* is placed at the front of the sanctuary alongside *a large pottery vessel* filled with water. The same pottery vessel used on Ash Wednesday to hold ashes can be used on Good Friday. At a specified point in the order of worship, a minister pours the water from the vessel into the basin and invites worshipers to come forward and *touch* the water as they renew their commitment to Christ.

In many traditions, the Good Friday worship service concludes with the *stripping of the altar*. Worshipers sit in silence as they watch everything removed from the altar—candlesticks, banners, and fabrics. When worship leaders pick up the lighted candle representing the life of Christ and carry it out of the sanctuary, the harsh reality of Christ's suffering and death is unmistakable. Once the altar is completely bare, someone hangs a large *black shroud* over it. The act signals the end of the service. Worshipers exit the sanctuary in silence, meditating on the pain and suffering that ensued because of people's opposition to the supreme revelation of God's love.

Sounds

❏ The Word of God

Old Testament	Psalm	Epistle	Gospel
Isa 52:13-53:12	22:1-18	Heb 4:14-16	John 18:1-19:42 or
		& 5:7-9	John 19:17-30

❏ Choral Literature

"O Sacred Head Now Wounded," Robert Leaf
"And With His Stripes We Are Healed," G. F. Handel
"Surely He Has Bourne Our Grief," C. H. Graun
"Surely He Has Bourne Our Griefs," Evan Copley
"Lamb of God," F. Melius Christensen

❑ Organ Literature

Adagio in g minor, Thomaso Albinoni (Organ transcription)
Choralvorspiel und Fugue uber "O Traurigkeit, O Herzeleid," *(Choral Prelude and fugue on "O Sorrow Deep"),* Brahms (Peters)
    O Welt, ich muss dich lassen (O World, I now must leave thee), Brahms (from *Eleven Chorale Preludes*)
    In Paradisium from *Requiem* by Gabriel Faure, Arr. Marcel Dupre (H. W. Gray-Belwin)

❑ Piano Literature

    "Moments Musicaux," Op 16, No. 3, Rachmaninoff
    "Sonata D Maj," 2nd Movement, Largo e sostenuto, Haydn

❑ Congregational Hymns

    "Ah, Holy Jesus, How Hast Thou Offended," Johann Heerman, Tr. Robert Bridges, HERZLIEBSTER JESU Johann Cruger
    "O Sacred Head, Now Wounded," Paul Gerhardt, Tr. James W. Alexander, PASSION CHORALE Hans Leo Hassler
    "Lift High the Cross," George W. Kitchin, Alt. Michael R. Newbolt CRUCIFER Sydney H. Nicholson
    "What Wondrous Love Is This," American Folk Hymn, WONDROUS LOVE William Walker's *Southern Harmony*
    "Ah, Holy Jesus, How Hast Thou Offended," Johann Heerman, Tr. Robert S. Bridges PASSION Johann Cruger
    "Alas, and Did My Saviour Bleed," Isaac Watts, AVON Hugh Wilson

❑ Homiletical Themes

    Suffering love; the silence of God; faith and fear; death; salvation; the crucifixion of Jesus as the revelation of our sin; the cost of discipleship; and the durability of grace.

❑ Sermon Titles

"Walking the Way of the Cross" (Willimon)
"Dealing With Broken Dreams" (Killinger)
"A Cry of Absence" (Gaddy)

❑ Prayers

It's early, Lord, awfully early. We are merely children in
the faith, beginners on our journey, early in the morning of
our spiritual lives just as not much passed dawn physically.
We are seeking to discover greatness in humbleness,
heal by hurting,
receive by giving,
live by dying.
It's late, Lord, later than we thought. Already we know
that before mid-afternoon today a Savior can be killed. We
already have learned our capacity for betrayal,
for rebellion,
for sin.
Come to us early and late, Lord, that we may know you in
every hour and walk with you and serve you all of our days.
We pray in the name of Christ our Lord. Amen.

_____   (Gaddy)

Great and Good God:
With Jesus' anguished cry of separation ringing in our
ears, how can we call this *good* Friday? What good is here—
that we crucified perfect love,
that we nailed to the cross one who came to give us
life?
What about that is good?
Still the rage in our world and the panic in our hearts that
we may hear your voice. We know that if you still speak to
us, you have not given up on us. Is this the good of the
day?
You took the worst action possible and brought redemption
out of it. You take the most despicable situations
imaginable and wring some admirable good from them. Surely

that is good.

You demonstrated on Good Friday that you will love us even while we are trying to shove you out of our lives.

You revealed on Good Friday that forgiveness is sometimes offered apart from the wrongdoers' request.

You did for us on Good Friday that which we could never do for ourselves.

O God, the good seems so distant, so difficult, so shrouded by the blackness of the grief caused by your death, so encrusted with layers of guilt.

But, the good is there! We see the good as we hear your voice.

Good God. Great God. Great and Good, God, thank you for the hope instilled by knowing you as the One who can take a bad Friday—a really bad Friday—and enshrine it in history as Good Friday.

We pray in the name of the one who on that Friday said, "It is finished" and commended himself to you. Amen.

———————— (Gaddy)

❑ Congregational Litanies

Leader: Slowly to the hill ascending
           Tis the deepest height to climb
People: Strange inversion of all value
           That the low should be sublime.
All: With the vertical unite us
           to God above: And here below
           the human by the horizontal
           Will cruciform completeness show.

———————— (Hendricks)

Sing: What wondrous love is this, O my soul, O my soul,
           What wondrous love is this, O my soul! What
           wondrous love is this that caused the Lord of bliss
           To bear the dreadful curse for my soul, for my
           soul, To bear the dreadful curse for my soul!
    Leader: God of amazing, wondrous love, forever doing a new

thing in this world: God of Abraham and Sarah, always summoning us to a new place: Feed our souls by the story of Jesus Christ who came to this place and gave everything for us through his life, death and resurrection.

People: **Expand our imaginations to experience what Jesus Christ reveals about you as a winsome, wooing God who weeps for us, and therefore about who we are as people so loved that all things are possible, even giving up where we are to move on to where you would have us be.**

Sing: To God and to the Lamb I will sing, I will sing, To God and to the Lamb I will sing; To God and to the Lamb, who is the great "I am," While millions join the theme, I will sing, I will sing, While millions join the theme, I will sing!

Leader: To the music that beats at the heart of creation, we join our song to the Lamb slain from the foundation of the world, whose blood has become the life that beats in our veins and ties us together with you, our sisters and brothers, and all creation.

People: **We thank you for the cup of the new covenant poured out for us through the chalice of Christ's being, so that we might be cleansed and healed and empowered to become the people you created us to be.**

Sing: And when from death I'm free, I'll sing on, I'll sing on, And when from death I'm free, I'll sing on; And when from death I'm free, I'll sing and joyful be, And through eternity I'll sing on, I'll sing on, And through eternity I'll sing on!

Leader: We thank you that in Christ's cup is life free from death in all its many shapes because he has entered into and overcome all things that bind us into hopelessness, and out of life's fullness.

People: **O God, transfuse us and transform us through the power of Christ's blood shed for us and shared with us, then send us to pick up our crosses and follow into the new thing of creation made whole and joyful.**

Sing: What wondrous love is this, O my soul, O my soul,
         What wondrous love is this, O my soul! What
         wondrous love is this that caused the Lord of bliss
         To bear the cross and bleed for my soul, To bear
         the cross and bleed for my soul!

Leader: God of eternity with the loving heart that bleeds
         for your children within time, in our hearts we
         hold the awareness of people everywhere who suffer,
         whose names you know even if we do not.

People: **For them and for ourselves we pray the cessation of
blood shed and tears spilled, and the dawn of a new
day when all our stories shall be woven together
into your story full of love.**

———————   (Penfield)

Leader: Broken are we,
         Crippled of mind and spirit,
         Limping and stumbling
         On our way to the Kingdom.

People: **The fragmented self,
Torn from its moorings,
Divorced from its end,
Deems itself whole.**

Leader: Preoccupied with the daily job,
         Busy with new investments,
         Devoted to family and self
         We ignore the call of wholeness
         To the community of forgiveness.

People: **We are the correct ones
Who prosper in our endeavors.
Satisfied with self-justification,
We have not time
To look into the mirror.**

Leader: There is evil here—
         Tis the work of those others.
         There is cause for our distrust,
         Justification for our aloofness.

People: **Yet, thanks be to God,
We may see ourselves
In the mirror of His Word,**

And see ourselves as He sees us.
Leader: Therein is our healing:
To see ourselves truly,
To know our brokenness.
People: **Acknowledging the burden of community**
Broken into shards,
Fractured in hope and dream,
We become the called—
Invited to share
The life of confession and healing.
All: **Thanks be unto Thee, O Lord,**
For Thou art patient with the impatient,
Healing the shattered with Thy wholeness.

_____

(Otto)

Reader 1: Now in essence he precedes us,
Goes beyond our time and space
Both with the thing to be united
And hell's power will he face.
Reader 2: His confinement seems a victory
For the farce of death and sin
Falter not, O weary pilgrim,
We shall see your face again.
Chorus: Lacrymose and
Comatose
Hold him close
Gloom and tomb
Exhume
All godly sorrow.
Watchers, waiters
Perpetrators
Wait tomorrow.

_____

(Hendricks)

Suggestions

• *Incorporate the ancient tenebrae service* into a Good Friday worship experience. The tenebrae service, which developed out of a monastic office, revolves around light, shadows, and the extinguishing of light. Place burning candles on the communion table. Though in the earliest tradition fifteen candles were used, in contemporary variations of the service worship planners determine the number of candles by the number of biblical texts to be read aloud. After each reading of the New Testament text related to the crucifixion of Christ, the reader extinguishes the flame of one of the candles. When the readings end, only one candle—a candle representing the life of Christ—remains lighted. Then, once the biblical account of Christ's actual death has been read or the *Benedictus* sung, a minister removes this final burning candle from the sight of the worshipers. Either the congregation can either depart in darkness or the still-burning candle, which had been taken out of sight, can be replaced on the altar as a sign of the hope of Christ's resurrection.

• *Invite and encourage people to renew their commitment to Christ,* which they demonstrated in their baptism. In one of our Good Friday services, we reminded worshipers of the importance of water in the lives of the people of God. I (DN) then said,

Having renewed our vows and recommitted ourselves to following Jesus Christ, we remember the first time we made those commitments and felt a sincere desire to live a worthy calling. After our rebirth by the Holy Spirit, we obediently entered the baptismal waters to participate in the death of Christ. Symbolically we died to the old way and rose again to the new way. The gift of water has had tremendous significance to the children of God. *Over* the water, the Spirit of God moved in creation. *Through* the water, God led the children of Israel out of bondage and into the promised land. *In* the water Christ received the baptism of John and an anointing by the Holy Spirit, which identified him as the Messiah who would lead people from bondage to sin into everlasting life. For many of us, entering the water of change in our lives occurred so long ago that we cannot remember the touch of that water and the feeling of being washed clean. Perhaps the level of our confessions to God and our recommitment to Christ could be even more profound if we could re-experience the touch of water. So, tonight here is water. If in feeling the water again, you can remember the moment when you first deeply and sincerely committed yourself as a follower of Christ, then come and be renewed; be refreshed by the covenant you made to be a child of God. There is water here and if it can strengthen your assurance, then come and be refreshed.

Following the statement, worshipers move at their own initiative to the basin filled with water. In our experience, some people gently touch the water and whisper a prayer while others completely submerge their hands in the water. Some individuals touch their lips with the water as others wash their faces and linger at the basin. Our congregation views this experience as a sacred moment in which we reflect on God's love and the gift of Christ.

- *Display instruments of the passion of Jesus* at the entrance to the sanctuary. Provide a related scripture text and a meditative comment or prayer along with each visual reminder of the events of the first Good Friday. Worshipers can find great meaning as they move among these presentations either prior to a Good Friday service or at their leisure during the day. Here are the fifteen stations we use along with the gospel text related to each one:

Objects	Text
coins	Matt 26:15
rooster	26:34
cup	26:38-46
lantern	John 18:3
rope	Matt 27:2
basin	27:24

purple robe	27:27-31
	John 19:1-5
crown of thorns	Matt 27:29
reed	27:48
nails	27:54-56
hammer	27:54-57
title board	John 19:19-21
dice	Mark 15:24
	John 19:23-25a
sponge	19:29-30
spear	19:34
ladder	19:38-42

- *Plan to move through the entirety of Holy Week without any mention of the resurrection of Jesus.* On Good Friday, face into the terror of the crucifixion of Christ while remaining silent about the glory of his resurrection. Though we certainly view the events of the passion from the perspective of the resurrection, we find it good discipline to look at the crucifixion of Jesus and all the controversial events leading up to it, as if we knew nothing about the resurrection. Not only does such an approach to Holy Week and Good Friday enhance our sense of the pathos of these days and greatly increase our eagerness for Easter, it also nurtures new dimensions and growth in our faith.

Holy Week Worship Service: The Easter Vigil of Holy Saturday

When worshipers exited the sanctuary following the Good Friday worship service, a sense of death filled the darkened room. Gathering for worship late on Holy Saturday evening, worshipers find that scene and sense unchanged.

We begin the Easter eve service much like we would a wake and conduct it in a manner similar to that used in a memorial service. Worshipers gather in a dimly lighted narthex, where they are requested to remain until everyone can enter the sanctuary together. The environment brings a hush to their voices.

At the appointed hour, the worship leaders join the gathering and, without announcement, the pastor begins the service reading words of comfort from Job 14. Another minister responds with a similar reading from Psalm 90. In the quietness that follows, I (WG) talk with those present about the purposes of the evening— to be together to do our grief work, to find comfort, and to take courage; to remember and reflect on the life of Christ; to give thanks to God for the gift and ministry of Jesus. After worshipers join in unison prayer, a tolling bell summons us into the sanctuary.

A processional forms behind the ministers and worshipers file into the darkened sanctuary, which has the feel of a tomb. People take their seats amid an antiphonal reading of Psalm 23.

A minister requests all present to think of stories related to Jesus' life and to feel free to share a story aloud if they so desire. We listen to dramatic monologues presented by individuals who represent characters who came in contact with Jesus during his ministry on earth: Pearl, a prostitute; the mother described in John 9; a leper who was cleansed by Jesus; and at least one who has encountered Jesus within the fellowship of our church. Other worshipers are provided an opportunity for spontaneous sharing.

After selected readings from the Prologue to the Fourth Gospel by another minister, I (DN) offer an attestation to our faith in Christ as the Light of the World. All worshipers are asked to find the candles that have been placed under every seat in the sanctuary, come forward with these candles and light them from "the Christ candle," and then leave the newly lighted candle—a symbol of the worshiper's life—setting in one of the window sashes of the room. Through this symbolic gesture, each participant can keep watch through the night and wait for the good news that belongs to tomorrow's dawn.

We depart in silence, and with great expectations!

Floral Arrangements

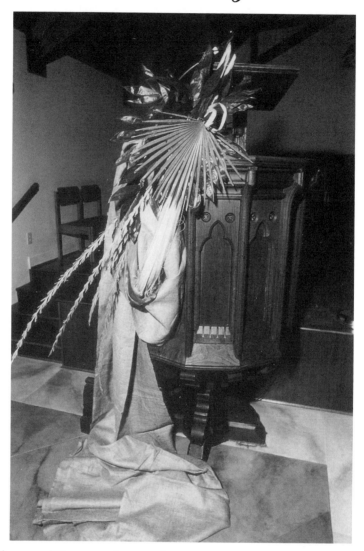

The carved German pulpit is enhanced with a variety of palm branches for the Sunday festival. The remains of dried palms frons clipped and burned to create the ashes for Ashe Wednesday create the bases for the arrangement. Sego, phoenix, palmetto, jade, and emerald make up the design of greenery. Lengths of burlap faced with purple gauze and cotton fabrics project pageantry of the day.

Worship Banners

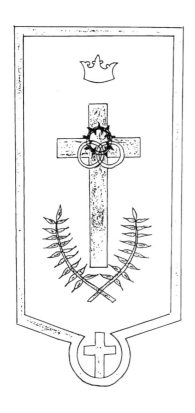

❑ **Holy Week: Passion** ❑

EASTER

Easter:
A Season of Celebration

A solitary whisper prompts a slightly louder response from a listener who, in turn, excitedly passes along the message to someone else. News travels from person to person with the speed and shock of an electric current. In a split second, or so it seems, the first individual's whisper has been replaced by the thunderous shout of a crowd whose words resonate with the beauty and clarity of a well-practiced chorus, "He is risen! He is risen! Christ is risen, indeed!"

History

Easter is the oldest and grandest of all Christian festivals. The earliest Easter celebrations embraced the full "fifty great days" from Easter Sunday to Pentecost. With joy, praise, and thanksgiving, Christians remembered the resurrection and ascension of Jesus and God's gift of the Holy Spirit. Symbolic of their irrepressible happiness, early Christians did not kneel during the entire Easter season.

Easter Day—also known as the Pasch, the Christian Passover, and the Day of the Resurrection—originally included both crucifixion and resurrection themes. Christians viewed the cross and the resurrection together as constituting "the new exodus," which Jesus made possible for all people.

Influenced by Jewish theology and liturgy, the first Christians began their celebration of Easter Sunday at sundown on Saturday. Though the vigil included the hope of the resurrection, worshipers recalled the crucifixion with thanksgiving—gratitude to God for the reconciliation with God made possible by this horrible event. At dawn, attention to the crucifixion gave way to a celebration of the resurrection through the baptism of new believers and participation in the Eucharist. After the development of Holy Week in the fourth century and the establishment of Good Friday as a time for remembering the crucifixion of Jesus, the focus of Easter narrowed to the resurrection of Jesus alone.

Even after the fourth century, the Saturday evening vigil remained an important part of the church's worship on Easter. A paschal candle was lit—"the new fire"—outside the worship center and in a processional brought into the sanctuary where it stood as a visible reminder of the presence of the risen Christ. After the blessing of the light (the paschal candle), Christians sang a song of praise called the "Exultet." The vigil proceeded with twelve readings from the Old Testament interspersed with psalms and prayers. At daybreak (cockcrow), new Christians were baptized as long-time Christians renewed their baptismal vows. Newly baptized believers were led into the sanctuary barefooted, carrying candles, and wearing white robes. There they joined the rest of the faithful in a joyful observance of Christian communion. As the light of Easter Day intensified, worshipers greeted each other with the ecstatic salutation, "Christ is risen!" "Christ is risen, indeed!"

Appreciative of the importance of celebrating the resurrection of Christ, Christians quickly established Sunday as a weekly celebration of the resurrection.

 *ensations* . . . .

Everything that matters in Christianity has roots that run deep into the mystery and truth at the center of Easter. Devoid of a reason to celebrate Easter, Christianity could claim no authority and offer no promise. The entire Christian Year would crumble like an old, discarded calendar because there would be no story of redemption to tell, no meaningful faith to nurture, and no holy pilgrimage to guide. A reason to celebrate Easter does exist, however; Christ is risen!

The news of Easter incites *joy*—irrepressible, unrestrainable, ecstatic joy—*excitement, hopefulness, confidence, faith,* and *grand expectations.* Easter shouts that *goodness matters* and *love prevails.* In the resurrection of Christ, as nowhere else, we see *God's sovereignty over life and death.* The resurrection displays a sovereignty that finds expression not in blatant acts of raw power but through quiet, sensitive ministries of compassion: *a power made perfect in weakness.* The resurrection of Jesus stands as a cosmic exclamation point after God's *affirmation of life.* God has not given up on creation, rather God continues to work through creation. Easter ushers us into a *whole new world.*

In recent years, a fascination with science, a dedication to reason, and a passion for the tangible have tempted worship leaders to turn sanctuaries into laboratories or lecture halls in an effort to "prove" the resurrection of Jesus. Outbursts of joyful praise have been replaced by attempts to amass rational arguments aimed at verifying spiritual truths. Marauders dedicated to scientific methodology have invaded the awesome realms of mystery and faith. What a serious mistake. Belief is not born of evidence. Positively responding to the resurrection of Christ requires an *act of faith.*

Sometimes Easter has been dubbed the "honeymoon season" for new Christians.[1] Just after baptism, a party begins. Easter begins a celebration of *realized hopes, accessible redemption,* and *the gift of eternal life.* Splashing around in the waters of baptism, dancing, singing, laughing, and *drinking the wine and eating the bread of communion* are the order of this season, a period in the Christian year intended to be every bit as happy as it is holy.

 *Sights*

After walking the road called Holy Week, sunrise on Easter morning incites unparalleled joy in Christian worshipers. Everything begins in darkness. *White fabric* on the communion table, pulpit, and other pieces of furniture, however, prevents absolute darkness. Only the excitement of watching light cover the earth equals the thrill of waiting for the first rays of light on Easter Sunday.

As the sun reveals its light, worship leaders ignite a *fire* and *light the paschal candle.* Worshipers join in a joyous processional to carry the flaming paschal candle into the sanctuary. Along the way, worshipers take light from the paschal candle and pass this light to others. Once the paschal candle has been placed in its holder, someone reads the biblical narrative of the miraculous resurrection of Christ and worshipers celebrate *communion.*

Worshipers in the early morning service then ready the sanctuary for the major worship hour of Easter Day. What a sight! Worshipers return to the worship center all the *paraments, banners, flowers, and altar candlesticks* that were taken away when the altar was stripped on the evening of Good Friday. Scents complement sights as freshly *polished brass, clean linens, spotless lilies, and fresh-baked bread* are brought into the sanctuary and set in their proper places. Splendor replaces starkness in the sanctuary as the sights and sounds of people offering themselves in preparation for worship stirs a corporate excitement. Once the last bit of preparation for Easter Sunday has been finished, the early morning worshipers enjoy an Easter breakfast together. All sense the same truth. The fast is over; the triumph is celebrated. Christ is risen!

As people arrive for worship on Easter Sunday, they should be aware that the day is unique. We drape the front entrance to the church with *bolts of white fabric* held in place by *hanging arrangements of white flowers*. *White blooming plants* fill the exterior urns. Inside the building, the narthex table contains *yards of unwound fabric, a single lily,* and a *large white angel,* which together tell the resurrection story visually.

White dominates the sanctuary, every item reflecting the purity of the risen Christ. *Tall arrangements of white flowers* line the center aisle—one on the end of each row—directing people's vision to the altar and the *cross:* the symbol of Christians' faith. A brass quintet plays as worshipers drink in the sights in the room and feel their spirits escalated to new heights. *Children, bells, brass, an organ,* and *a choir* contribute to the thrill of this day when everyone present focuses on the same purpose.

❑ Flowers

The flowers of Easter must convey new life. This can be done with a presentation of *young bulbs* with their *tender foliage* breaking through a *container or scape of moss and dirt.*

Floral displays containing various sizes of *cracked-open egg shells* convey a message about the new life that stands at the center of Easter truth. Using a variety of *egg shells from birds, ostriches, and chickens* creates interesting variations in both texture and color.

Budding trees form the height of the arrangement while items associated with the resurrection fill the covered base: a basket filled with *pomegranates* at various stages of development; a bird's nest, and open shells. In the tree, *preserved butterflies* can be seen. Also attractive is the incorporation into this scene of a *pet bird in a cage*. This kind of floral arrangement sets off pleasant responses among children and broadcasts the good news of new life to all present.

❏ Banners

The most outstanding banner(s) of the Christian year should be reserved for this most important day on the liturgical calendar. Easter banners can be constructed of *crepe or gauze fabric*, presented in *irregular shapes* without any symbols. These banners, suspended on large "T" shaped poles, can be set in walkways, around entrances, and even at the edge of the parking lot to create a festive focus among arriving worshipers.

Banners can also be hung along the side aisles of a sanctuary if the height of the ceiling permits. These banners too can be created without the use of symbols and displayed as pieces of abstract artistic expressions. No banner should be a distraction or cause confusion. Every banner should contribute to the overall enhancement of congregational worship by elevating the jubilation.

People who desire banners containing symbols have numerous symbols from which to choose. For centuries, *trumpet lilies* have symbolized Easter. The purity of their white color represents the glory of the resurrection. Additionally, this majestic flower rises from what appears to be a dead bulb, recalling the death and resurrection of Christ. Another symbol frequently used on Easter banners is *a lamb bearing a cross* symbolizing victory over death. The lamb usually has a three-rayed nimbus around its head. Other *symbols* commonly used as designs on Easter banners include:

A *butterfly* representative of the resurrection; *crowns* that denote victory and kingly estates; *a laurel wreath* indicative of victory; *a tomb* related to the gospel accounts of the resurrection; *ivy* as a symbol of immortality and eternal life; *a peacock* whose flesh (according to legend) cannot decay and thus represents immortality;

a phoenix—also from legend—signifies resurrection; and *a pome-granate*, which indicates immortality.

The altar banner is the most glorious banner in the room, con-taining numerous symbols that proclaim the message of Easter. This banner is constructed of *the finest materials in whites and golds*. Easter banners can be as simple as *large lengths of white linen* cut in shapes along the bottom edge and suspended with several lengths of *white satin ribbon*.

I (DN) have found that banners without words communicate more effectively than those containing a text or single words. Without words, interpretations of the banner have no boundaries—both a positive and a negative factor. Sometimes people perceive a banner to communicate more than it was even conceived to con-vey. Thus, the design of a banner should be carefully decided and detailed so the basic intention of the banner can be communicated.

If text seems vital to a banner's design, however, several *phrases* present themselves as possibilities:

"Christ the Lord is risen today"; "I am the resurrection and the life"; "Believe and never die"; "I am the alpha and the Omega"; "I am the beginning and the end"; "O death where is thy sting? O grave where is thy victory?"; "The strife is o'er, the battle is done"; "I know that my redeemer lives—glory hallelujah"; "Thine is the glory, risen conquering son"; "Endless victory"; "Risen savior"; and "Rejoice and sing."

Single *words* that contribute substantially to Easter banners include: "Allelujah"; "Resurrection"; "Alive"; Victorious"; "Triumphant."

Sounds . . . . ❧

❑ The Word of God

Old Testament	Psalm	Epistle	Historical	Gospel
Isa 25:6-9	118:14-24	1 Cor 15:1-11	Acts 10:34-43	John 20:1-18
Isa 65:17-25		1 Cor 15:19-26		Mark 16:1-8
Jer 31:1-6		Col 3:1-11		Luke 24:11-12
				Matt 28:1-10

❑ Organ Literature

Entrata Festiva (For Brass quartet, tympani, and organ) Flor Peters
Christ lag in Todesbanden (*Christ Lay in the Bonds of Death*) *and Christ is erstanden* (*Christ is arisen*), J. S. Bach from *Orgelbuchlein*

❑ Piano Literature

"Preludio" from "Bachianas Brasileiras No. 4," H. Villa-Lobos
"Sonata E Major," K. 380, L. 23, Scarlatti

❑ Congregational Hymns

"Christ, the Lord, is Risen Today," Charles Wesley, EASTER HYMN *Lyra Davidica*, 1708
"The Strife is O'er," Latin, Tr. Francis Pott, VICTORY G.P. Palestrina
"Welcome, Happy Morning," Venantius Honorious Fortunatus, Tr. John Ellerton, FORTUNATUS Arthur S. Sullivan
"Thine Be the Glory," Edmond L. Budry, Trans. R. Birch Hoyle, HARMONIA SACRA Arr. from G. F. Handel
"Christ Is Alive," Brian Wren, TRURO *Psalmodia Evangelica*
"On the Day of Resurrection," Michael Peterson, EMMAUS Mark Sedio, Harm. Charles H. Webb

❏ Homiletical Themes

The resurrection of Christ; the resurrection of the believer—now and later; the resurrection and the world's crucifixions; resurrection and renewal; life after death; the indomitable power of God; the glory of life; hope that is invincible; Christ in us and in our world; ingenuous mercy; the triumph of love; the intrusive grace of God; rebirth; and the shock of Easter.

❏ Sermon Titles

"Surprised by God" (Willimon)
"The Laughter of God" (Claypool)
"If I Should Wake Before I Die" (Sehested)
"Easter and the Cultivation of Courage" (Claypool)
"God Doesn't Have Any Orphans" (Killinger)
"Is the Gospel Your Good News?" (1 Cor 15:1-11) (Cox)
"Living the Life to Come—Now!" (Killinger)
"The Final Reality" (Gaddy)

❏ Prayers

Great God, we recognize you and praise you as the Power of the Resurrection, the One able to bring life from death and redemption from destruction.

Early in the morning, late in the evening, in a garden, beside the expressway, at the office, Your Son comes to us, O God.

Forgive us if we call him by the wrong name.
Pardon us if we don't quite recognize him.
God, we're not accustomed to resurrections.
Grant to us the ability to follow him.
Instill within us the grace to serve alongside him.
Enable us to be his disciples.

God, we're trying to take in the meaning of his resurrection.

That he comes to us is such good news. That he walks the streets of our town is a realization of great comfort. That

he wills to live within us is a fact of exultant joy.
    On this resurrection morning, thanks be to you, O God, for
the gift of your risen, living Son who makes us aware that
we too can live—really live. In his name, we praise you. Amen.
                            _____
                                                        (Gaddy)

God of Life and Death:
    We hardly know how to pray to you right now. Quite
honestly, you caught us completely off guard with the
resurrection. We are as thankful for it as we are surprised
by it. But, we are surprised. We thought it was all over.
We understood evil to be the winner, death the victor.
    Now, how do we pray? When should we expect reversals?
How should we anticipate surprises? Do you want to know all
that we want to ask?
    We have some reversals in mind, God. Would you change
our national goals? Would you reassert the necessity of
justice, peace, and equality in our society? More
personally, would you rid us of all fear and anxiety? We
desire to be rid of suffering, all suffering.
    So, how should we pray, God? Should we just ask? Do you
have time for all reversals? Can your divine energy be
harnessed by our human agendas?
    Caring God, we now pray the prayer that got it all
started—crucifixion and resurrection. We offer it with the
confidence that you always act in wisdom and love.
    Abba, God, you know our wills; but we pray not that our
wills may be done, but that your will may done on earth as
it is in heaven. Amen.
                            _____
                                                        (Gaddy)

❑ Congregational Litanies

Leader: Why do we stand weeping in the darkness of Good
                Friday?
            Why do you seek the living among the dead?
            He is not here. He has risen!
            Xpistos Anesti*—Christ is risen!
                Alithos Anesti*—Truly, He is risen!

People: **Christ is risen! He is risen indeed!**
Leader: The Man of Sorrows has become the resurrected,
                victorious Savior!
            The Head that once was crowned with thorns is now
                crowned with glory!
People: **Let us crown Him King of kings and Lord of lords!**
        Christ is risen! Alleluia!

                                    _____   *Phonetic Greek (Findley)

Minister: We celebrate good news; Jesus Christ is risen!
People: **God is our strength and our song; God is our**
        salvation.
Minister: When we have locked ourselves away in the upper
             rooms of our lives, Christ's presence has come to
             us with a word of peace
People: **. . . a word that sends us out of our hiding**
        places with strength and power.
Minister: When believing does not come easily and we are
             more skeptical than faith-full, Christ's presence
             has come to us with a word of assurance
People: **. . . a word that transforms our anxiety to**
        comfort and turns our mourning into joyful dance.
Minister: When tears cloud our eyes so that we cannot see
             signs of the Resurrection, Christ's presence
             comes to us with a word of hope
People: **. . . a word that reminds us of the evidence of**
        new life all around us—even within us.
Minister: Christ is risen!
People: **Christ is risen indeed!**

                                                    (Sledge)

Minister: On this day of resurrection, do you renew your
             profession of Christ as your Lord and Savior?
People: **With joy and thankfulness for God's gift of grace**
        to me, and in the joy of the resurrection of my
        Lord and Savior, Jesus Christ, I do confess my
        faith and remember the joy of my new birth and
        baptism.
Minister: May the God of all grace, who has given us new

birth by water and the Holy Spirit, and bestowed
upon us the forgiveness of sins, keep you all in
newness of life. Amen. Alleluia!
Remember your baptism and be thankful!

—————— (Findley)

First   Alleluia and love, alleluia and love.
Reader: From his throne above
               God spoke, death revoked.
               A new thing in earth and heaven
               Light and salt and active leaven.
               Now replace his side so riven
               that the water and the blood from them
               Have slaked the thirst of dying men.
               Alleluia and love, alleluia and love.
Second   Alleluia and joy, alleluia and joy
Reader: Let triumphant Mary's boy
               Emerge into our world anew
               And unambiguously attest
               The victory of God's Goodness.
               And the undeserved largess
               From the bounty of God's grace
               And the fullness of His face
               Alleluia and joy, alleluia and joy.
Third   Alleluia and peace, alleluia and peace
Reader: Let all our vain anxiety cease
               Cast now on Him your every care
               For in the cross, the godly snare
               Begins creation to repair
               On blessed resurrection day
               Unite our hearts in faith to say
               Alleluia and peace, alleluia and peace.
All   Love, joy, peace
Readers: Alleluia, alleluia
               Love, joy, peace.

—————— (Hendricks)

Leader: Risen Christ, you have given yourself to us.
People: Now we give ourselves for others.

Leader: As people who live in a Good Friday world with
            Easter faith, we celebrate as we leave this place. You
            have raised us with Christ and made us a new people.
People: **As people of the resurrection, we will serve you
            with joy.**
Leader: Go in peace to love and serve the Risen Lord.
All: **We are sent in the power of Christ's resurrection.
            Alleluia!**

_____   (Findley)

Suggestions

- *Involve as many worshipers as possible* in as many ways as
  possible in the worship service on Easter morning. Include children by having them bring individual cuttings of flowers from
  their own gardens at home. These flowers can be gathered during the Sunday School hour and arranged around the door
  frames at the entrance to the sanctuary. A pre-constructed
  frame covered in chicken or crawfish wire and set within a
  door, provides a mechanic to hold these beautiful offerings.

- *Set a similar construction in the form of a cross* near the chancel area. Have children bring forward their flowers during the
  service. Guild members can receive these floral offerings and
  place them in the cross.

- Another possibility is to *ask children to bring forward flowers*
  (suggest all white blooms) during the early part of the service;
  perhaps during the festive processional. As children arrive at
  the chancel with their flowers, designers can receive the flowers and arrange them in oasis cages and a base of greenery set
  along the chancel aisle.

- *Enhance the processional by using a dancer* draped in white
  directly behind the children and in front of the processional
  cross. As brass instruments and the organ introduce the

processional hymn, children skip with joy, flower petals flutter through the air, and white clad dancers create shapes that communicate a spirit of joy. As congregants and members of the choir lift their voices to express their praise, carry the processional cross through the intermingling sights, sounds, and smells of joy that fill the moment. Few, if any one, will doubt that a celebration of Christ's resurrection is underway.

- Still another alternative involves *the creation of an aisle of flowers* through which the processional cross can pass on this day of celebration. Position the smallest children at the front of the procession creating "a way of petals" for the cross as they strew white flower petals along the aisle (much as they had strewn palm branches a week earlier).

- *Plan a dramatic presentation of a piece of art* that proclaims the Easter message. The set of batiks on "the Stations of the Cross," which we secured for a Lenten exhibit, contains a fifteenth batik on the theme of the resurrection. This batik is an addition not usually found in artistic presentations of "the Stations of the Cross." We did not display this piece until Easter morning. Because of its size (12 ft. high) and its need for light to move through it, the positioning of the work was crucial. In the Easter Sunday service, after the call to worship and a reading of the New Testament's account of the women's findings during their early morning visit to the tomb of Jesus, the large banner rose from behind the altar revealing the victorious, risen Christ. An air of excitement shot through members of the congregation. Easter had arrived for all of us. During the next two weeks, people revisited the church building to see the completion of the artistic collection.

- *Celebrate communion as part of the Easter worship celebration.* We once conducted this part of the worship service outside under the great dome of the sky. One Easter Sunday, after celebrating communion around a table set up on the edge of the parking lot, each worshiper released a white helium balloon to symbolize their soul's overwhelming joy. This act provided a means of emotional release befitting the climax of the jubilant celebration—a release that could not find expression in words.

Notes

[1]John H. Westerhoff III, *A Pilgrim People: Learning Through the Church Year* (Minneapolis MN: The Seabury Press, 1984) 21.

Floral Arrangements

The floral pulpit hanging consists of white trumpetor Easter lillies, casablanca lilly buds, and white and champagne roses. Corkscrew and kiwi vines give a natural dimension to the base of green salal for this Easter design.

The main aisle is arrayed with stanchions of white larkspur, white stock, and bridal veil. The communion table is filled with a natural design of white potted phalaenopsis orchids. Rising above the altar is a twelve foot batik of the resurrected Christ created by a European artist.

Worship Banners

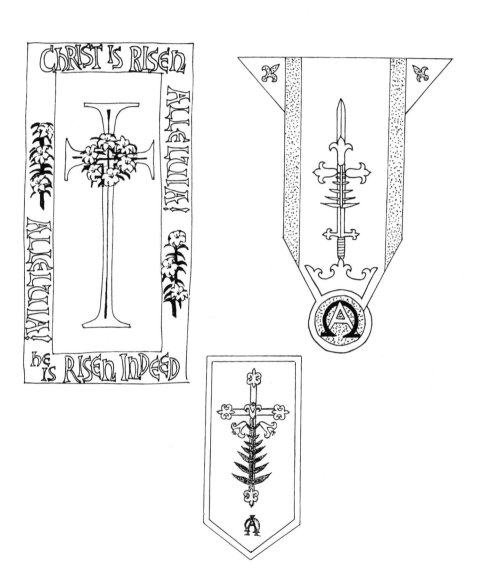

❏ Easter: Celebration ❏

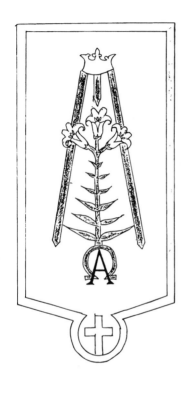

❑ Additional Banners for Easter ❑

PENTECOST

Pentecost:
A Season of Fire

Fire! Fire! The whole world is on fire!

In a split second, confusion and commotion meld into a singular declaration. Everybody sees flames at the same time and shouts, "Fire!" People run into each other. Words collide. Or, is it worlds? Panic prevails. Tongues of fire sweep across the chaos, leap into the air, and dance from person to person. Amazingly, though, this fire from heaven heals rather than harms, builds rather than destroys, and melts chaos into communion as it sears people's lips, opens their ears, and fills their hearts with passion.

Pentecost is a season of fire. The fire is the Holy Spirit.

History

The Christian festival of Pentecost borrows its name and date from the ancient Jewish festival called the Feast of Weeks (Exod 23:16) and also referred to as Pentecost. This Hebrew holy day, which celebrated the wheat harvest, marked the end of the harvest season just as Passover marked its beginning. The festival day was the fiftieth day, the day after a "week of weeks." During Pentecost, Jews celebrated the renewal of the covenant and the giving of the Law.

Following the crucifixion and resurrection of Jesus, multitudes of people gathered in Jerusalem for the observance of the Jewish festival of Pentecost. Christians celebrate Pentecost because the power of God's Holy Spirit came upon the disciples of Christ on Pentecost and the Christian church was born. In the early church, the term "Pentecost" often applied to the entire period made up of the fifty days after the Passover and not to the fiftieth day only. Church leaders considered these fifty days as a time of uninterrupted rejoicing. By the end of the second century, fasting and kneeling in prayer were forbidden during this period.

Some traditions refer to Pentecost as Whitsunday, a term which the English coined in association with the white robes of baptism. English Christians viewed Pentecost as a time for making financial contributions for the upkeep of church buildings.

Sensations . . . .

Pentecost arrives like *a rush of wind that takes our breaths away*. The truth of the day is staggering; its implications lead to unrestrained rejoicing.

Initially, the situation was difficult. After the ascension of Christ, followers of Christ *feared* they were alone; alone and facing a mission as big as the world itself. *Despair* seemed to be a realistic option. How could people do the work of Jesus if Jesus were no longer in their midst? Could followers of Christ ever hope to experience the kind of unity essential for carrying out Christ's great commission?

God responded to people's anxieties and needs by keeping Jesus' promise of the gift of the Holy Spirit. The arrival of God's Spirit provided incontrovertible evidence that the movement began in Jesus would not be stopped. Along with God's gift of the Holy Spirit came *the birth of the church* and *empowerment for members of the Christian community.*

We experience the biblical story personally. A letdown follows Easter, emotionally and spiritually. The grand party of life is over. Spirits sag. After celebrating Christ's life to the best of our ability, we seem to have little energy left to continue Christ's ministry in the world. Pentecost arrives with the announcement of *strength from God* and *a supportive, encouraging community of believers* with whom to work. We are not alone! God's spirit is within us and God's people are around us.

During Pentecost, Christians—one by one and in congregations —do well to ask: "Will we wait on God's Spirit to guide us and strengthen us in our lives or will we seek to go it alone, buying into the myth of self-sufficiency?" and "How can we hope to experience unity apart from living as a community of the Spirit?"

Out of such questions come crucial actions. Pentecost is a time for *church renewal* and *rededication among individual Christians.* The season of Pentecost is also a time for examining the relationship between unity and diversity in local congregations and within the larger Christian family.

Baptisms also befit Pentecost. Recalling the early Christians baptism by God's Spirit, contemporary Christians gather to celebrate individuals' commitment to the lordship of Christ through baptisms by water.

All who understand Pentecost realize that regardless of the chronology marked by a calendar, the gift of God's Spirit presents Christians with *a new day.*

Sights

The visuals of worship on Pentecost should enable worshipers to catch a glimpse of as well as feel the components of that day when God's Holy Spirit came and the church of Christ was born. Sights and sounds of the day include wind, fire, tongues of flame, confusion moving toward union, diversity contributing to unity, vigorous energy, sweeping courage, common goals, inclusiveness, power, and a commission.

Sensations merge in the worship experience of a Pentecost Sunday. Relatively abstract sounds, somewhat quiet and mysterious in tonality, begin the service. Worshipers sense tension within themselves as they try to interpret the meaning of these prophetic sounds for the rest of the service.

The choir, placed in the narthex out of sight from worshipers, begins to speak. In various languages and unfixed tempos, phrases from the Shema (Deut 6) sound. Rather than remaining in an orderly processional as usual, members of the choir enter the room moving in several different directions. Soon the choir surrounds the congregation and engulfs them in a confusion of sounds spinning from numerous locations in the room. As members of the choir approach the chancel, they move to the center aisle. When the individuals begin to unite with each other, the sounds also unite. Suddenly everyone in the congregation can hear and understand the words of the Shema being chanted in English. Pentecost begins with the choir sharing its essential message by both sight and sound—the gift of the Spirit comes from God who is One.

High drama accompanies the processional hymn. *Dancers*, each dressed in one of the colors found in a *multi-colored flower arrangement* at the front of the room, enter the sanctuary bearing *torches of flame*. When the dancers arrive at the chancel, they rhythmically move together interweaving the colors that they wear and thus merging their flames. To climax the dance, the dancers move to the flower arrangements and ignite flames within them. Worshipers see power, energy, and beauty as the torch is passed to the children of God. Once again worshipers realize the coming of God's Spirit.

❏ Flowers

A strong, vivid arrangement of flowers adorns the altar. *Bright orange, fire red, and brilliant yellow flowers* are used to create the impression of tongues of fire. A *stem of gladiolus* most effectively presents a flame-like appearance. *Lapping green unopened buds* extending beyond the *colorful florets* provide a convincing design of flowers.

Disguised within each of the four flower arrangements are individual stands, approximately 36 inches high and tripod in shape, to hold shallow, iron bowls filled with sterno (a flaming material used for heating food). The flowers completely cover the stand so that once lighted only flames will appear at the top of each arrangement.

❏ Banners

The word *flame* best captures the intensity and brilliance appropriate for a Pentecost banner. *Reds, yellows, gold,* and *oranges* on the banner create a contagious sense of the congregation's envelopment by the Spirit. To depict the energy of the Spirit, the banner's edges can be done in a jagged design to suggest the lapping of fire.

A processional banner works well on Pentecost Sunday, allowing tongues of fire to dance into the room. The construction of such a banner is not complicated, but its effect is powerful. Start with a 30 to 36 inch bamboo pole. Attach a piece of ecru ribbon (1" by 48") following the circumference of the pole. Tape on two over-lapping rows of light yellow ribbons. Layer a row of dark yellow, then a row of talisman, a row of orange, a row of rust, and a row of red. As these colors graduate outward the width of the ribbon can increase so the final row of red conceals the other colors.

The effectiveness of the processional banner is increased significantly when it is carried by a dancer who sweeps the tongues of fire across the congregation. This banner can be placed across the front of the pulpit and left there as a visual enhancement to the rest of the worship service. Other designs can adorn a Pentecost banner as well. Common *symbols* associated with Pentecost include:

> a dove, representing the descent of the Holy Spirit; flames as indications of the Spirit; a Jewish menorah signifying for Christians the seven gifts of the Spirit.

Meaningful *phrases* can appear on the Pentecost banner:

> "like the rush of a mighty wind"; "as of fire, distributed and resting on each one"; "veni creator spiritus"; "spirit of light"; "spirit of truth"; "spirit of all grace"; "come down O love divine"; "tongues of fire and hearts of love."

The banner can also be built around a single *word*: "Comforter"; "Counselor"; "Rejoice"; "Inflamed"; "Prophetic Fire"; "Celestial Dove"; "Paraclete."

Sounds

❑ The Word of God

Old Testament	Psalm	Historical	Epistle	Gospel
Isa 44:1-8	104:24-34	Acts 2:1-21	1 Cor 12;	John 20:19-23
Ezek 37:1-14		Rom 8:14-17	3b-13	& 7:37-39
Gen 11:1-9				John 15:26-27
				& 16:4b-15

❏ Choral Literature

"Peace I Leave With You," Walter Pelz
"I Will Sing With the Spirit," John Rutter
"Witness," Jack Halloran
"Pentecost," Hal Hopson
"Upon This Rock," John Ness Beck

❏ Organ Literature

Fanfare to the Tongues of Fire, Larry King (Hinshaw) in *Majestic Trumpet for Organ*
Settings of the plainchant melody *Veni Creator*
Fantasy upon Komm heiliger Geist, Herre Gott, J. S. Bach
Chorale, "*Komm Gott, Schopfer, Heiliger Geist*," ("Come God, Creator, Holy Spirit") BWV 667, J. S. Bach
(Bach, *Orgelwerke*, Serie IV, Band 2, Pp 94-97. Leipzig: Deutscher Verlag Fur Musik)
Finale (From Choral Varie on "Veni Creator," Opus 4), Maurice Durufle
(Durufle, Maurice. *Prelude, Adagio et Chorale Varie*, Opus 4. Paris: Editions Durand et cie.)
Hymn-Prelude, "Come Down, O Love Divine," DOWN AMPNEY Wilbur Held
Hymn-Prelude, "Crown Him with many Crowns," DIADEMATA Wilbur Held
(Both of the above are available in Held, Wilbur. *Hymns for the Pentecost Season*, St. Louis, MO: Concordia Publishing House 97-5517)

❏ Piano Literature

Chorale II "Jesu meine Freude," Willard Palmer, from *Contemporary Album for the Young*, Publ. Alfred
"Ogive I," Erik Satie

❏ Congregational Hymns

"Come Down, O Love Divine," Bianco da Siena, DOWN AMPNEY Ralph Vaughan Williams

"Come, O Creator Spirit," Latin, Tr. Robert Bridges, VENI CREATOR SPIRITUS Plainsong

"Spirit of God, Descend Upon My Heart," George Croly MORE-CAMBE Frederick C. Atkinson

"O Spirit of the Living God," Henry H. Tweedy, FOREST GREEN Trad. English melody, Arr. Ralph Vaughn Williams

"Filled with the Spirit's Power," John R. Peacey, SHELDONIAN Cyril V. Taylor

❏ Homiletical Themes

The descent of the Spirit; the empowerment of the Spirit; the birth of the church through the Spirit; revelation; the universal scope of the gospel; church renewal; the mission of the church; being a holy priesthood; Holy Spirit; the Holy Spirit in the church; the Holy Spirit in the individual Christian; creativity and regeneration; and the world as parish.

❏ Sermon Titles

"The Fire Next Time" (Willimon and Killinger)
"Babel and Pentecost" (Claypool)
"Help of the Helpless" (Rom 8:22-27) (Cox)
"Learning to Wait" (Claypool)
"Patchworks of Possibility" (Sehested)
"How Come I Can Hear You?" (Willimon)
"The Church That God Wants" (Killinger)
"Angels at the Crossroads" (Acts 12:1-7) (Sehested)
"Knowing and Doing" (Claypool)

❏ Prayers

We pray, O Merciful God,
For the descent of the Dove.
May Thy Spirit hover over the chaos of our minds,
Calling Thy image out of the void in which we have lost
    ourselves.
Renew our minds, O Holy Spirit,
In the likeness of the mind of Christ.
Grant us His mind that the courage of doing good,
    the strength of turning the other cheek, the power of
    crucifixion
May continue to be moments of sobriety in a world staggering
    in the drunkenness of violent hate.
Come, Holy Spirit,
Fill us with the warmth of God's love for all God's
    creatures. Amen.

—————   (Otto)

O God, our Creator; O Christ our Savior and Redeemer; O Holy
Spirit:

In this glorious season of Pentecost, renew us again by blowing
Pentecostal winds and blazing flames of fire. Protect us, O God, like a
father, with your strong arms of protection. Comfort us, O God, like a
mother with your gentle hands of comfort. Greet us this morning as our
songs of praise rise to thee. And as you have called us to be your people,
grant us the courage we need to fulfill our high and holy calling. Use us
as servants and prophets, and give us the endurance and tenacity to
stand for truth, right, and justice in our world. Amen.

—————   (Findley)

Holy God, Giver of the Holy Spirit:
You have promised us that when we pray the Holy Spirit will
make intercession for us, communicating to you thoughts and
actions too profound to be captured in our words.
    Hear the unmitigated praise of our unspeakable joy.
    Receive the penitent pain of one who is wrong.
    Accept the nervous concern of persons preoccupied with
        the suffering of others.

Embrace the vulnerable openness of those who seek
    direction.
Respond in love to those who seek to overcome doubt with
    faith.
Loving God:
We cannot always articulate our thoughts or translate our
emotions into simple sentences. Sometimes we can only smile
or cry, groan or ache. We trust you to understand us and to
respond to us.
    In these moments, accept us as we are and receive the
    intercession of the Holy Spirit on our behalf.
        Fill us with your grace.
        Direct us in your paths.
We pray in the name of the One who promised us the ministry
of the Comforter. Amen.

_____

(Gaddy)

    Our hope, O Lord, is in Thy Kingdom,
That mighty, ever flowing stream
Of justice and compassion.
For our eyes are on street people;
Our hearts go out to those
Fallen at the side of the road.
    Help us to see Thy Christ
In the least in our midst,
That we might worship Thee
In spirit and truth.
    Help us to serve Caesar
By damning and praising him
In the name of Christ.
Then are we in the world,
But not of it,
Giving to God
What belongs to God.

_____

(Otto)

❑ Congregational Litanies

Leader: Come, and write the commandments of God on your hearts.

**People: Our eyes shall behold the world through their light; our hands
shall carry them with us on our journey.**

Leader: You shall teach them to your children as you sit in your
homes and, again, as you walk in the way.

**People: We shall dream of them when we lie down and talk of them
when we rise up.**

Leader: From generation to generation, we will tell of the faithfulness
of God. From everlasting to everlasting, the Lord will journey
with us on our way.

——————

(Sledge)

Leader: Come, Holy Spirit, Light of God,
Rest upon us;
Lead us unto the Truth
That comes from His speaking.

**People: We long for
The resting of Thy Spirit
Upon us.
Then may we know
The end and the why
Of our being in His image.**

Leader: Come, Holy Spirit, Love of God,
Rest upon us;
That we may not be strangers
In the world of Thy hands.

**People: Come, Holy Spirit, Grace of God,
Inflame our hearts
That we may be the instruments
Of that divine love
Which seeks out
The poor and broken hearted.**

Leader: Come, Holy Spirit, power of God,
Raise our spirits
From the death
Into which we are born.

**People: O Resurrection life of God,
Empower us**

To walk in His way,
Fearful of no person nor dominion.

Leader: Feed us, O Spirit of God,
That we may bring
Good News to the poor,
That we may bind up
The broken hearted,
That we may open prisons
And comfort the mourning.

All: Come, Holy Spirit,
Bless us
With what we can not provide,
That our faint spirits
May be revived with and in praise!

_____

(Otto)

Leader: The Lord be with you.
People: And with your Spirit.
Leader: Lift up your hearts.
People: We lift them up to the Lord.
All: We believe in a continually creating God
who calls us to costly love.
We believe in a continually caring Christ
whose example encourages us to risk ourselves
for the sake of the gospel.
We believe in a continually healing Holy Spirit
whose power enables us to share one
another's burdens.
We believe in a continually caring community
called the church which is the presence of
Christ in our world.
We believe in a continually growing relationship
between ourselves and the God whom we
come to worship here.

_____

(Sledge)

Leader: Come, Holy Spirit,
Presence of Christ.
Invade this week

And make it His.
Blow upon us
The miracle of re-creation.
People: Consume our hearts
With God's love for us.
Call us from the grave,
Empowered to be disciples of Him
Who promised to be with us
To the end of the world.

─────────

(Otto)

Suggestions

- To celebrate God's gift of the Spirit to the church, *produce a festival of gifts,* celebrating the talents and abilities embodied in the congregation. Call attention to the diversity out of which the church is formed. Plan a gala in which members of the congregation display examples of their unique talents and the numerous different ways in which the Spirit has gifted them. Construct booths or set up tables for individuals to use in exhibiting their offerings. Concerts, artistic demonstrations, and displays of various kinds provide excellent insight into the meaning of inspiration. At the end of the day, invite a designer to express thanks to God for the many individual gifts exhibited and for the contribution to the life of the church made by each of the artists.

- *Organize a festival of the arts to celebrate Pentecost.* Devote the entire weekend to educating and stimulating members of the congregation regarding the impressive and multiple ways in which the arts can assist in the mission of the church. Though not every event takes place within a context of worship, the whole experience contributes to the enhanced quality of the church's worship. We scheduled such an event with an itinerary as follows:

Friday Evening

*3:00-4:00 An exhibition of floral interpretations for each season of the Christian Year
*4:30-5:30 A lecture or seminar on the transforming and liberating power that flowers convey as works of art communicating the gospel
*7:00 "Looking for Beauty"—a lecture on the church and the arts given by a guest (Dr. William Hendricks)
*7:45 "A Tasteful Palate"—a delicious experience featuring the culinary artistry of preparing and presenting desserts
*8:00 "The World of Carl Sandburg"—a readers' theater production focused on the works of one of America's greatest treasures

Saturday Morning and Afternoon

*7:30-10:00 "Cambridge Passage"—patterned after London's famous Camdon Passage, a fleamarket of artists and their wares, featuring painters (water color and oil), sculptors, weavers, collage artists, faux finishers, and photographers
*10:00 "On Being a Sensual Christian"—a lecture on the importance of the senses in worship and discipleship by our weekend guest
*2:00 A recital featuring violin (Mr. Ye Tao), violincello (Ms. Mao-Mao Zhang), and piano (Mrs. Marjorie Stricklin)
*3:00 "Let Us Dance"—a lecture by Dr. Hendricks and an open dialogue concerning the church and various artistic expressions
*4:00 Vespers—a service of thanksgiving for the mystic vision led by the Chancel Choir of our church and based entirely upon choral literature written about the artistry of the afterlife

• *Sponsor an ecumenical presentation* on how various religious congregations celebrate the major times of transition in their member's lives. Ask each participating congregation to present a museum-like exhibit depicting the manner of worship (if any) with which they address various stages of life—birth, baby dedication, baptism, confirmation, education, bar/bat mitzvah, weddings, house dedications, and funerals. Docents should be available with each display to explain the significance of the articles exhibited. Also host a lunch during which ministers in the participating congregations discuss differences and similarities between their communities' approach to the various seasons of life.

• *Sponsor a similar ecumenical presentation on seasonal worship traditions* within a variety of different congregations. Use the same format as that of the "Seasons of Life" event. Our experience with such a project resulted in overwhelmingly positive responses. Our congregation joined with Methodist, Greek Orthodox, Roman Catholic, and Jewish congregations for a "Seasons of Holiness" study. We developed a book of worship traditions (for comparison) and made it available to each participating congregation. Participants discovered an amazing number of similarities between all the celebrations: Advent, Christmas, Hanukkah, Epiphany, Ash Wednesday, Lent, Holy Week, Easter, Rosh Hashana, Yom Kippur, Sukkoth, Pesach, Shabuoth, Pentecost, and the Sundays after Pentecost. What better way to celebrate the life and mission of the children of God fleshed out on Pentecost?

Floral Arrangements

The asymmetrical design at the base of the antique English brass lectern is an interpretation of the tongues of fire. The floral design consists of red, yellow, orange gladioli, and corkscrew. The colors are graduated to visualize the image of the flames.

Worship Banners

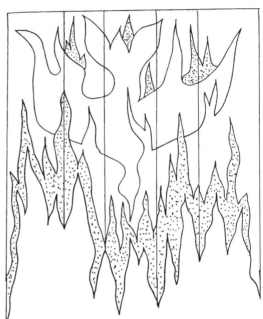

❏ Pentecost: Fire ❏

The Sundays After Pentecost:
A Season of Growth

Reality. Cold, hard reality. Routines. Ordinary days filled with common tasks. From the high moments of grand celebration set off by the resurrection of Jesus and the descent of the Holy Spirit, worshipers move back into the somewhat mundane schedules of average days. Questions surface, profoundly important questions: What does it all mean? What difference does it make to us as individuals and in the world at large that Jesus of Nazareth lived, taught, healed, suffered, died, and rose again? We do not live back then or over there, but here and now. What we must do is go to work every day, raise the children as best we can, pay off our debts, try to have a little fun, and get some rest.

These questions and concerns make up the matters of faith during the Sundays after Pentecost.

History

Unlike the liturgical seasons prior to Pentecost, the last and longest part of the Christian year developed without early liturgical intentionality. People considered the stretch of days between Pentecost and Advent as the rest of the year—the long period of time following the church's careful commemoration of the life and ministry of Jesus. Not until late in the eighth century did the church give organizational form to this period and consider it a new season in the Christian year—the season after Pentecost.

Church leaders devoted the first half of the Christian year to revisiting and reliving the birth, earthly ministry, passion, death and resurrection of Jesus as well as the coming of the Holy Spirit as Jesus promised. Subsequently, Christians dedicated the second half of the church year to a consideration of how individuals live as faithful followers of Christ in the daily routines of their lives.

Traditionally (since 1334), the Sundays after Pentecost—twenty-six in number—begin with Trinity Sunday, the first Sunday after Pentecost in the Western church. Eastern churches observe this day as a festival of Holy Martyrs. Distinct from event-based celebrations oriented to the history of salvation, Trinity Sunday became an occasion for theological thinking, and pondering the nature of God. On Trinity Sunday, Christians focused on the meaning of the total revelation of God—God as Creator, God as Redeemer, and God as Spirit (Comforter and Sanctifier). Because large portions of the suggested gospel readings for this extended period focus on the kingdom of God, many denominations have referred to the days after Pentecost as "Kingdomtide."

Today many liturgists do not consider the time between Pentecost and Advent a season, referring to it instead as the Sundays after Pentecost or Ordinary Time. Understandably, this lengthy period differs significantly from the well-defined, clearly-focused seasons that precede it. No one theme dominates worship during these days. Rather, a variety of themes offers each congregation an opportunity to choose the focus most applicable to its interests and needs. Lectionary suggestions during this period do not offer four complementary readings for each Sunday, but four different biblical texts from which one can be chosen for a Sunday.

 . . . .

Most of us feel more at home in the season after Pentecost than during the peaks and valleys of the preceding holy days. Few of us reside amid the lofty spiritual peaks of Christmas and Easter or down in the dangerously low valleys of Lent and Holy Week. We know best "ordinary time." So, when we enter the days after Pentecost, the terrain looks familiar and we have a sense of belonging. This is where and how we live.

Individuals gather for corporate worship during the season after Pentecost devoid of either too great a sorrow or exalted anticipation but with firm resolves: to *learn to live as the people of God,* to *study the implications of Christian discipleship for every realm of life,* and to *translate a personal commitment to Christ into practical forms of social ministry in Christ's name.* Frankly, at points along the way, the season seems exceptionally long and unduly tiring. At such times, *prayer* becomes an important dimension of public worship as do *inspirational reminders of God's provisions* for servant people and *encouraging words from Jesus.*

Praying for *God's rule on earth* incites considerations of very practical issues and raises questions about a disciple's personal responsibilities in relation to these issues. A dominant question pervades experiences of worship and meditations on discipleship: As a disciple of Christ committed to the sovereignty of God, how am I to engage in family life, work, recreation, politics, community action agencies, international evangelical missions, and services to the poor and imprisoned?

Many different themes emerge during the Sundays after Pentecost, pinpointing specific visuals for worship becomes problematic. Because individual congregations tend to choose very diverse emphases, visual components in worship vary from church to church.

❏ Colors

Green is the most common color associated with the time after Pentecost; it is a time for the greening or growth of the church. Worship leaders, however, traditionally use *white* as the dominant color on Trinity Sunday and "Christ the King" Sunday (the Sundays that bracket this time period). White is also the primary color for worship on All Saints Day or in any service recognizing saints who were not martyrs. *Red* symbolizes Christian martyrs. Red also denotes the Holy Spirit and the evangelical task of the church.

The long expanse of worship services during this season provides a good opportunity for experimentation and invention when it comes to communicating the gospel through colors. Each congregation should incorporate into its worship specific colors that have special meaning for the people involved. Incorporating new colors into a congregation's worship services signals the good news that the church is alive, well, fresh, and creative.

A few colors contain a sense of energy that conveys the life of the church in a richer manner than is possible with more basic colors. Among these colors are: *copper, mustard, emerald, sapphire, rust, lime,* and *blue-green.*

❏ Banners

Worship planners can choose from an infinite variety of patterns and styles in constructing banners for the Sundays after Pentecost.

Perhaps preparing a banner for Trinity Sunday offers the greatest challenge. Symbols for the Trinity are limited because of the difficulty of communicating this mysterious theological truth. Traditionally, geometric designs have been popular symbols of the Trinity. Triangles and triparted forms denote the mystery of the doctrine and the day. Some congregations use shamrock and *fleur-de-lis,* or circles and trefoils. Other shapes that often appear on banners in a trinitarian form include three intertwined circles and three fish in a triangle.

Banners for the other Sundays in the period after Pentecost can be constructed around a number of *symbols* which have been significant in the history of the church:

> The hand of God descending with three rays of light depicts the power of God; FISH is used to convey the name of Christ; a rock brings to mind the divine presence; a unicorn serves as a mythical reminder of the offering of Christ; a boat or a ship symbolizes the church and its journey; a globe or a picture of the world reminds the church of its expansive mission.

Denominational *logos* and general ecclesiastical *symbols* include: crosses, circles, flames, globes, doves, hands, and fish combined to convey the work of the church.

Specific *phrases* can be used such as:

> "Holy, holy, holy is the Lord God Almighty, Who was and is and
> is to come"; "Go ye therefore and teach all nations"; "Come Holy
> Spirit our souls inspire"; "The Spirit hovering her wings over the
> church"; "Other foundations can no man lay than that which is
> laid on Jesus Christ"; "For, behold, the kingdom of God is within
> you"; "So send I you"; "If not us, then who?"; "The harvest is
> great but the laborers are few"; "He comes to us . . . and says fol-
> low me"; "Thy kingdom come, thy will be done"; "The Lord of
> hosts is with us, the God of Jacob is our refuge"; and "Now unto
> the King eternal be honor and glory forever."

Sounds . . . .

❑ The Word of God

Two different approaches to this season has equal value. The use of lectionary readings provides guidance for a corporate pilgrimage through
passages of the Word of God which enlighten, instruct, and direct Christian disciples. Alternatively, a more topical approach to worship brings
into focus a series of specific biblical teachings aimed at nurturing spiritual growth. With minor modifications in planning, the two approaches
can be combined. Below are lectionary readings for one year of the Sundays after Pentecost followed by suggested biblical passages related to
topics appropriate for extended consideration in worship.

Lectionary readings for one year:

Old Testament	Psalms	Epistle	Gospel
1 Sam 16:1-13	20	2 Cor 4:5-12	Mark 2:23-3:6
1 Sam 16:14-23	57	2 Cor 4:13-5:1	Mark 3:20-35
2 Sam 1:1-17	46	2 Cor 5: 6-10, 14-17	Mark 4:26-34
2 Sam 5:1-5	48	2 Cor 5:18-6:2	Mark 4:35-41
2 Sam 6:1-15	24	2 Cor 8:7-15	Mark 5:21-43
2 Sam 7:1-7	89:20-37	2 Cor 12:1-10	Mark 6:1-6

2 Sam 7:18-29	132:11-18	Eph 1:1-10	Mark 6:7-13
2 Sam 11:1-15	53	Eph 2:11-22	Mark 6:30-34
2 Sam 12:1-14	32	Eph 3:14-21	John 6:1-15
2 Sam 12:15b-24	34:11-22	Eph 4:1-6	John 6:24-35
2 Sam 18:1, 5, 9-15	143:1-8	Eph 4:25-5:2	John 6:35, 41-51
2 Sam 18:24-33	102:1-12	Eph 5:15-20	John 6:51-58
2 Sam 23:1-7	67	Eph 6:1-4	John 6:55-69
1 Kgs 2:1-4, 10-12	121	Eph 6:10-20	Mark 7:1-8, 14-15, 21-23
Prov 2:1-8	119:129-136	Jas 1:17-27	Mark 7:31-37
Prov 22:1-2, 8-9	125	Jas 2:1-5, 8-10, 14-17	Mark 8:27-38
Job 28:20-28	27:1-6	Jas 3:3-18	Mark 9:30-37
Job 42:1-6	27:7-14	Jas 4:13-17, 5:7-11	Mark 9:38-50
Gen 2:18-24	128	Heb 1:1-4, 2:9-11	Mark 10:2-16
Gen 3:8-19	90:1-12	Heb 4:1-3, 9-13	Mark 10:17-30
Isa 53:7-12	35:17-28	Heb 4:14-16	Mark 10:35-45
Jer 31:7-9	126	Heb 5:1-6	Mark 10:46-52
Deut 6:1-9	119:33-48	Heb 7:23-28	Mark 12:28-34
1 Kgs 17:8-16	146	Heb 9:24-28	Mark 12:38-44
Dan 7:9-14	145:8-13	Heb 10:11-18	Mark 13:24-32
Jer 23:1-6	93	Rev 1:4b-8	John 18:33-37

Texts for topical emphases:

Exod 20:1-17 (Ten Sundays on the Ten Commandments)
Matt 5:3-11 (Nine Sundays on the Beatitudes)
Matt 5-7   (Ten to Twenty Sundays on The Sermon on the Mount)
Matt 6:9-13 (Nine Sundays on the Lord's Prayer)
(The Parables of Jesus):

Matthew	Mark	Luke	Topic
13:3-8	4:3-8	8:5-8	Sower
	4:26-29		Patient Husbandman
	4:30-32	13:18f	Mustard Seed
21:33-44	12:1-11	20:9-18	Wicked Husbandmen

24:32f	3:28f	21:29-31	Budding Fig Tree
	13:33-37	12:35-38	Doorkeeper
5:25f		12:58f	Before the Judge
11:16-19		7:31-35	Children Playing
12:43-45		11:24-26	Unclean Spirits
13:24-30			Tares and Wheat
13:33		13:20f	Leaven
13:44			Treasure
13:45f			Pearl
13:47f			Seine-net
18:12-14		15:4-7	Lost Sheep
18:23-35			Unmerciful Servant
20:1-16			Good Employer
21:28-32			Two Sons
22:1-10		14:6-24	Great Supper
22:11-14			Guest at Wedding
24:43f		12:39f	Burglar
24:45-51		12:42-46	Servant/Steward
25:1-13			Ten Virgins
25:14-30		19:12-27	Talents
25:31-46			Last Judgment
		7:41-43	Two Debtors
		10:25-37	Good Samaritan
		11:5-8	Help at Night
		12:16-21	Rich Fool
		13:6-9	Barren Fig Tree
		13:24-30	Closed Door
		14:7-11	Places at Table
		14:28-32	Planning
		15:8-10	Lost Drachma
		15:11-32	Prodigal Son
		16:1-8	Unjust Steward
		16:19-31	Lazarus and Rich Man
		17:7-10	Servant's Reward
		18:1-8	Unjust Judge
		18:9-14	Pharisee and Publican

❏ Choral Literature

"Steal Away to Jesus," Dale Adelmann
"The Lord's Prayer," Maurice Durufle
"Saul," Egil Havland
"O How Amiable," Ralph Vaughn Williams
"With a Voice of Singing," Kenneth Jennings
"God of Grace and God of Glory," Paul Langston
"Yonder Came Day," Arr. William Appling
"You Must Have That True Religion," Arr. Roland Carter
"Let Me Fly," Arr. Robert Decormier
"The Promise of Living," Aaron Copland
"Many Gifts One Spirit," Allen Pote
"At the River," Aaron Copland
"Hark, I Hear the Harps Eternal," Arr. Alice Parker
"Ride the Chariot," Arr. William H. Smith
"Soon—Ah Will Be Done," William Dawson
"Great Day," Brazil Dennard
"O Be Joyful in the Lord," John Rutter
"O Be Joyful in the Lord," Charles Beaudrot
"Built on the Rock," Arr. Melius Christiansen

❏ Piano Literature

"Scenes from Childhood," Op. 15, Schumann
    No. 12 "Child Falling Asleep"
    No. 13 "The Poet Speaks"
"In Evening Air," Copland
"Etude" Op. 2, No. 1, Scriabin
"Prelude in E Major," Op. 11, No. 9, Scriabin
"Prelude in C# Minor," Op. 11, No. 10, Scriabin
"Prelude in C Minor," Op. 8, No. 1, Pachulski
"Prelude in E Minor," Op. 28, No. 4, Chopin
"Prelude in B Minor," Op. 28, No. 6, Chopin
"Sarabande," Brahms
"Nocturne in G Minor," Op. 37, No. 1, Chopin
"Nocturne in E Flat Major," Op. 9, No. 2, Chopin
"Songs Without Words," Op. 19, No. 4, Mendelssohn

"Largo," "Aria," "Sarabande," from *Elegance in Style* by Jeanine Yeager, Publ. Kjos
"VIII Nocturne," Poulene
"Arioso," J. S. Bach
"Passacaglia," C. F. Witt

(If a longer prelude or meditation is needed, some of the above pieces with similar styles and key relationships can be joined together. Conversely, many of these pieces have effective eight-bar phrases if only a short response is needed.)

❑ Homiletical Themes

The edification of the church; thinking about the Christian faith; consideration of various issues in the light of the gospel; the kingdom of God; growth in grace; the nature of the Christian life; healing; forgiveness; peace and justice; prayer; obedience; service; and love.

❑ Sermon Titles

"Patience for the Long Haul" (Claypool)
"The Real Test of Your Religion" (Killinger)
"The Dog Days of Pentecost" (Willimon)
"The Truth About Jesus Christ" (John 16:12-15) (Cox)
"An Ordinary Day With an Extraordinary Savior" (Willimon)
"A Yearning Heart" (1 Kgs 3:16-27) (Sehested)
"The Keys of the Kingdom" (Claypool)
"When It's Time to Adjust Your Sights" (Killinger)
"When It Is Tough to be a Disciple" (Willimon)
"David and Bathsheba and Safe Sex" (2 Sam 11) (Sehested)
"Genuine Religion" (Luke 7:36-8:3) (Cox)
"Loving Self and Loving Others" (Claypool)
"On Selling One's Self to Evil" (I Kgs 21:1-14) (Cox)
"Kissing Feet and Forgiving" (Luke 7:36-50) (Sehested)
"If You Don't Know Where You're Going You May Already Have Passed Your Stop" (Killinger)
"A Full Life in Christ" (Col 2:6-19) (Cox)

"Who is to Blame for the Pain?" (Luke 13:1-5) (Sehested)
"Bringing Division in the Name of Jesus" (Luke 12:49-53)
(Sehested)
"Measuring One's Growth" (Claypool)

❑ Prayers

Oh, Lord God, whose sovereignty rules also over the grave;
We, who bear the name of Death,
Have heard Him speak, "Lazarus, come forth."
We praise Thee
For the newness of life
In which we may walk.
Vicit agnus noster; eum sequamur.
"Our Lamb has conquered; let us follow Him." Amen.

_____   (Otto)

Understanding and Helping God:
Sometimes our enthusiasm outruns our reason and eagerness
    out-distances wisdom. What we desire is good, but we
    desire it too badly.
Instill patience within us so that we will not settle for
    too little.
Enable us not to accept hope without reality,
                salvation without faith,
                forgiveness without grace,
                peace without justice,
                love without commitment,
                belief without integrity.
Help us, God. We mean well. We want to do well. Please
    push us if we need a push in order to prevent us from
    stopping short, from experiencing a partial joy and
    thinking we know the whole thing, from getting near the
    kingdom and believing we are in the kingdom.
We pray in the name of the One who would not be satisfied with
anything less than a whole, abundant life; the One who, by his
death, made such life possible for all of us, Jesus the Christ. Amen.

_____   (Gaddy)

Leader: O God, who loves us in the midst of our doubts and deepest worries, be with us in the midst of life's storms.

People: Save us and help us, O Lord.

Leader: So inspire us by the vision of your heavenly power that we might set aside our faithlessness and fear.

People: The storm is strong, O Lord. We face the winds of change. Is there no mercy for us, no sense of peace and calm?

Leader: Forgive us for our little faith. Forgive us when we are caught midway between faith and doubt. We are afraid.

People: O God, keep us safe one more time.

Leader: In times of doubt and questioning, when the vision of your power seems faded and we feel buffeted by winds of change that challenge our faith and our understanding, give us peace and still our storms.

(Findley)

God, our creator! Make us discontent with things the way they are in the world and in our lives. Teach us to blush again for: our tawdry deals; our arrogant but courteous prejudice; our willing use of the rights and privileges others are unfairly denied.

Jar our complacency; expose our excuses; get us involved in the life of our churches, our communities, our world, and help us to find integrity once again that we may in some way keep within reach of the Christ whom we claim to follow. Amen.

(Leonard)

Minister: O God of mystery and love, whose grace is so freely bestowed upon us, thank you for Christ who unites all people and all things. We confess, as individuals and as a congregation, that we are often engaged in those actions which separate.

People: We confess, O God that we are often uncomfortable with the thought of being united with some people. We do not want to walk among the poor and the homeless. We are reluctant to care, to tend those whose diseases might affect us. We often insulate ourselves from people who remind us of our own mortality and the transience of the life we know. Our fear prevents us from making our world more like your kingdom. Our fear prevents us

from opening our hearts and souls that your kingdom might form within us. Forgive us. Help us to make room in our hearts that you may form your image within us, and that our every impulse and action might help your kingdom to come in this world. Amen.

$$\rule{3cm}{0.4pt}$$ (Findley)

O God our Help, the more helpless we find ourselves in life, the greater is our recognition of your power to help us. We have learned that your strength is indeed made perfect in our weakness. We cherish the words of our Savior, "He that loseth his life shall find it" as we seek your comfort just now. Amen.

$$\rule{3cm}{0.4pt}$$ (Gaddy)

> O God, what is your vision for us?
> Is it to be witnesses of your Word?
>   peacemakers in the world?
>   friends to the lonely?
>   caregivers to one another?
>   reflections of your love?
> Show us how you would use our gifts
> to bring your kingdom into
> this world. Amen.

$$\rule{3cm}{0.4pt}$$ (Sledge)

❑ Congregational Litanies

Leader: Who are you?

People: We are people with a hundred histories yet to be told and a million songs that haven't yet been sung! We are sometimes winners and sometimes losers.

Leader: Your faces look pleasant enough to me, and mostly contented.

People: Don't be fooled! We have learned how to fake people out . . . It doesn't take much to disguise ourselves . . . to cover our pain with a smile . . . to hide our shame with cheerfulness . . . to conceal our boredom with frantic activity.

Leader: Then who are you . . . really?

People: Some say we are SHEEP; others that we are WOLVES; still others say that we are a little lower than the ANGELS, the children of God.

Leader: And, why are you here?

People: To find out which we really are, perhaps, or to discover that we are all of these things and more . . . AND to consider the idea of confronting God.

Leader: To consider it only?

People: Most of us, yes! It is dangerous to do more. Yet we may hear something worth hearing, think something worth thinking, feel something genuine, or even pray something real, and thus draw closer to confronting God.

Leader: Then, if we ARE ready, let us present ourselves AS WE ARE to GOD . . . we shall dare to call upon God's name and then we shall wait, for God will not be rushed!

All: God, help us to understand.

_____

(Leonard)

Right Side: O God, the source of our common life, when we are dry and scattered, when we are divided and alone, we long for community . . . we long to know our neighbors.

Left Side: With those we live beside, who are often strange to us, whom we may be afraid to approach, yet who have riches of friendship to share . . . we long for community; we long to know our neighbors.

Right: With those we have only heard of, who see with different eyes, whose struggles we try to imagine, whose fierce joy we wish we could grasp, we long for community . . . we long to know our neighbors.

Left: With those we shall never know, who speak languages we do not understand and whose nations are separated from ours by borders we have imposed, we long for community . . . we long to know our neighbors.

All: Exhuberant Spirit of God, breathe compassion into your world through us. Let the winds of your Spirit cross the barriers of our divisions to fill the earth with justice and joy.

_____

(Sledge)

Leader: The new life, O Lord, is it merely a dream,
            A fantasy hidden in a celestial beam?
            Our "heavenly commonwealth," the apostle states,
            Life "hidden with Christ in God," he relates.
People: Come now, let the new life be seen.
            Let it burst through with heavenly sheen.
            Let transcendence transect the earthly plane.
            Let things on earth be raised to heavenly vein.
Leader: But how? Is it possible to contemplate-
            That "things heavenly" can "things earthly"
            penetrate?
            Is this not reserved for some future date
            When God His plan for all will consummate?
People: Nay, perhaps at least it has been begun.
            Perhaps in Christ some small vict'ry was won
            Which will embark us on a heavenly way
            And emit some signs in the life of every day.
Leader: What signs? The old man and his habits cast away,
            Unchecked lust of the flesh no longer holding
            sway,
            Covetous desire for things, idolatry,
            And raging thought and tongue bridled
            constantly.
People: What others? The new man with new habits imbued,
            Understanding in *imago Dei* renewed,
            Gentile and Jew, slave and free no longer separate,
            For the all in all is Christ, our mighty
            Potentate.
Leader: What garments now dignify beloved saints?
            What entreaties are foremost among their
            plaints?
            What thoughts and words well up from guileless
            hearts and lips,
            What aims and acts bedeck their terrestrial
            ships?
People: Let love divine, the perfect bond, o'er all else
            prevail.
            Let compassion and kindness under it unfurl
            sail.
            Let the stout wood of humility stay the
            mast.

Let patience and forgiveness seal against the
blast.

All: Let the peace of Christ reign richly in all our
hearts

Let the one body be fitly joined in all its
parts.

Let joy abound through psalm and song and chord.

Let all be done, in word or deed, in Jesus
Christ, the Lord. (Col 3:1-17)

(Hinson)

———

Leader: How blest are those who know their need of God; the kingdom of heaven is theirs.

People: How blest are the sorrowful; they shall find consolation.

Leader: How blest are those of a gentle spirit; they shall have the
earth for their possession.

People: How blest are those whose hearts are pure; they shall see God.

Leader: How blest are those who suffer for the cause of right; the
kingdom of heaven is theirs.

All: Store up treasure in heaven . . . for where your treasure is, there
will your heart be also.

(Leonard)

———

Leader: O God of great mercy, all of us have made mistakes.

People: Yet your grace, God, sees within us and works with the person
hidden inside.

Leader: The ships on the sea, moved by the strongest winds, are
guided by the smallest rudder . . . going wherever the will of
the pilot directs.

People: But we are human beings, God. We resist your direction.

Leader: We refuse the purity and goodness that you would place
within our hearts. Our own words and acts betray us. At one
moment we speak words of blessing, and then at another
moment our mouths speak words that wound and hurt. Our
actions injure others and create self-conflict within.

People: Yet your grace, God, knows the evil *and the goodness* that live
within our divided hearts. And even though you know the
truth about us, you accept us as we are and offer us unconditional love and forgiveness.

Leader: God of mercy, thank you for choosing us, in spite of our-
              selves, to be your people—loved, forgiven, graced with an
              honored place in your Kingdom. We are astonished that we
              are the very ones chosen for your holiest of destinies.
People: O God of second chances, and third and fourth and fifth . . .
         Forgive us. Help us to accept ourselves, and to trust ourselves
         one more time because you have trusted us.

                              _____   (Findley)

Leader: We believe that God is in the world; God the creator was and
              is and will be forevermore.
People: God reigns over all the earth!
Leader: We believe that Christ came to earth to show us God's vision
              for the world.
People: God reigns over all the earth!
Leader: We believe that as the sisters and brothers of Jesus Christ we
              are the signs of a new world, called to be faithful in this time
              and place.
People: God reigns over all the earth!
Leader: We believe that the Spirit of God moves among God's people
              and invites the world into God's realm.
All: We believe that the world can change, that peace and wholeness
        can come and that the new world of God's realm can arrive.
        God reigns over all the earth!

                              _____   (Sledge)

Suggestions

• *Be at your creative best during this period.* Do not, however,
  lose sight of the purpose of what you are doing. A variety of
  biblical-theological themes prompts various approaches to worship and innumerable components that can contribute to
  worship. Keep in mind, though, that every ingredient in worship must be a medium of truth that contributes to the purpose
  of worship—not just a component in worship for aesthetic
  enjoyment alone.

- *Plan several worship experiences* that will contribute to the congregation's spiritual strength and growth. Possibilities include: concerts, art exhibits, lectures, exploration of social concerns, discussion of social ministries, ecumenical experiences, and ethnic and cultural studies.

- *Choose a topic related to the reign of God* in people's lives and flesh out this topic in worship. Possibilities include: "Words without Actions"; "Hunger for Righteousness"; "Fields of Labor"; "To Follow"; and "Loving our Neighbors."

- *Create visual displays* of broken ships, fields of wheat, forgotten nets, contents of a crisis closet, and empty food containers. Each display will prompt thoughts about an important dimension of Christian discipleship.

- *Set up an exhibit on a table in the narthex* to confront entering worshipers with imagery that suggests what Christians should convey by their lives. A cup of water speaks of Christians' responsibility to reach out to others. Use a rock or a stone to remind worshipers of what they must avoid—a means of harm, a burden, or an enemy of freedom; A shaker of salt calls to mind Christians' Christ-mandated functions as a flavor, a preservative, and a distinctive in life.

- *Provide exhibits of black and white photographs* that focus on the needs of people in a specific community.

- *Sponsor a program of liturgical dance,* interpreting the struggles and prejudices that all people encounter. This program could be accompanied by a choral presentation of spirituals.

- *Focus a worship experience on exclusion* and the reasons why people choose to practice exclusion. This could lead to a study of neglected opportunities for ministry among alcoholics, artists, welfare recipients, homeless persons, and hungry people. An open discussion of such possibilities can help destroy barriers and open the church to people with sincere desires to be full participants in the fellowship.

• *Plan a "Renewal of Commitment"* Such a service is designed to consider seriously the purpose of the church and the congregation's involvements related to that purpose. At the conclusion of the service, provide everyone present an opportunity to renew their commitment to being a part of the body. Such a serious reevaluation of the church and each individual's involvement in it can create more effective ministries, more active participation by a greater number of members, and a more truthful attempt to reveal the gospel.

Special Occasions That Present Opportunities for Christian Worship

❑ Religious Days

The Christian year does not include all the religious celebrations valued by the church. Beyond its retelling of the gospel of Christ and challenging persons to grow as disciples of Christ by means of the Christian calendar, the church—at least certain parts of it—observes other days of religious significance. Two of these occur within the season after Pentecost and provide occasions for focusing on themes important to the Christian pilgrimage.

Reformation Sunday

Following the Reformation that swept through Europe in the sixteenth century, certain segments of the church decided to commemorate this event. Reformation Sunday became a time for remembering the ministry of Martin Luther, reasserting the primacy of the Bible in the life of the church, reaffirming the centrality of faith in a Christian's experience, and recounting the major errors in the church corrected by the early reformers. The day also acknowledges the need for a continuing reformation.

Since Vatican II, some church leaders have recommended the discontinuance of Reformation Sunday celebrations, suggesting that these occasions continue an emphasis on divisiveness within the church. Others, however, see Reformation Sunday observances as valuable opportunities to affirm the importance of perpetual reform within ecclesiastical institutions and to celebrate the centrality of the Bible, the sufficiency of faith, and the leadership of the laity within the church.

Memories of Luther's Ninety-five Theses and the beginning of the great division within the church produce a variety of visual enhancements to worship. Posting *theses* on the entrance doors to the worship center immediately sensitizes worshipers to the significance of the day. *Banners* composed of lamps symbolizing Christian knowledge hang throughout the sanctuary.

One year I (WG) presented the sermon on Reformation Sunday in five different sections. Each section contributed to an overall statement of Ninety-five Theses of importance to our church. When I completed each portion of the message, I walked to the communion table and laid on top of it a copy of the these just presented, inviting the church's continued consideration and discussion of these issues.

❑ The Word of God

Old Testament Lessons	New Testament Lessons	Gospel
Psalm 46	Rom 3:19-28	John 8:31-36
Jer 31:31-34		

❑ Choral Literature

(A Festival of Psalms based on Psalm 46)
"A Mighty Fortress Is Our God," Mark Hayes
"Glorious Everlasting," Thomas Cousins
"Lord, Thou Hast Been Our Refuge," Ralph Vaughan Williams

❑ Piano Literature

"Passacaglia," Handel

❑ Congregational Hymns

"The Church's One Foundation," Samuel J. Stone, AURELIA S. S. Wesley

"A Mighty Fortress Is Our God," Martin Luther, Tr. F. H. Hodge, EIN FESTE BURG Martin Luther

"I Greet Thee, Who My Sure Redeemer Art," Abridged from Psalm 124, Trans. Elizabeth Smith, TOULON Genevan Psalter

"Call Jehovah Your Salvation," Based on Psalm 91, James Montgomery, HYFRYDOL Rowland H. Pritchard

"Cast Your Burden on the Lord," Rowland Hill, SAVANNAH Foundery Collection

❑ Homiletical Themes

Inspiration of the Bible; the priesthood of all believers; faith and works; renewal; liberty; conscientious courage; nature of the church; prophetic voices.

❑ Sermon Titles

"The Unfulfilled Promise of the Reformation" (Gaddy)
"Continuing the Reformation" (Gaddy)
"Faith Alone: Reformation Heresy or Biblical Truth?" (Gaddy)

❑ Prayers

God of Redemption and Renewal:
As we remember with gratitude the Reformation of the past,
we pray for certain reforms in the present. Instill within
each of us the most important dimensions of the Reformation
dynamic   a love for the Bible
            an interest in interpretation
            a commitment to the centrality of faith
            support for congregational worship
            a recognition of the ministry of all persons
            a passion for the church.
Reproduce in us the convictions about salvation and the
courage for reformation that righted the course of the
church in the sixteenth century.
We offer ourselves now
            to be renewed by your Spirit,
            to become agents of renewal in your church, and
            to serve as ambassadors of the One who can make
               all things new.
We pray in the name of Christ. Amen.

             ————————   (Gaddy)

God of Abraham and Sarah, Joan of Arc and Martin Luther:
We want to praise you
        with words and deeds,
        with thoughts and emotions,
        with prayers and hymns,
        with community and commitment.
We want to praise you, God.
Please understand, though, that we also want to insulate
ourselves from change. Even the evil in the familiar seems
more attractive than the good in the unknown.
So, God, as you accept our praise, tear down the defenses in
our lives that we may be transformed, changed, reformed,
reborn.
May our praise find its highest expression in our openness
to transformation.
We pray, fearfully but honestly, in the name of Christ. Amen.

             ————————   (Gaddy)

❑ Congregational Litany

Leader: Let us call upon the spirits of our sisters and brothers of reformation, a host of witnesses who surround us.

Jeanne d'Albert:

I am Jeanne d'Albret, daughter of Margaret of Navarre, one of the Huguenots, born to her in 1528. Following in my mother's footsteps, I was scholar, poet, and religious reformer. As Queen of Navarre, I withstood the Inquisition, which was invoked against me in 1563, and I established Protestantism throughout the country. New religious ideas were studied at my palace. In my free time, I worked a series of tapestries with religious liberty as their theme.

Argula Von Grumbach:

I am Argula Von Grumbach. I lived in Bavaria during the sixteenth century. Here is what you should know about me: I led worship services in my home, conducted funerals without authorization, and—no surprise —was imprisoned for my outspoken support of Martin Luther.

People: We are Reformation People. We proclaim our spiritual power. We are healers, priests, and prophets. We affirm our responsibility to break bread and lift the cup of blessing in the name of liberation.

John Smyth:

I am John Smyth. I have often been called the first Baptist. I was also called a divisive man because, as they say, my preaching was "socking it to" men in high places! I suppose I was somewhat a religious refugee, for I needed more fresh air for my soul than the English atmosphere could provide. I went over to Holland and taught and preached there what came to be known as basic Baptist distinctives. My message was a continual plea for liberty of conscience and I could never abide a state enforced religion. The freedom of the human spirit is well worth saving! I thought it was my calling to save it.

Thomas Helwys:

My name is Thomas Helwys, another religious refugee in Holland with my friend Smyth. We parted ways eventually, with some strong disagreements, but also because of my compulsion to return to England to minister to the people of my native land. In 1612, I organized the first Baptist congregation on English soil. Unfortunately, I was a man of political rashness. I suppose that my publication, which was the first in England to demand full religious liberty, was a perilous and fanatical concept. I was, they say, one of the leading fanatics! It is no wonder that I ended up behind prison bars.

People: **We are Reformation People. We proclaim our political power as voters and agents of change. We affirm our responsibility to influence public policy, to build a new world, to nurture the struggling poor, to liberate those who are oppressed.**

Marguerite Kellis:

I am Marguerite Kellis, a member of the Shinnecock Indian Tribe and a weaver of baskets. I used my knowledge of the healing properties of roots and berries to bring comfort to the elderly and the dying. I was the midwife for the births of many Shinnecock babies. My family said I was like a great boulder weathered by many storms but remaining constant in my faith. I lived into my eighties and am very proud of my niece, Elizabeth Haile, the first Native American clergywoman ordained in the Presbyterian Church.

Martin Luther:

I am Martin Luther. While many say I was the initiator of the Protestant Reformation, I assert that I have done nothing. I have let the Word of God act. When I was twenty years old, I had not yet seen a Bible. Finally, I found a Bible in the library and forthwith I took it with me to the monastery. I began to read, and re-read, and read it over again. I was threatened with excommunication and at times became very despondent. Always reminded of the powers of the Church over me, I was warned that the day would come when my supporters would desert me. "Where will you be then?" they asked me. And I answered my enemies with the only answer I could give with certain faith. "Then, as now, I will be in the hands of the Almighty."

People: **We are Reformation People, creators of new life and new birth. From the work of our hands, from the prompting of our hearts, from the imagination of our minds, we re-form God's church into new and fresh images of redemption and reconciliation, that all who find their way into our community will find new life.**

_____   (Findley)

All Saints Day/All Souls Day

The early church sought a time to honor the many Christian martyrs and devout disciples of Christ not consistently honored in some manner. Thus, by the fourth century, Christians in Antioch commemorated all such predecessors in the faith on the first Sunday after Pentecost, closely associating the deaths of these saints with Christ's victory over death as celebrated on Easter. An annual "All Saints" festival developed throughout most of Christendom. In the ninth century, 1 November became the day officially designated for this observance. This day was formerly known in Great Britain as All Hallows Day.

As a means of commemorating the deaths of faithful Christians who were neither martyrs nor especially distinguished disciples, an Abbott of Cluny, named Saint Odilo, started the observance of All Souls Day on the day after All Saints Day in 998 A.D. Though the church conducted funerals for individual Christians at the time of their deaths, All Souls Day became an important occasion for remembering all those people who had died in Christ.

Believing that every disciple of Christ qualifies as a saint, most congregations in the free church tradition refuse to ascribe the title of "saint" to only a few people. Even Christians in this tradition, however, welcome opportunities to memorialize their predecessors in the faith. Some congregations observe All Saints Day or All Souls Day for that purpose. Others choose the national patriotic holiday known as Memorial Day. Memorial Day was originally a time set aside to honor service men who lost their lives in the Civil War. By the time it became a legal holiday in 1971, however, the day expanded in scope to honor persons who died for their country during one of the nation's other wars) for this purpose. Still others select an altogether different time to give thanks to God for their fathers and mothers in the faith.

Sights

Though *white* is the generally accepted liturgical color for these days, we find powerful symbolism in displaying an *empty black urn* set atop *a black pedestal* in our place of worship. This visual communicates vacancy, the absence of those whom we love who have died.

Sounds

❑ The Word of God

Old Testament Lessons	New Testament Lessons	Gospel
Dan 7:1-3, 15-18	Rev 7:9-17	Matt 5:1-12
Ps 24:1-6	Col 1:9-14	John 11:32-44
Ps 149	Eph 1:11-23	Luke 6:20-36
Prov 34:1-10	1 John 3:1-3	

❑ Piano Literature

"Elegie," Op. 10, Mossenet

❑ Choral Literature

"How Lovely are the Messengers," Mendlessohn, ed. Donald Neuen
"Ain'a That Good News," Hall Johnson
"Festival Piece on Saint Anne," Eugene Butler
"Holy God We Praise Thy Name," John Ferguson
"Hark I Hear the Harps Eternal," Arr. Alice Parker

❏ Congregational Hymns

"For All the Saints," William Walsham How, SINE NOMINE Ralph Vaughan Williams

"Ye Holy Angels Bright," J. H. Gurney, DARWALL John Darwall

"Jerusalem the Golden," Bernard of Cluny, Trans. J. M. Neale, EWING Alexander Ewing

"Holy, Holy, Holy," Richard Heber, NICEA J. B. Dykes

❏ Homiletical Themes

Authentic piety; saints and sinners; the impact of a life; seedy saints; the church as "a royal priesthood"; life as gift; death and faith; memory and hope.

❏ Sermon Titles

"Where are the Saints?" (Gaddy)

"Counsel for Saints" (Gaddy)

"An Aspiration to Sainthood" (Gaddy)

❏ Prayers

We are saints a-borning by your grace, O God.
    Without your help we will not become what we long to be.
This day we pray that you will go on changing us by grace.
Generate in us a still stronger desire not to be successful
    but to be faithful.
Create in us a still greater strength to keep on despite
    discouragement.
Fill us with dreams that can renew us and others in an age
    of pessimism and despair.
Heighten our longing to dare and to be daring.
Stir within us the deep desire to commune ever more fully
    with you.
Through Jesus Christ we pray. Amen.
                                            —————   (Hinson)

God of History:
This morning we are conscious of our predecessors in the
    faith.
From them we have received abundantly—
    Translations of scripture offering God's Word in
        English
    Writings in theology making plain the truths we affirm
    Examples of courageous faithfulness inspiring us in
        commitment.
Through them we have perceived your face, heard your voice,
    and learned your will.
        They have incarnated divine truth in various
            situations.
        They have spoken authoritatively, pastorally, and
            prophetically, convinced of knowing your Word.
        They have lived as you wanted and as we desire to live.
Thanks be to you, O God, for persons who have preceded us in
    the faith.
        For those who built this house of worship
        For those who taught us as children
        For those who modeled faith for us
        For those who cared about the integrity of our
            spiritual lives.
Sovereign God, we feel blessed. We stand in a tradition of
    privilege. Make us responsible stewards of that that we
    have received.
Enable us to live in a manner that allows us to pass on to
    those who succeed us a faith, an ethic, an obedience that
    are true to Scripture, helpful to all who follow, and
    pleasing to you.
We pray in the name of the Pioneer, Jesus the Christ. Amen.

───────────

(Gaddy)

Each day is an occasion for giving thanks for life. But on this day, O
God, we pause to thank you for particular lives. We thank you for the
people whose deaths brought to our souls the dark night of sorrow and
whose living memories now bring us the light of day. Each of them
possessed something worth remembering, something loved, something
sacred, something honorable, something good. For the lives of each of
these persons, and for the lives of all those who have no one to remember
their names, we give you thanks.

We thank you, O God, for holding in our care those you sent ahead of us. They prepared a road, marking its pitfalls, digging wells for our thirst, building shelters for our rest. Not always did they know who would follow them, but they pressed on. Sometimes they stumbled, many times they were injured, but they went on carrying a spark of the divine.

Now we travel that road, which is different, yet the same. Now that we are preparing the way for those who will come after us, we are awed by the responsibility. Help us by your Spirit to mark a clear path for our children and their children. May our faith give a small light to their way. Amen.

———————   (Findley)

❏ Congregational Litanies

Leader: God, our Creator, we praise you for the saints: for saints who have gone before us; for saints who are alive today; for saints in our midst; for the sainthood in us all.

People: God of love, we thank you for saints who have loved us, for families through whom we were created, for the people who taught us of your love.

Leader: For matriarchs and patriarchs, prophets and priests; for disciples, apostles, leaders and servants.

People: For pastors and missionaries, educators and healers, clerks and cooks.

Leader: God, to whom we come in faith, we thank you for the faith of the saints:

People: For Abraham and Sarah, Mary and Joseph; for Hannah and Elijah, Elizabeth and John.

Leader: For Martin Luther and Teresa of Avila; for John Calvin and Margaret of Navarre.

People: God, whose forgiveness brings us hope, we remember the saints who experienced hope:

Leader: Jacob and Samuel, Ruth and Naomi, for Augustine and Elizabeth Seton.

People: God of justice and peace, we honor saints whose peaceful ways give vision of your realm:

Leader: Archbishop Oscar Romero, Bishop Tutu, Sojourner Truth, and Ghandi; Martin Luther King, Jr. and Rosa Parks, Dietrich Bonhoeffer and Clarence Jordan.

Unison: God, we are renewed by the courage of the saints of history. We are inspired by the saints who walk among us today. May your Spirit move each of us to be healers and preachers, teachers and peacemakers, visionary sculptors and potters who continually create a new dream of your church on this earth. May we sense the presence of the great cloud of witnesses that surrounds us as we live our lives. As they heard your call and courageously proclaimed their faith, may we also hear your call and respond faithfully.

_____   (Findley)

Leader: The saints who still live among us call our attention to God in unexpected ways and at unexpected times. They enable us to see faith and life in new ways. They help us find our way a little, not so much by pointing it out to us, as by the way they themselves walk in the world.

People: And the great cloud of witnesses around us . . . The saints triumphant in glory. Their witness calls forth in us belief and hope and strength; helps us lay aside every encumbrance and sin that entangles us; and lets us run with endurance the race that is set before us.

Leader: Sisters and Brothers, saints of God, as we honor the saints who are now walking with us on this journey, inspiring us to press on; and as we bear witness to the great multitude that has gone before us, we remember them as those who taught us to hold fast to our faith.

People: Let us stand together during this time of remembrance and join our hearts in a prayer of thanksgiving for those we have called "saints"—whose lives have pointed us toward God.

Leader: (Reads the names of deceased persons to be remembered with thankfulness.)

_____   (Findley)

❏ Civil Holidays

During the season after Pentecost, several different dates on the civil calendar present potent opportunities for meaningful services of Christian worship. No reason exists to avoid an acknowledgment of these days in worship or to shy away from treating their themes from a Christian perspective. As long as worshipers understand the important distinction between civil holidays (memorials and anniversaries of significance to a nation) and traditional Christian holy days (feast days and fast days that help share the truth of the gospel), the church can use civil observances as "teachable moments" for the celebration of Christian truths. Such a purpose squares nicely with the liturgical intent and common themes of the season after Pentecost.

Independence Day

Since 1776, in the North American colonies and later throughout the whole of the United States, churches have celebrated the independence of this nation. Though the source, intent, and activities of Independence Day festivities are clearly political in nature, a national focus on independence provides a prime opportunity for Christians to consider the relationship between church and state, between religion and government, and between faithful Christian discipleship and responsible Christian citizenship.

Caution must be exercised lest Christian worship become politicized and the government Christianized. Any attempted synthesis of national patriotism and Christian discipleship produces a civil religion that may pass for a form of Christianity but in reality functions as an enemy of authentic Christianity.

Sounds . . . .

❏ The Word of God

Old Testament Lessons	New Testament Lessons	Gospel
Deut 8:18-20	1 Tim 2:1-3	Luke 4:18-19
Amos 5:24	1 Pet 2:13-14	Matt 22:15-21
Prov 14:34	Gal 5:1, 13	
Mic 4:1-4	2 Cor 3:17	

Psalm 33:12   Rom 13:1-7
                               Rev 13:1-8

❏ Piano Literature

"Important Event," Op, No. 6, Schumann

❏ Choral Literature

"Battle Hymn of the Republic," Roy Ringwald
"If You Will Only Let God Guide You," David Schwoebel
"God of Grace and God of Glory," Paul Langston

❏ Congregational Hymns

"Eternal God, Whose Power Holds," Henry Hallem Tweedy, FOREST GREEN Ralph Vaughan Williams
"God of our Fathers, Whose Almighty Hand," Daniel C. Roberts NATIONAL HYMN George W. Warren
"Once to Every Man and Nation," Jame Russell Lowell, EBENEZOR Thomas John Williams
"God of the Nations," Fred Pratt Green, TOULON Claude Goudimel

❏ Homiletical Themes

Christian patriotism; responsible Christian citizenship; church-state relations; Christians and political action; rulers as servants of God; national righteousness.

❑ Sermon Titles

"I Pledge Allegiance" (Gaddy)
"Proclaim Liberty" (Gaddy)
"Righteousness Exalts a Nation" (Gaddy)
"The New Politics" (Gaddy)
"When Kings Die" (Gaddy)

❑ Prayers

God of Deliverance, Lover and Provider of Liberty:
We pray for people for whom doors are shut, shut tightly and
      locked though the light of freedom has come to our world.
We pray for people smothering in slavery, people who know no
      freedom. You know their names, God.
            Release those people plagued by oppressive governments.
            Set free individuals whose religion has wrapped their
                  hearts and minds in chains.
      Unloose persons enslaved by their own prejudices.
      Undo the bindings of unrealistic personal expectations and
            social pressures and allow the bound to experience liberty.
      Tear down the prisons constructed by ignorance and let
            the captives know the joy of enlightenment.
Today, we give thanks to you, O God, for the freedom we
            enjoy and ask for forgiveness for those times when we
      seem to forfeit freedom for security or orthodoxy or
      conformity. We confess to you our grateful reception of
      this unearned blessing, a freedom that is ours because of
            our place of birth.
This morning, God, grant at least a vision of freedom to all
      who cannot make peace with bondage.
Set before the world the good news of freedom through Christ
      and use us as the messengers and facilitators of that
      Word, if you so desire.
Amid our celebrations of political freedom, call us back to
      an enduring commitment to the One Whom to serve is to be
      set free.
We pray in the name of the Liberator. Amen.

                    ————————
                                              (Gaddy)

Amid our celebrations of political freedom, call us back to
an enduring commitment to the One Whom to serve is to be
set free.
We pray in the name of the Liberator. Amen.

——————————

(Gaddy)

God of all Nations, Sovereign of Creation:
We pray for wisdom and courage that we may respond in
obedience to the admonition of our brother Paul of Tarsus
who admonished us to let our politics be worthy of the
gospel of Christ. Amen.

——————————

(Gaddy)

❑ Congregational Litanies

Leader: "The Lord God said, 'It is not good that a human being
should be alone.' " (Gen 1:18)

People: **Gracious God, we thank you for our story of origin that
calls us to partnership in order to be complete.**

Leader: "Then I looked and I heard the voice of many angels
surrounding the throne and the living creatures and the
elders; they numbered myriads of myriads and thousands
of thousands, singing together with full voice; and every
creature in heaven and on earth and under the earth and
in the sea, and all that is in then, singing." (Rev 5:11, 13)

People: **Even more do we thank you for our story of destiny that
summons us to a multi-cultural, multi-hued, multidi-
mensional weaving of all that is into one harmonious
whole.**

Leader: Yet, "when people began to multiply on the face of the
ground . . . the Lord God saw that the wickedness of
humankind was great on the earth, and that every incli-
nation of their thoughts was only evil continually . . . and
it grieved God to the heart." (Gen 6:1, 5, 6)

People: **But in between where we came from and where we are
going we confess that we are caught in the confines of the
human condition, between the will of partnership with
the will to power over, and community is splintered.**

Leader:	"In Christ all things hold together . . . and you who were once estranged and hostile in mind, doing evil deeds, Christ has now reconciled in his fleshly body through death." (Col 1:17, 21-22)
People:	**We thank you that also with us in the in between is Jesus Christ, whose cross is the link between creation and consummation, opening to us a new way of being together.**
Leader:	"As many of you as were baptized into Christ Jesus have clothed yourselves with Christ. There is no longer Jew or Greek, there is no longer slave or free, there is no longer male and female; for you are all one in Christ Jesus . . . heirs according to the promise." (Gal 3:28-29)
People:	**And we thank you that the Holy Spirit, knowing that we are lineal, sequential thinkers, is dealing with us slowly, inexorably, one issue at a time, to weave us into one glorious whole.**
All:	**Lord our God, we thank you that we are here and now with these our sisters and brothers. Stretch us as Christ was stretched on the cross to hold things together, until the strands of our separateness are woven together into the fabric of community that glorifies you.**

————————
(Penfield)

Leader:	"God is our refuge and strength, a very present help in trouble."
People:	**"Blessed is the nation whose God is the Lord." (Ps 33:12)**
Leader:	"The nations rage, the kingdoms totter."
People:	**"Righteousness exalts a nation, but sin is a reproach to any people." (Prov 14:34)**
Leader:	"The Lord of hosts is with us; the God of Jacob is our refuge."
People:	**"Let your manner of life, your citizenship, be worthy of the gospel of Christ." (Phil 1:27)**
Leader:	"Be still, and know that I am God. I am exalted among the nations, I am exalted in the earth!"
People:	**"Render to Caesar the things that are Caesar's, and to God the things that are God's." (Mark 12:17)**
All:	**"The Lord of hosts is with us; the God of Jacob is our refuge." (Based on Ps 46)**

————————
(Gaddy)

Thanksgiving Day

In 1863, President Abraham Lincoln proclaimed Thanksgiving Day as a national holiday. In 1941, the United States Congress decreed that Thanksgiving Day always be observed on the fourth Thursday of November.

Precedents for Thanksgiving Day probably reach back into the practices of the seventeenth century Puritans in England and Holland, who provided so many of the first settlers in North America. These pietists set aside certain days to fast and others to feast in an attempt to conform to the providential will of God. Only occasional times of thanksgiving (no prescribed days) were observed.

After their first severe winter in the new land, a harsh period in which nearly half the Pilgrims died, the pioneering settlers saw signs that better days lay ahead. The next fall, residents of Plymouth joined native Americans in a three-day period of rejoicing and giving thanks. Though this celebration apparently had no formal religious significance, the very idea of communally thanking God for the gifts of harvest and life caught on and continued.

Sights

Seeking to draw all causes for thanksgiving into consideration, I (DN) use four urns set at the corners of our communion table as voices for the various divisions of the earth. Each offers praise. One urn contains *flowers*—beauty. The composition is formed out of dried materials gathered from church members' gardens. The second urn is filled with *grains. Wild grasses, wheat, oats, sorghrum,* and *dock* make up the display. In the third urn, a design of *fruits and vegetables* using natural *vines* and *harvest baskets* is used. The fourth urn contains water offerings such as *shells, corrals,* and *sponges.*

◀🎶 · *Sounds*

❑ The Word of God

Old Testament Lessons	New Testament Lessons	Gospel
Joel 2:21-27	1 Tim 2:1-7	Matt 6:25-33
Ps 126	Phil 4:4-9	John 6:25-35
Deut 26:1-11	2 Cor 9:6-15	Luke 17:11-19
Ps 100		
Ps 65		
Deut 8:7-18		

❑ Choral Literature

"The Promise of Living," Aaron Copland
"Te Deum," John Rutter
"O Clap Your Hands," John Rutter
"Let the People Praise Thee, O God," William Mathias
"O Clap Your Hands," Ralph Vaughan Williams
"Thanks Be To Thee," Joseph Haydn, ed. Wamer Imig
"The Old Hundredth Psalm Tune," Ralph Vaughan Williams
"Now Thank We All Our God," J. Cruger, Arr. Noble Cain

❑ Congregational Hymns

"Praise My Soul the King of Heaven," Henry F. Lyte, LAUDA ANI-MA Mark Andrews
"For the Beauty of the Earth," F. S. Pierpoint, DIX C. Kocher
"Now Thank We All Our God," M. Richckart/Catherine Winkworth, NUN DANKET J. Cruger/Mendlessohn
"All Creatures of Our God and King," St. Francis of Assisi, LASST UNS ERFREUEN Harmonized by Ralph Vaughan Williams

❏ Homiletical Themes

Grace; the meaning of gifts; gratitude; blessings; the eucharistic; ethics; affluence and responsibility; praise.

❏ Sermon Titles

"It *is* Good to Give Thanks" (Gaddy)
"The Ministry of Thanksgiving" (Gaddy)
"Beyond Thanksgiving—Thanksliving" (Gaddy)

❏ Prayers

(One year, on the Sunday before Thanksgiving Day, I (DN) asked each member of our congregation to write a prayer for Thanksgiving Day and to share a copy of that prayer with me. Selecting from those printed prayers of thanksgiving, I composed the following prayer that three other readers and I offered to God during a worship service on the morning of Thanksgiving Day.)

Reader 1: Let us say our prayers.
            Eternal God,
Reader 2: the Alpha and Omega,
Reader 3: who sees the end from the beginning,
Reader 4: from whom we come, to whom we belong, and in whose service we find our peace.
Reader 1: Once more in this place we would be still and know that you are our God.
Reader 3: You have led us in the journey
Reader 4: And followed behind to nurture and sustain during the fearful times
Reader 2: And laid your hands upon each of us and all of us together as we have struggled to be your people in this world.
Reader 1: With awe and reverence we now come to meditate upon the thoughts of our God. O God, how good it would be if, on this day, we could express our gratitude and love for your goodness. Words fail us, yet our hearts are lifted up with the

highest and richest appreciation that we are given the possibilities of loving you with all that we are and hope to be.

Reader 4: O God, we do not recognize that every goodness flows from you,

Reader 2: that all of life-centering peace comes from you,

Reader 3: that light itself has its origin and receives its radiance from your presence.

Reader 1: Forgive our foolish ways and accept our gratefulness for the opportunity of realizing the truth of life and the chance to express our counted and uncounted blessings.

(All readers move to the communion table)

We mostly come in the spirit of thanksgiving neither for the gifts that you have given nor for the deeds that you have done . . .

Reader 4: We come first in gratitude because you are God. You are the center of our world and you give unity and meaning and purpose to life. Without you, O Lord, we would have no aim and purpose. Your omnipresence gives to us the courage to face the offerings of this life.

Reader 3: We thank you that you are also the Father and Mother of our greatest and best gift—Christ our Lord—and for the revelation and reconciliation that is ours through Christ.

Reader 2: We thank you that you are also the God of Calvary. We do not fully know or understand its explanation, but comprehension is with you.

Reader 1: Thanks be to you, O God, for the assurance and confidence that we have through the victory of Jesus Christ. O God, even this day, give us continued victories over our social evils and sins—and rise again to triumph to save us. We confess O Lord . . .

Reader 3: that churches are barely Christian

Reader 4: that industries are barely just

Reader 2: that nations are unpeaceful and many of our relationships are without love.

Reader 1: Bring us back to the appreciation of this day and give to us the desire to be images and reflections of our Lord. You have formed us in your own image and given us this world. You have loved us from the beginning of time and remembered us when we chose a way other than yours. We praise you, O God, for your faithful mercies.

Reader 4: Your grace that has sustained us

Reader 2: Your discipline that has corrected us

Reader 3: Your patience and love that have redeemed us.

Reader 1: Help us to love you and to be thankful for all your gifts by serving you and delighting in doing your will. We celebrate and give thanks for a place where freedom is not a tragedy but is more than a conqueror.

Reader 4: A place where rebels are not embittered but rather embraced.

Reader 2: A people who do not walk in the safe middle protected on both ends but rather are possessed by the challenge to lead with imagination and meaning.

Reader 3: A place that teaches unconditional love not condemnation as the final word at the story's end.

Reader 1: O God, save us from the smallness of being religious. Give to us the desire to be Christ-like and to be your people even if it means rejection by others and death. Dear Lord, we would not fail to give you praise for our homes on this earth and for the joy of living,

Reader 3: For good health and strength enabling us to enlarge the harvest . . . and good minds that help us grasp knowledge and seek truth,

Reader 2: for food in generous portions . . . supplies beyond our needs and rations that surpass our emptiness,

Reader 4: for work, for the courage and pride of believing in our dreams and a determination to fulfill them, for the skill and enterprise of manipulating this world's resources for the improvement of daily living,

Reader 2: for people with whom we come into contact who are authentic and whose love is real.

Reader 1: God of life, accept our thanksgiving for the graces of daily life—for routine, repetitious tasks and the process of decision-making. Grant us a zeal to live and work where and as we should—seeking to find your kingdom wherever we find ourselves.

Reader 3: For our country, we pray. Give us guidance and give us wisdom. Give us the grace of strong conviction along with a sympathetic understanding of those who differ from us. Renew our spirit of goodwill and give us the desire to stand for truth, liberty, and justice for all.

Reader 1:   Now, O God, we would not forget to pray for those this day
            who are so burdened with life and living that they cannot
            comprehend or find gratitude or words of thanksgiving. Help
            us know that this day there are people who can not say their
            own prayers and for them we voice their condition and sit-
            uations. Send to those in need your presence and if we can
            be the channel through which your call can flow, give us the
            courage and understanding to minister. These are our
            prayers, O Lord.

            (Readers two, three, and four conclude the prayer while
            moving back to their seats)

Reader 3:   forgive our mistakes,
Reader 4:   lift our visions,
Reader 2:   continue your indwelling love
Reader 1:   and grant to us wisdom and strength and courage for facing
            the tomorrows of our lives. Through the grace of Jesus Christ
            our Lord, we pray. Amen.

                            ————————   (Nixon)

❏ Congregational Litanies

Leader: Thanks be to you, O God, for bringing us to this
            table.
People: **Yes. Thanks be to you, O God.**
Leader: As we eat this bread, we give thanks.
People: **for the "house of bread"—Bethlehem,**
Choir: for the "bread of life"—who was born there,
People: **for corn bread, light bread, sourdough bread, wheat
            bread—which satisfy our hunger and allow us to feed
            others who are hungry.**
Leader: As we drink from this cup, we give thanks
People: **for "the living water"—which quenches our thirst
            for life,**
Choir: for the community of faith that is nurtured in
            this act of communion,
People: **for the holy wetness that falls when spiritual
            aridness scorches our lives.**

All: **Thanks be to you, O God, for bringing us to this table and gifting us with bread and wine.**

            ————————   (Gaddy)

Leader: Let us give thanks to God for Jesus.

Left: **We give thanks for the events of Jesus' life that make up our past—**
           His teaching that instructed us.
           His praying that inspired us.
           His death that saved us.
           His resurrection that assured us.

Right: *We give thanks for the presence of Jesus' life, which fills our present—*
           His comfort for all who labor and grow weary.
           His consolation for all who grieve.
           His love for all who exist.
           His peace for all who are at war with themselves or with others.
           His salvation for each person who seeks it.

All: **We give thanks for the promise of Jesus' life, which gives hope to our future—**
           His assurance that we will not be left alone.
           His explanation that discipleship is not dependent on dating his final return.
           His pledge to be with us always—in all situations and at all times.

Leader: Thanks be to you, O God, for Jesus—for his life in the past, present, and future; for his life, which gives us life.

            ————————   (Gaddy)

Floral Arrangements

The 19th century marble gallery statue is adorned in a garland of box-wood and myrtle. The design consists of garden pink and purple hydrangea enhanced by rose celosia. The above composition was used for an arts festival and is appropriate for the second Sunday of Advent.

Floral arrangements can enhance any corner of the church and communicate the message for the day. The arrangement above focuses members' attention on baptism.

Fresh fruits and vegetables, arranged in seasonal vines and accented with shafts of wheat, communicate God's bountiful grace in this Thanksgiving harvest design.

Worship Banners

❑ **Sundays After Pentecost** ❑

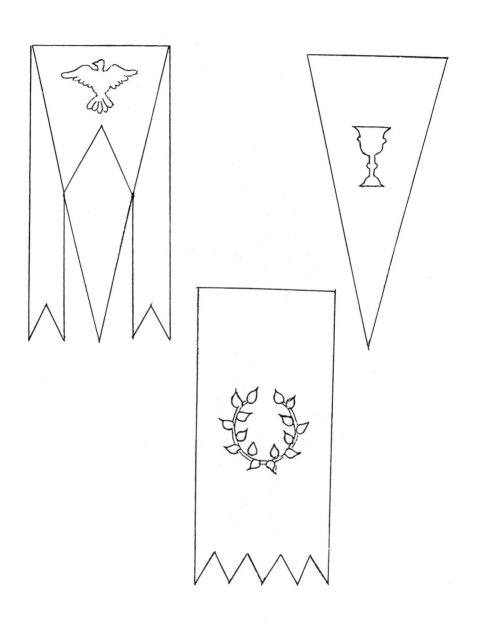

❑ **Additional Banners** ❑

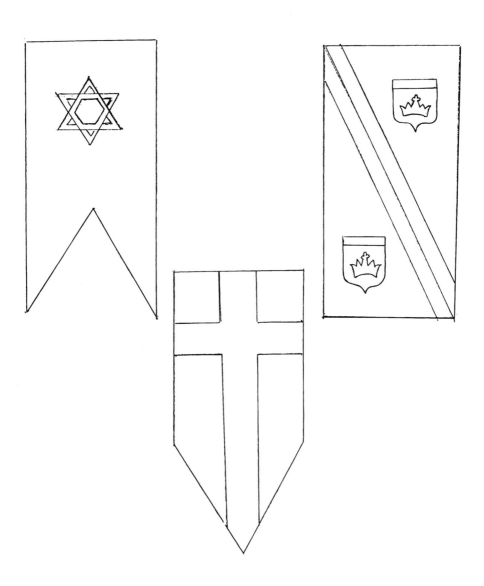

❏ **Additional Banners** ❏

Christian Worship

Appendix:
Further Resources

Annotated Orders of Worship

The Worship of God
Northminster Church
The Twenty-fourth Sunday after Pentecost

The Prelude to Worship
    The sounds of the organ (and/or piano) establish the mood of the
    worship experience.

The Prologue   S. Carracciolo
                        Jesus, I Adore Thee
    From the rear of the sanctuary or in the narthex, the choir presents
    a musical synopsis of the entire service. Hearing "The Prologue,"
    gives worshipers an insight into the major theme of this particular
    service.

The Call to Worship
    A litany in which people state the life-situations, needs, and expecta-
    tions that they bring to worship as they commit themselves to an
    encounter with God.

The Introit   J. Allen
                        Open My Eyes
    This brief piece of music (again sung from the back of the sanctuary)
    introduces the nature of the processional hymn and prepares the con-
    gregation to sing it.

The Prayer of Praise and Adoration
    A member of the congregation offers to God audible statements of
    reverence, devotion, and commitment.

The Processional Hymn   NICAEA
                Holy, Holy, Holy! Lord God Almighty
    Members of the choir and ministers of the congregation enter and
    take their positions in the sanctuary during this hymn. Unless the

season dictates a different spirit, this hymn is usually majestic and filled with praise.

The Old Testament Lesson Jeremiah 37:17a

> Leader: This is the word of the Lord.
> **People: Thanks be to God.**

The Meditation   M. Ryan-Wenger
In the Beginning Was the Word
The choir responds to the reading of the Old Testament with a piece of music, which moves worshipers to openness to the New Testament as well.

Pastoral Prayer
Though not included every Sunday, this prayer gathers the concerns of the congregation and sets them before God with a request for divine help.

The New Testament Lesson   1 Thessalonians 2:9-13, 17-20

> Leader: This is the word of the Lord.
> **People: Thanks be to God.**

A New Testament lesson is read in every service. Often a reading from the gospel occurs as well. When the gospel is read, members of the congregation are requested to stand. A gospel reading is followed by the reader stating, "This is the Holy Gospel of our Lord Jesus Christ" and the congregation responding with, "Praise to Thee, O Christ."

The Hymn   AUSTRIAN HYMN
Word of God, Across the Ages
The Litany
A responsive reading that prepares the congregation for the sermon.

The Sermon
"Is There a Word From God?"
The Anthem   N. Sleeth
Spread Joy

Because the sermon concluded with a joy-inducing promise, the choir picks up that theme and proclaims it chorally.

The Offering of Our Lives and Labors unto God
A time of decision-making and offering related to the stewardship of all of life.

The Meditation
An instrumental presentation that serves as a transition into communion. Those who will lead communion move to the lectern during this time.

The Service of Communion

The Call to Confession
Worshipers are reminded of the importance of confession before God and invited to confess their sins.

The Prayer of Confession
A printed prayer of confession allows worshipers to confess their sins in unison.

The Assurance of Forgiveness
A reiteration of God's promise of forgiveness to all the penitent.

The Communion Prayer and Lord's Prayer
One of the persons who will serve communion offers a prayer, which leads into members of the congregation joining in the Lord's Prayer.

The Distribution of Elements
Members of the congregation come forward to the chancel to receive the bread and the wine of communion.

The Meditation   *Canon of Praise*   Pachelbel
The choir sings as members of the congregation receive communion.

The Time of Invitation
The Commission
The pastor invites new members into the church and voices the commission for God's people to minister in the world.

The Recessional Hymn   FESTAL SONG

The Benediction
  Sometimes spoken and at other times sung, the benediction comes
  from the back of the sanctuary.

The Postlude

The Worship of God
Christmas Eve

The Organ Voluntary
The Processional Hymn   IRBY
              Once in Royal David's City

The Bidding Prayer
The Carol   *Of the Father's Love Begotten*   DIVINUM
                                                         MYSTERIUM

— The Lessons of Prophecy —

Isaiah 40:1-8
Jeremiah 23:5-6
Zechariah 9:9-10
The Carol   *Lo, How a Rose E'er Blooming*   ES IST EIN' ROS'

Micah 5:2-4
The Carol   *O Little Town of Bethlehem*   ST. LOUIS

— The Coming of Christ —

Luke 1:26-35
The Carol   GABRIEL'S MESSAGE
          The Angel Gabriel from Heaven Came   Basque Carol

Matthew 1:18-25
The Carol   *Song of the Crib*   15th c. German

Luke 2:1-8

The Carol   *Away in a Manger*   MUELLER
                                                                  19th c. American

Luke 2:8-12

The Carol   *The First Noel, the Angel Did Say* THE FIRST NOEL
                                                      Traditional English

Luke 2:13-14

The Carol   *Angels We Have Heard on High*   GLORIA
                                                      19th c. French Carol

Luke 2:15-20

The Carol   *What Child Is This, Who,*   GREENSLEAVES
                              Laid to Rest   16th c. English

The Revelation   John 1:1-14
The Homily
The Dispersal of Light

The Carol   *Silent Night! Holy Night!*   STILLE NACHT
                                                          19th c. German

The Commission
The Recessional Carol   IN DULCI JUBILO
                        Good Christian Men, Rejoice   Medieval Carol

The Benediction
The Postlude

❧❦❧

The Worship of God
Ash Wednesday

The Prelude to Worship
The Prologue   Mueller
                   Create in Me A Clean Heart

The Call to Worship
 A brief invitation to a unique experience of worship beginning a
 pilgrimage to the cross.

The Processional Hymn   BEACH SPRING
             Come, Ye Sinners, Poor and Needy

The Prayer of Praise and Adoration
The Psalm   Psalm 51:1-12

The Elements of Worship
 An explanation of the meaning of Ash Wednesday in the Christian
 year is given: the significance of ashes in Christian tradition, the symbolism of bearing a sign of the cross imposed with ashes, and the
 importance of confession and repentance as well as praise and adoration on the church's journey to the crucifixion and resurrection of
 Jesus.

The Call to Confession
 A summons to acknowledge personal sins before God in a spirit of
 penitence.

The Prayer of Confession
 A printed prayer that worshipers offer in unison.

The Response   ST. MARGARET
             O Love That Wilt Not Let Me Go
             (stanza one)

The Assurance of Forgiveness
 A reminder from one of the ministers that God hears our confessions
 of sin and with love and grace offers forgiveness.

The Imposition of Ashes
 The symbolic use of ashes upon the forehead is an Old Testament tradition conveying a sign of penitence, grief, and mourning. The sign
 with ashes is a reminder to each of us, "Remember O people, Thou
 art dust, and unto dust thou shalt return." As New Testament Christians, let the ashes be for us a visual reminder that "As in Adam all
 die so in Christ shall all be made alive." So let us mark with the sign

of Christ, a cross, on each other's forehead and convey to the world our sincere desire to take up our cross and follow the Son of God.

The Commission
A statement from a minister reminding worshipers of Christians' responsibility to live like and for Christ in the world.

The Recessional Hymn ELLESDIE
Jesus, I My Cross Have Taken

The Worship of God
Maundy Thursday

With the exception of the ministers' spoken assurance of God's forgiveness and words of grace while serving the bread and wine of communion, this entire service proceeds in silence. Worshipers move through the order of service at an individual pace. The printed order of service that follows provides directions for every aspect of the worship experience.

The Prelude to Worship
Silence.

The Call to Worship
A printed paragraph invites the worshiper to consider Christ's call to discipleship and to participation in the body of Christ.

The Prayer of Invocation
A printed prayer helps the worshiper to pray, bringing to mind the faithful service and unconditional love so integral to the significance of this evening.

The Hymn
A printed paragraph for meditation enables the worshiper to get in touch with the inarticulate, inaudible music of the soul.

A Moment of Personal Reflection
> In the quietness of the moment, reflect on your personal journey with the Christ of this world. Seriously examine your commitment, repent of your weaknesses, and discover new possibilities for a closer relationship with God. This is a night for laying aside our fears, hatreds, and alienations so that God's love may reign.

The Collect for The Word
> A prayer of preparation for receiving God's Word in the biblical text for the evening.

The Lesson   Luke 22:7-20
> A printed copy of the New Testament text.

The Invitation
> A reminder of Jesus' invitation to the Lord's Supper and the meaning of accepting this invitation.

The Call to Confession
> A word of instruction regarding the importance of offering confessions to God, especially in preparation for the service of communion.

The Prayer of Confession
> A printed prayer of confession.

> *Following the prayer of confession, you are invited to come to the front of the nave. A minister will share words of assurance and offer the elements of remembrance. After participation in communion, please return to your seat for further reflection and meditation.*

The Reflection
> Words that enable each worshiper to understand the meaning of what has taken place. Special attention is devoted to the gifts of Christ found at Christ's table.

The Commission
> Words of instruction that help the worshiper translate the sentiments of this service into acts of mercy in the world. Members of the church are reminded of the nature of the body of Christ and of the importance of Christ's commandment, "Love one another, as I have loved you."

The Recessional
Silence.

The Worship of God
Good Friday

The Opening Sentences
In the narthex
A brief explanation of the content and significance of the Good Friday worship service.

The Call to Worship
A litany that identifies the major characters in the Good Friday drama and encourages everyone present—including the betrayers and the deserters—to hear again the story of God's grace.

The Processional
As the congregation moves into the sanctuary for worship, please join in the singing of the hymns.

Alas and Did My Savior Bleed	AVON
When I Survey the Wondrous Cross	HAMBURG
I Stand Amazed in the Presence	MY SAVIOR'S LOVE

The Prayer for Illumination
A request to God for enlightenment as a result of this worship experience.

The Hymn   REDHEAD
                              Go to Dark Gethsemane

The Shadow of Desertion
The Lesson   Matthew 26:30-46
The Hymn   OLIVE'S BROW
                         Tis Midnight and on Olive's Brow

The Shadow of Betrayal
The Lesson   Matthew 26:47-50, 55-56

The Meditation   J. Cruegar
                        Ah, Holy Jesus
                              solo

                    The Shadow of Accusation
The Lesson   Matthew 26:57-68
The Hymn   WONDROUS LOVE
                    What Wondrous Love Is This

                        The Shadow of Denial
The Lesson   Matthew 26:69-75
The Litany
    A litany identifying the One betrayed and denied and the ones, then
    and now, leveling the charges against him.

The Hymn   GORDON
                        My Jesus, I Love Thee
The Prayer
    A pastoral prayer.

The Confession   *(Congregation in unison)*
    O Lamb of god, that takes away the sins of the world,
    have mercy upon us and forgive us of our sins. Amen.

The Reconciliation
The Words of Assurance
The Hymn   ST. MARGARET
                O Love That Wilt Not Let Me God

The Prophecy   Isaiah 53

                    The Shadow of Crucifixion
The Lesson   Matthew 27:27-44
The Homily
    A brief message on the meaning of the crucifixion of Christ.

The Hymn   PASSION CHORALE
                    O Sacred Head Now Wounded
                      The Shadow of Death
The Lesson   Luke 23:44-46
                              Mark 15:39

The Remembrance
During this moment of silent meditation, reflect upon the depth of God's love and the sacrifice of Christ in order that reconciliation and salvation could exist.

The Shadow of The Tomb

The Lesson   John 19:38-40

The Desolation

The Hymn   WERE YOU THERE

Were You There
verse 3, solo

The Silent Meditation
The Tolling
During the tolling worshipers are requested to leave quietly and in a mood of reverence.

The Worship of God
Holy Saturday: The Easter Vigil

The Words of Comfort from Prophets and Psalms
Job 14
Psalm 90

The Opening Sentences

A pastoral statement recognizing the presence of sorrow in our midst and inviting each person present to meet God and find comfort in this experience of worship. After an acknowledgment of the death of Christ, the pastor requests prayers from the people and encourages all worshipers to watch for the dawning of the third day.

The Prayer for Illumination
congregation in unison

In this unison prayer, members of the congregation confess the difficulties involved in accepting death and letting go of those we love who have

died. We ask for the gift of divine grace in the presence of death that we
might worship and grow in trust.

The Entrance

The tolling of bells will call the worshipers together.
Antiphonal Psalm 23

The Remembrance of the Life of Jesus Christ

*Many of us have known this Jesus Christ of Nazareth and have exper-
ienced the stories associated with his life. As we give thanks for what
he did while he was on this earth, some of you may relate those memories to the others of us gathered here.*

Pearl
The Mother in John 9
Amazing Grace v 1
solo

The Leper
A Member of Northminster Church
My Faith Has Found a Resting Place v 1
solo

The Proclamation

A very brief statement acknowledging the death of Christ as a sacrificial
death akin to that of a Passover lamb that has been slain; comparing this
evening with the night on which the pillar of fire destroyed darkness;
and confessing the reality of grace that brings the offer of forgiveness and
freedom to all people. Worshipers are encouraged to view this eerie
evening as a blessed night because of its promise of redemption.

The Lesson

Listen to the word of God. (John 1)
In the beginning was the Word, and the Word was with God, and the
Word was God. In Him was life, and the life was the light of all people.
The light shines in the darkness and the darkness has not overcome it.

The Attestation of Faith

The Light of Christ rises in its glorious state overcoming the darkness of death. As we wait the final hours for salvation's story to be complete, let us divide the flame so that the darkness is conquered, others are given hope and the Christ of the Morning Star will find our lights bravely burning—waiting in faith for the victory of salvation to be complete.

The Return

Come, then, and with this new fire renew your commitment as a follower of Christ. As you depart, place your light, symbolic of your life in one of the window sashes around the nave of this room. Leave with the light a portion of your spirit as it keeps watch through the remaining hours of the night and waits for the break in tomorrow's dawn. So come, that your hearts and minds might be kindled with the holy desire to shine forth with the brightness of Christ's rising.

At the conclusion of this service, share the peace of God with the other followers of Jesus Christ who have worshiped here; then go to wait for tomorrow's dawn.

Christian Symbols
Traditional Symbols in the Christian Year

Advent

Advent Wreath. A circle, representing the unending love of God, constructed out of fresh evergreens, symbolic of eternal life. The wreath contains four candles within the circle and a larger "Christ candle" in the middle of the circle. Some traditions use four purple or blue candles. Other traditions use three candles of purple or blue and one of pink or rose (the "gaudete" candle), which is lighted on the third Sunday of Advent. Interpretations of the symbolic significance of each candle varies. Typically, however, lighting the first candle represents hope and expectation; the second, peace and proclamation; the third, joy and rejoicing; and the fourth, love and purity. In all traditions, lighting the white candle in the center of the circle represents Christ, the Light of the World.

Chi Rho. The first two letters in the Greek spelling of Christ.

Jesse Tree. A small tree, commonly an evergreen, which represents the genealogy of Jesus who descended from Jesse, the father of David. The prophecy of Isaiah 11:1-2 inspired the idea of the Jesse Tree, which frequently is displayed with an off-shoot growing from its trunk.

Messianic Rose. A five-petalled, white rose with a center highlighted in red representing Isaiah the prophet's reference to the kingdom (35:1). "The wilderness and the solitary place shall be glad for them and the desert shall rejoice and blossom as a rose."

Tau Cross. The T-shaped cross often associated with the Old Testament generally and Moses particularly.

Christmas

Angels. Messengers of the birth of Christ often depicted with wings symbolizing their divine mission.

Apples. The fruit of paradise symbolizing Christ as the Second Adam.

Candles. Symbols of Christ as the light of the World; the fulfill-ment of prophecy: Those who walk in darkness will see a great light.

Creche. Figures representing the major characters of the nativity of Christ. Typically a creche includes: the babe of the manger, Mary, Joseph, angels, shepherds, and animals. Some people delay displaying the three kings until Epiphany.

Daisies. Floral symbols of Jesus, the"sun of righteousness," which visually declare the innocence of the Christ child.

The Star of Bethlehem. A species of white flowers with a petal design resembling the five points of a star. These commonly used flowers bloom late in the season.

The Swallow. A bird that represents the Incarnation. Medieval paintings of the nativity frequently included this symbol.

Epiphany

Chest, Caskets, and Cruses. Containers which represent the treasures —gifts of gold, frankincense, and myrrh—brought to Jesus by the three kings from the East.

Shells. Symbols of water which have become associated with baptism. Epiphany worship gives detailed attention Jesus' baptism.

Star of the East. A symbol of the five-pointed star which directed Eastern royalty to Jesus.

Three Kings. Representatives of Gentiles, also recipients of God's gift of Jesus.

Water Jars. Symbols of Jesus' first miracle during a wedding in Cana of Galilee. This event revelatory of the divinity of Christ receives special attention during Epiphany.

Ash Wednesday and Lent

Gourds. Symbols of resurrection and renewal drawn from the Old Testament story of Jonah.

Pansies. Flowers that symbolize meditation and remembrance.

Sack Cloth and Ashes. Signs of penitence derived from religious practices described in the Old Testament.

Thistle. A symbol of the great sorrow which results from personal sinfulness generally and of the passion of Jesus specifically. This thorny representation of earthly sorrow appeared first in the Genesis account of God's judgment related to Adam.

Violets. Flowers that symbolize humility.

Holy Week

Dandelion. A bitter herb often associated with the passion of Jesus.

Goldfinch. A bird commonly associated with the passion of Jesus because of its propensity to eat thorns and thistles. Many artists have included the goldfinch in paintings of Christ as a means of demonstrating the close connection between the Incarnation and the passion.

Instruments of Passion. Items associated with the suffering of Jesus—the cross, the crown of thorns, nails, a spear, the reed, a sponge, the scourge, the purple robe, coins, dice, and a hammer.

Rooster. A fowl symbolic of Peter's denial of Christ and the desertion of Christ by Christ's friends.

Palm Branches. Green leaves traditionally viewed as symbols of victory. Artists often place palm branches in the hands of martyrs they depict to declare their triumph over death. According to the gospels, the people in Jerusalem threw palm branches in the path of Jesus as he entered that city at the beginning of the last week of his public ministry.

Pelican. A bird associated with the loving sacrifice of Christ for all people. Legend has it that pelicans exceed all other creatures in loving their offspring. A pelican will pierce its own breast to provide blood for feeding its young if necessary.

Easter

Anchor. This nautical tool symbolizes steadfast, undying hope and thus believers' faith in the resurrection of Christ.

Butterfly. Often a symbol of the resurrection of Christ because of the three stages of its life cycle. The caterpillar, which becomes a chrysalis and then a butterfly, brings to mind the life, death, and resurrection of Christ.

Crown. A sign of victory and royalty often associated with Christ's completed sovereignty over life and death.

Eggs. Colored, hard-boiled eggs symbolize the resurrection of Christ and new life. In the Middle Ages, Easter Sunday was sometimes called Egg Sunday.

Peacock. A beautiful bird symbolic of immortality.

Phoenix. A symbol of the resurrection that commonly appears in connection with the crucifixion of Christ. The phoenix is a mythical bird that burned itself upon a funeral pyre, rose from its own ashes, and, restored and refreshed, began a new life.

Pomegranates. Christian symbols of hope in immortality and resurrection probably derived from a pagan myth associated with the return of spring and the rejuvenation of the earth.

Pentecost

Dove. A symbol of peace and purity often associated with, or descriptive of, the Holy Spirit.

Tongues of Fire. A symbol of religious fervor also used to depict the presence of the Holy Spirit.

Additional Symbols

Banner	Victory	**Mirror**	Justice and truth
Book	Knowledge	**Moon**	The Virgin Mary
Candelabra (seven)	Christ/Light of the World	**Oil**	Anointing
		Pillar &	Scourging of
Circles	Wholeness, eternity	**Cord**	Jesus
Eye	Enlightenment; the all seeing nature of God	**Pearl**	Word of God
		River	The four gospels
Fish Net	The church	**Salt**	Superiority
Fountain	Eternal life	**Scales**	Justice
Hands	God	**Seven**	A sacred number,
Honey	Goodness		perfect number
Keys	Spiritual power	**Ship**	The church
Ladder	Christ's descent from the cross	**Skull**	Penance
Lantern	Judas' betrayal of Jesus		
Lion	Christ (because of its royal dignity)		

Colors with Symbolic Significance

Color	Symbolic Meaning
Black	Mourning, penance, death (Good Friday)
Black and White	Humility, purity in life, penance
Blue	Heaven, loyalty, devotion, spiritual love, truth, constancy, fidelity (often associated with Mary the Mother of Jesus)
Brown and Grey	Mourning, humility (Ash Wednesday)
Gold	Kingship, divine royalty, illumination, fruits of the Spirit
Green	Hope, regeneration, life, fertility, victory (Trinity in the Sundays after Pentecost)
Purple and Violet	Love, truth, suffering (Advent and Lent)
Red	Passion (Pentecost and Sundays related to saints and martyrs)
Silver	Purity, chastity
White	Purity, light, joy, faith, glory (Christmas, Easter)
Yellow	Sun, God, divinity, truth

Floral Symbols

Flowers	Christian Significance
Amaryllis	Pride
Anthurium	Love of God (heart-like shape)
Azalea	Devotion, Love
Bird of Paradise	Majesty
Camellia	Purity
Carnation	Divinity, Divine Love, Faithfulness
Chrysanthemum	Fruitfulness, Long Life, Constancy, Dignity, Joy, Reliability
Cornflower	Love
Crocus	Joy, Gladness, Authority
Cyclamen	Death
Daffodil	Resurrection, Benevolence, Joy
Daisy	Innocence, Cheerfulness, Faithfulness, Sympathy
Dandelion	Bitter sorrow of Christ's passion, Wisdom
Delphinium	Beauty, Sweetness
Dogwood	Continuity, Cross, Penitence
Evergreens	Life
Fern	Humility, Grace
Forsythia	Submissiveness
Fressia	Innocence
Gardenia	Purity
Gladiolus	Incarnation, Word of God, abundance, Beauty, Generosity, Sword of the Lord
Goldenrod	Encouragement
Hyacinth	Constancy
Hydrangea	Conceit
Holly	Crown, Goodwill, (sometimes associated with sin and evil)
Iris	Mary (especially her sorrow),

	Health
Ivy	Faithfulness, Eternity, Fidelity, Love
Lily	Resurrection, Redemption
Narcissus	Self-love
Orchid	Nobility, Purity
Poinsettia	Messianic promise
Pansy	Meditation, Remembrance, Friendship, Love
Peony	Stability, Wealth
Rose	Friendship, Kingdom of God (or reign of God), Messianic promise, Rejoicing
Snapdragon	Arrogance
Stock	Eternity
Sunflower	Turning to God, Adoration, Respect
Thistle	Sorrow, Independence
Tulip	Benevolence, Charity, Kindness
Zinnia	Remembrance

Plants with Symbolic Significance

Plants	Christian Significance
Bamboo	Abundance, Constancy, Devotion, Endurance, Friendship, Life, Steadfastness
Bittersweet	Truth
Broom	Humility
Cherry Branch	Virtue
Cyprus	Mourning
Eucalyptus	Temptation
Evergreens	Life
Gerbera	Sadness
Hosta	Devotion
Laurel	Accomplishment, Eternity, Glory
Magnolia	Virtue
Maple Leaves	Faithfulness
Myrtle	Life, Peace, Love
Oak	Force, Forgiveness
Olive Branch	Peace, Abundance, Hope
Palm Branch	Paradise, Christ's passion
Plum Branch	Duty
Pine	Contentment, Endurance, Integrity, Loyalty, Power
Smilax	Memory
Thorns	Crown
Reed	Anxiety, Greatness
Vines	God's Love
Wheat	Bountiful, Resurrection
Willow Branch	Grace, God's Promise, Mercy
Yew	Immortality

Fruits with Symbolic Significance

Fruits	Christian Significance
Apple	Original Sin, Justice, Righteousness, Salvation
Apricot	Distrust
Blueberry	Prayer
Cherry	Works (Fruit of Paradise)
Fig	Fertility, Love
Grapes	Holy Communion
Lemon	Fidelity, Love
Peach	Congeniality, Wisdom, Silence
Pear	Christ's Love, Mary, Love
Plum	Fidelity
Pomegranate	Fertility, Hope, Resurrection, Unity of Church
Strawberry	Righteousness, (trilobed leaves represent the Trinity)

Banners

Construction and Designs

❑ Fabric

Felt is the easiest fabric with which to work when making a banner. This material is not difficult to cut into patterned pieces or to pin into place prior to permanently fusing it onto the banner. Another advantage to using felt is that it comes in a wide variety of colors.

Cream-colored felt works well as the body of a banner. Even white patterned pieces stand out clearly against such a background. Using a hot glue-gun, attach to the banner black cording for outlining and gold roping for borders.

❑ Colors

We have not suggested specific colors for each part of the banners depicted here. Banner artists can use whatever colors best convey the biblical truths involved for them or the colors of the fabrics most readily available to them. Traditionally, liturgical banners require the use of red, gold, blue, black, green, pink, brown, and straw colored felt for the words and symbols attached to a banner as well as white or cream colored felt for the background of the banner itself.

If one color dominates the worship center in which a banner will be displayed, worship planners may wish to use that color as the border for all their banners. If not, hot gluing a thick, metallic gold roping around the edge of a banner can give it a very distinctive look.

❏ Designs

Use an overhead projector to blow up designs for the banner. Project the blown-up designs (in any size you desire) onto butcher paper or craft paper, which has been taped to a wall. Trace the images and cut them out to use as patterns. Designs projected in large images produce irregular drawings though the irregular lines can be smoothed out when cutting the patterns from the paper.

Draw the designs to a scale of one inch equals one foot to construct a 3 x 6 foot banner. Of course, you can produce a smaller size by reducing the magnification displayed by the overhead projector.

Outlining the cut felt pieces with black cording really helps the designs stand out and gives the entire banner a finished look. On metallic pieces—crowns and trumpets—outlining the gold felt with black cording and then gluing gold metallic cording inside the black cording creates a rich, regal look.

❏ Finish

Sew loops of felt across the top of the banner so it can hang from a dowel rod.

Seasonal Sounds
Suggestions for
Instrumental Musicians

Special sounds capture the spirit and substance associated with each season of the Christian year. Below is a list of recommendations for particular sounds, the musical instruments to produce them (other than organ and piano), and specific pieces of music for each of these instruments that can help create the appropriate mood for each of the major seasons on the Christian calendar.

Advent

❑ First Sunday: Hope
Instrument: Cello
Literature:
    Sarabande, Suite No. 2 in D Minor, J.S. Bach
    Sarabande, Suite No. 1 in G Major, J.S. Bach
    Sonata No. 5 in E Minor (slow movement) A. Vivaldi
    Concerto in B Flat Major (slow movement) Baccherini
Adagio, J. S. Bach
Transcription/Arrangement
Four Pieces in Folk-Style (Langsam), Schumann

❑ Second Sunday: Peace
Instrument: Harp
Literature:
    Prelude in C, J.S. Bach
    He Shall Feed His Flock (from *The Messiah*), G.F. Handel

❑ Third Sunday: Joy
Instruments: Percussion and Speaker
Literature:
    Psalm Collage, James Moore
    (Percussion instrumentation is divided into three areas:
    Membranes, Metallic Instruments, and Keyboard Percussion.)
    (The text is taken from Psalms 47:1; 149:3; 150:5; 29:3-4; 100:1-5)

❏ Fourth Sunday: Love

Instruments: Flute and Guitar
Literature: *Mountain Songs*, "Hush You Bye," Robert Beaser

Christmas

Instrument: Recorder Quartet

Epiphany

Instrument: Keyboard Percussion
Literature:
> *In the Name of the Lord*, Walter B. Saul II
> (A meditation on several of the names ascribed to Christ from holy texts: Alpha, the Holy Child, the Bright Morning Star, the Good Shepherd, Love, a Friend of Tax Collectors and Sinners, the Lamb of God, the Resurrection, and Omega)
> *Jesu, Joy of Man's Desiring*, J. S. Bach, Arr. Andre Marchetti

Lent

Instrument: Violin
Literature:
> *Sonata and Partita for Solo Violin*, J. S. Bach
> First Sonata in G Minor (Adagio)
> Second Sonata in A Minor (Andanta)
> Second Partita in D (Allemnade and Sarabande)
> Third Partita in E (Loure)
> *Fantasies for Violin*, Teleman
> Seventh Fantasy in E flat (Largo)
> Sixth Fantasy in E Minor (Grave and Siciliana)
> *Adagio in E Major, K. 261 for Violin*, W.A. Handel
> *Largetto for Violin*, G. F. Handel, Arr. Jeno
> *Largo for Violin*, Veracini

Palm Sunday

Instrument: French Horn
Literature:
> *Day Profundis*, Gardner Reed
> *Kirken Aria*, Stradella

Good Friday

Instruments: String Quartet
Literature:
> *Ave Verum Corpus*, W.A. Mozart
> *Sarabande*, Buxtehude, Arr. Paul Gordon
> *Diveriminto*, L. Mozart, Arr. Paul Whear
> *Cannon in D*, J. Pachebel
> *Passacaglia*, G. F. Handel
> *Concerto No. 13 in D*, Alvison, Arr. A. Milner
> *Air, J. S. Bach*, Arr. A Stoesell
> *Largo*, Purcell
> *Golden Sonata*, E. Clark
> *Panis Angelicus*, C. Frank, Arr. Digullian

❑ Saturday Vigil

Instrument: Oboe
Literature:
> *The Winter's Past*, Wayne Barlow
> *Evening Piece*, W. Benson
> *Elegy*, J. Massanet
> *On Wings of Day*, F. Bartholdy-Mendelssohn

Easter

Instruments: Brass Quintet
> *March Triumphant* (Based on NUN DANKET), Sigrid Karg Elert, Arr. G. Olson
> *Canzon Cornetto*, Schitz, Arr. G. Olson
> *Tocata*, A. Bonelli, Ed. Robert King
> *Cantate Domino*, Han Hassler, Ed. G. R. Belden and Don Little
> *My Spirit Be Joyful*, J. S. Bach, Arr. H. Herforth

Pentecost

Instrument: Trumpet

Credit for works of art according to season:

Advent: Alinari/Art Resource, NY: S0063794/AL48708/B&W Print; Pontormo, Jacopo. Visitation. S. Michele, Carmignano, Italy.

Christmas: Giraudon/Art Resource, NY: S0063806/PE4935/B&W Print; Limbourg Brothers. Nativity. Musee Conde, Chantilly, France.

Epiphany: Alinari/Art Resource, NY: S0063851/AL58307/B&W Print; Crucifixion and Adoration of the Magi. Ivory plaque. Bargello, Florence, Italy.

Lent: Giraudon/Art Resource, NY: S0063801/PF126/B&W Print; Crucifixion. Reliquary said to belong to Pepin of Aquitaine. Musee Aveyron, Conques, France.

Holy Week: Alinari/Art Resource, NY: S0063799/AL65005/B&W Print; Duccio. Entry of Christ into Jerusalem. Detail from Maesta Altar. Museo dell'Opera Metropolitana, Siena, Italy.

Easter: Alinari/Art Resource, NY: S0044122/LA19131/B&W Print; Mantegna, Andrea. Resurrection of Christ, detail. PRINT SLIGHTLY RIPPED AT THE BOTTOM. Musee des Beaux-Arts, Tours, France.

Pentecost: Foto Marburg/Art Resource, NY; S0063802/29078/B&W Print; Pentecost. Wooden relief, c. 1521.

Sundays after Pentecost: Foto Marburg/Art Resource, NY: S0007777/X192.353/B&W Print; Rembrandt Harmensz. van Rijn. Christ Teaching ("La Petite Tombe"). Etching. Staedtliche Kunstsammlung.